Praise for *Smart Collaboration*

"Gardner has done the hard work of looking at what actually happens within law firms to make a persuasive and factual case that partners who master the art of collaboration are the ones who will thrive in today's complex market."

—**STEPHEN J. IMMELT**, CEO, Hogan Lovells

"Gardner presents a powerful empirical case for smart collaboration in a VUCA (volatile, uncertain, complex, and ambiguous) world. This book is a must-read for law firm leaders and partners committed to improving client relationships globally."

—**WIM DEJONGHE,** Senior Partner, Allen & Overy

"Gardner's book should be mandatory for everyone working in professional services. Buy the book, share it with your partners, and if you haven't already, start practicing its principles today."

—**NILS H. THOMMESSEN**, Managing Partner, Wiersholm

"In *Smart Collaboration,* Gardner describes the value of collaborative expertise in solving problems. In today's world, problems are so complicated and sophisticated that no single expert is in the position to solve them without smart collaboration."

—**JOSEPH C. SHENKER**, Chairman, Sullivan & Cromwell LLP

"Gardner dissects the concept of collaboration and reveals its true nature, from a soft skill we all preach but don't take too seriously into a key performance indicator that all professional service firms should place at the very top of their list—one that has greater impact on the success and sustainability of firms than any of the other popular KPIs. A must-read for anyone, not just top leaders, in knowledge-based organizations."

—**EDUARDO C. LEITE**, Chairman, Baker & McKenzie

"In this groundbreaking work, Gardner advises firms to embrace the brave new world of offering expert cross-fertilization and true multifunctional cooperation for at least two compelling reasons: better service and more revenue."

—**BEN HEINEMAN JR.,** Senior Fellow, Harvard Law School and Harvard's Kennedy School of Government; former Senior Vice President and General Counsel, General Electric

"A must-read for any ambitious professional and the single best book I would recommend to any professional service firm leader."

—**CLAUDIO FERNÁNDEZ-ARÁOZ**, Senior Adviser, Egon Zehnder; author, *It's Not the How or the What but the Who*

"Gardner's *Smart Collaboration* draws on an astounding data set to paint a picture of today's—and tomorrow's—professional service firms. She demonstrates that effective collaboration, a skill that must be ingrained as a part of the firm's DNA, is necessary to succeed in the twenty-first century."

—**DAVID W. RIVKIN**, President, International Bar Association; Co-Chair, Debevoise & Plimpton LLP

"An outstanding tool for enhancing quality, efficiency, and results in law firms and for improving individual and group skills. *Smart Collaboration* is an enjoyable must-read for lawyers around the world."

—**HORACIO BERNARDES-NETO**, Partner, Motta, Fernandes Rocha Advogados; Secretary General, International Bar Association

"This book and the thinking in it can help you bring collaborative behaviors alive within your business."

—**MARK RIGOTTI,** CEO and Partner, Herbert Smith Freehills

"Not sure that collaboration will make your professionals more effective and your firm more profitable? Read chapter 6 of *Smart Collaboration*. Believe me, you'll read the rest."

—**ROGER MELTZER,** Partner and Global Cochairman, DLA Piper

"Professor Gardner's research proves that collaboration as a core value in professional service firms is much more than an ancillary value. Gardner provides powerful evidence that a collaborative culture leads directly to superior client service, and a law firm that is better off, both financially and strategically."

—**PAUL W. THEISS,** Chairman, Mayer Brown LLP

SMART
COLLABORATION

How Professionals and Their Firms

Succeed by Breaking Down Silos

SMART
COLLABORATION

HEIDI K. GARDNER

Harvard Business Review Press

Boston, Massachusetts

The web addresses referenced in this book were live and correct at the time of the book's publication but may be subject to change.

Library of Congress Cataloging-in-Publication Data
Gardner, Heidi K., author.
Smart collaboration : how professionals and their firms succeed by
    breaking down silos / Heidi Gardner.
Boston, Massachusetts : Harvard Business Review Press, [2016]
ISBN 9781633691100 (hardcover)
Professional corporations. | Cooperation. | Institutional cooperation.
    | Globalization. | Interdisciplinary approach to knowledge.
LCC HD62.65.G37 2017 | DDC 658.4/6–dc23
LC record available at https://lccn.loc.gov/2016026317

CONTENTS

PREFACE

Why are some teams so much better—or worse—than others at using experts' knowledge to crack tough problems?

I first became intrigued by this question when I was a management consultant for McKinsey & Company in London, Johannesburg, and New York. At McKinsey, we approached nearly every client engagement with a team. Many of my teammates had not just solid business training but also fascinating backgrounds—astrophysicists, medical doctors, former lawyers, and military officers—that gave them unique perspectives on our work. But on multiple occasions, I wound up asking myself very similar questions: *Is this collaboration producing exemplary results? Are we integrating all our unique knowledge to create a whole that is more than the sum of its parts?*

Certainly, those questions took root years earlier, while I was at the London School of Economics working on my master's thesis, which focused on leaders' roles in promoting teamwork in knowledge-based firms. But now, my work experience cast a new light on these issues. I sensed that some of our consulting teams weren't firing on all cylinders. Sometimes the right players weren't in the room. Sometimes they were, but even so, we weren't always successful at surfacing and applying our team members' specialized expertise to the problem. Yet sometimes we were brilliant.

Eventually, I left the business world in pursuit of an academic career. I earned my PhD from the London Business School, with a dissertation focused on answering some of the questions that had vexed me about my McKinsey teams. I subsequently spent six years on the Harvard Business School faculty, where I continued conducting research to address that puzzle. I also sharpened my questions somewhat. In my HBS executive education classes, I often heard participants tell me, in so many words, "Sure, project teams are hard enough. But you should see what happens when we try to get the *partners* to work together!"

It didn't matter if they were in architecture or accounting firms or think tanks; massive global organizations or ones with a dozen partners; publicly traded companies, limited-liability partnerships, or the government; headquartered in Copenhagen, Chicago, or Cairo; global or domestic. A common challenge faced by the senior partners across all these knowledge-based organizations was convincing their high-powered experts to collaborate with other equally autonomous colleagues.

I decided to explore this challenge in a sustained and systematic way, as described in the introduction that follows.

Writing a book about collaboration was, as it turned out, a collaborative endeavor. As I discussed and tested my ideas over the years, I was astonished by the groundswell of interest those ideas prompted, and by the number of people who asked, "How can I help you?" Several months into writing the manuscript, I hit on a new idea to tap into this enthusiasm. I created what I called a *board of contributors*, and invited those people who had expressed a passion for the subject of collaboration to periodically review early-stage ideas for this book. I posted rough drafts a few paragraphs at a time, and board members posted their critiques, challenged my ideas (and sometimes each other's), and provided nitty-gritty examples from their own experiences. Although I didn't plan it this way, the book has turned out to be a testament to the power of surfacing and integrating the work of specialized experts. Their voices show up throughout the book, and I'm grateful for them.

The search continues for even more powerful ways to collaborate on tough problems in knowledge-based organizations, including the subset of that universe that includes professional service firms. I invite you to read my current thoughts on the subject, and contribute to the next generation of those ideas.

ACKNOWLEDGMENTS

Writing this book about collaboration was itself a highly collaborative endeavor. Through my research, teaching, and speaking over the last decade, I've had the privilege of working with thousands of incredibly talented professionals, and I'm deeply grateful for their input, feedback, and support. I hope that this book serves as a testament to the power of uncovering and integrating the knowledge of specialized experts. Beyond that—and true to my research findings—many of the people who started collaborating on the content have now become close colleagues and personal friends.

First, I thank the research participants: leaders, professionals, and staff across the many professional service firms, and executives and board members of the client organizations I studied. All were generous with their time and insights—and most important, with their trust in providing me with sensitive data, candid interviews, and other confidential inputs. To keep your confidence, I refrain from naming you, but I am humbled and indebted to you. Early in the writing phase, I formed a board of contributors, comprising all sorts of professionals who shared my passion for the topic of collaboration and helped to significantly improve this book by providing their critiques, examples, and ideas. Thank you!

My students (JDs, LLMs, MBAs, and PhDs) and executive education participants at Harvard Law School and Harvard Business School were also invaluable sources of ideas, feedback, and inspiration. Many times I presented and tested early-stage ideas in the classroom, and I appreciate my Harvard faculty colleagues who created those teaching opportunities and encouraged me to stretch my wings: Jay Lorsch, Bob Eccles, Boris Groysberg, David Wilkins, and Scott Westfahl.

I am grateful to my colleagues and the Advisory Board members at Harvard Law School's Center on the Legal Profession for providing me a "research home" and many opportunities to present and refine my ideas. The initial parts of this research were supported by the Division of Research at Harvard Business School. Across both institutions, a tremendously capable group of research associates have supported this effort, including Erin McFee, John Ng, Danielle Wedde, Shuli Wang, and Audrey Bloom. The research also benefited from robust peer challenge provided by participants in Harvard's GroupsGroup seminars; the initiative's founder, the late J. Richard Hackman, continues to inspire my research efforts. I hope I've done him proud.

The thinking behind this book evolved through some joint research and writing projects with other academics, and I have been blessed with coauthors who live the collaborative ideals: incredibly tough in the realm of ideas but personally warm and encouraging. This group includes Anand Narasimhan, Tim Morris, Ruth Wageman, Mark Mortensen, Stuart Bunderson, Melissa Valentine, Lisa Kwan, Jonathan Cromwell, Silvia Hodges Silverstein, Forrest Briscoe, Andrew von Nordenflycht, Madeline King, and Rebecca Normand-Hochman. Each of you pushes me to aim higher, and you make work fun.

I have also benefited enormously from the wisdom, insights, critiques, and encouragement of mentors and colleagues who played a role in this book and my life along the way. I couldn't possibly name everyone, but some of these vital influences include Ian Davis, Claudio Fernández-Aráoz, Ben Heineman, Jim Hever, James Lam, Patti Milligan Tsedal Neeley, Raymond Oldfield, Aric Press, Charles O'Donnell, Joe Macrae, Randall Peterson, Barrett Rollins, Søren Røssel, Sara Singer, John Soroko, and Nils Thommessen. Thank you from the bottom of my heart.

Those people who helped make this book a reality deserve thanks, too. I especially thank my copyeditor Jeff Cruikshank, whose monumental experience, wit, and patience were a godsend. Tim Sullivan of Harvard Business Review Press and his highly talented team gave this first-time book author guidance, confidence, and all sorts of support, for which I'm deeply grateful.

Finally, my family deserves enormous credit for the many, many ways they helped this book come to life. My husband, Ivan Matviak, has been an intellectual sounding board, constantly comparing my emerging findings to his observations about work inside professional service firms and financial institutions. Moreover, Ivan's love, support, and patience were vital throughout this journey. Our young daughters, Zoe and Anya, have grown up with this book; they've accompanied me across the globe for research trips and speaking engagements, not just listened to but also participated in countless dinner conversations about the ideas, and made the whole process fun for me. Both sets of parents—Phyllis and Bill Gardner, and Carla and Greg Matviak—have jumped at the chance to support my research by helping to make sure all of us stayed healthy and happy during my long days and heavy travel. I love you all.

I'm passionate about the potential for collaboration to bring about a more inclusive work environment, where people can contribute to their fullest potential even when they're not part of the established in-crowd, or their ways of working diverge from traditional ones. My research carries on, and I recognize that we have much work remaining. I hope readers will be inspired to become part of our ongoing collaborative journey.

Why Collaborate?

The greatest asset in any knowledge-based organization is the expertise of its professionals—the engineers and architects at a design-build firm, the scientists at a research institute, the lawyers and accountants at their respective firms, and so on.

The most important challenge faced by any such organization is bringing that collective expertise to bear on problems that, increasingly, are so complicated and so sophisticated that no single expert—no matter how smart or hardworking—is in a position to solve them.

Today's problems simply demand that specialists in the context of professional service firms—the central focus of this book—work together to integrate their separate knowledge bases and skill sets to forge coherent, unified solutions. They have to collaborate, in efficient and effective ways. I call it *smart collaboration*.

Defining "smart collaboration"

Smart collaboration is a *means to an end*, rather than an end in itself: knowledge workers integrate their individual, specialized expertise in order to deliver high-quality, customized outcomes on complex issues. Or they team up to develop an innovative approach to a thorny issue. Or they rely on an expert from a different domain who can efficiently transport a best practice across industries rather than reinventing a solution from scratch. These relationships typically extend over time, and across discrete projects, as the participants identify new approaches and initiate further engagements. In addition to offering up their expertise, these professionals also help, advise, stimulate, and counterbalance each other. By truly collaborating, a team of knowledge professionals is able to address issues that none could tackle individually.

But teamwork isn't cheap—the risks, coordination effort, and startup costs are real—so unless you know why you're collaborating, it may not be smart at all.

In these ways, smart collaboration is different from the mere assembly of experts' individual pieces after each has contributed to a "divide and conquer" approach. It's also different from sequential teamwork, in which one expert builds on others' prior contributions and then hands the project off to the next person. Although collaboration may not involve direct, face-to-face work, it *does* require repeated interactions that, over time, allow the creative recombination of different people's information, perspectives, and expertise.

The type of collaboration that I'm advocating isn't cross-selling. Cross-selling happens when, for example, the lead partner introduces a colleague to his client so that the newcomer can provide additional, discrete services. Although the lead partner may provide some general oversight or quality control, he doesn't get deeply involved. It's merely a referral, or a handoff.[1]

Put simply, cross-selling is the professional equivalent of what you've surely heard at the register at McDonald's: "Do you want fries with that?" As the chapters that follow will clearly show, collaboration—especially *smart* collaboration—is truly different.[2]

Hard evidence for collaboration

Collaboration is a means toward achieving the penultimate goal of solving complex, interesting problems—and the ultimate goal of giving firms a strategic, sustainable, and profitable platform. While there are many feel-good arguments in favor of collaboration, the real justification for effective collaboration in the knowledge sector can be found in the bottom line. Done right, collaboration makes your firm more successful—in the war for clients, and in the war for talent. This book provides the hard evidence for what has so far been considered a soft subject. "What the Data Says about Collaboration" shows how much more revenues increase from clients served by multiple disciplines.

What the data says about collaboration

Here's a simple example drawn from my research. This figure, with data from three different law firms, shows the effect on revenues of cross-practice collaboration: in each firm, clients served by two practice groups generate multiple times more revenue than those the firm serves with a single practice. You can see that this nearly exponential revenue growth continues as more practice groups are involved.

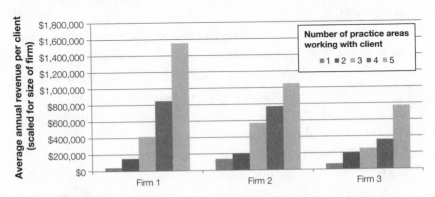

Source: Adapted from H. K. Gardner, "Why It Pays to Collaborate," *American Lawyer,* March 2015.

Until recently, professional service firms could make a strategic choice about whether to pursue the kinds of work that require effective internal collaboration. Given the inherent challenges of collaboration, some opted out.

But today, opting out is an increasingly unattractive option. The market for professional services is bifurcating into high-profit, customized work versus lower-end, routine work. Many professional sectors—indeed, much of the broader universe of knowledge work—have already approached, or will soon arrive at, an hourglass shape. Firms that want to capture, or even just maintain, their share of high-profit, customized work simply must foster collaboration among their experts. Collaboration has gone from a nice-to-have to a strategic imperative.

At the same time, collaboration is no less important for firms pursuing work that is fairly standardized. Standardized tasks increasingly require new flavors of collaboration—for example, joint problem solving that is more supported by and intertwined with technology. Any firm that hopes to differentiate itself in this end of the market needs even *more* refined, *more* efficient collaboration among its professionals.

Keep in mind that there may be no viable alternative. A pretty consistent theme across all kinds of professional service firms over the past few decades has been increased productivity and profitability extracted mostly from their star performers. Yes, that has been one way to establish and eke out a competitive advantage—but it is ultimately a self-limiting strategy. As one managing partner recently put it: "We can no longer squeeze additional productivity from individual partners—can't ask them to work harder or longer. Instead, we need to find ways to help them to do higher-value work more efficiently and effectively. Our clients tell us that if our lawyers truly collaborated across internal siloes, it would differentiate us from competitors."[3]

In short, multiple trends are pushing the market toward collaboration, which every day becomes both more essential and more complicated. Let's look a little more closely at two corollary trends that are fueling the rise of collaboration: expertise specialization and the increasing complexity of today's problems.

The drive for specialization

Because knowledge is changing ever faster, professionals across nearly every domain must specialize to keep current.

This trend is simply a massive acceleration of a process that's been going on for centuries.[4]

"In all professional fields," as Geoffrey C. Hazard Jr., a legal scholar, observes, "research and practical experimentation yield new knowledge and new methodologies by the minute." The consequences of this knowledge explosion, Hazard continues, are clear: "There are limits to the depth of knowledge and skill that can be achieved by anyone, except an occasional Renaissance Man, so that we all must specialize to stay abreast."[5] Think about the changes in surgery over the centuries: from barbers, who also doubled as surgeons, to today's specialists, who practice not just in pediatrics or tumors or the thyroid gland but in a confluence of all three.

It used to be that the professional's power over his or her clients stemmed from an *expertise gap*—the same kind of gap that arises when a naive owner of a car goes into a shady auto-repair shop. As the car owner, you may well get talked into expensive repairs that you don't need, simply because you don't know much about cars.

That gap has largely gone away in the contemporary professional services context. Sophisticated clients are harder to impress. Yes, they hire the firm that they think can provide a solid solution. In most cases, however, they're expecting an outcome beyond the "tried and true." In fact, among the clients I interviewed as part of my recent research, *innovation* was among the top ten reasons that they cared about their professional advisers' ability to collaborate: they strongly believed, based on their own experiences and observations, that collaborative teams of experts were more likely to deliver novel, advanced solutions.

If you think that you're in a line of work where clients don't expect innovation, consider this: For many clients, innovation doesn't necessarily mean a cutting-edge, never-before-seen solution. Instead, they expect their professional advisers to innovate by taking the standard technical approach and meticulously tailoring it to the very specific needs of the client's business. One client explained to me in a research interview the instructions he gives his consultants: "Don't give me the 100 percent technically right answer; I'd rather have it 80 percent bullet-proof and 100 percent applicable . . . otherwise it's zero percent useful."

The drive for specialization happens on two levels: the individual and the firm level. Most savvy and ambitious professionals today understand that it's in their economic interest to become *truly expert* at one particular topic. Ideally, that one topic is both arcane (in the sense of not being easily learned) and critically important (meaning there's a market for this skill). If these people are successful, their specialization becomes their "three-word brand" that allows people to tap their expertise in precisely the ways where they can add the most value. Clients can seek them out with the most burning questions on that topic, colleagues can refer work that is exactly in their sweet spot (so they can add tremendous value with minimal investment of precious hours), conference organizers will place them on the panels where they can add the pithiest insights, journalists will see them as the go-to expert when their niche area hits the headlines, and so on.

This trend has been happening for decades, and not only among the global elite. And the failure to recognize it can have serious consequences for knowledge-based firms. In one case, the New York law firm of Jackson & Nash lured away a partner, Victoria A. Stewart, from a competitor with the offer for her to develop a specialized practice in environmental law. When the work failed to materialize, Stewart claimed that she was then put to work on general litigation matters. According to Stewart's complaint, her "career objective—continuing to specialize in environmental law—was thwarted and grossly undermined during her employment with Jackson." She sued her former employer, claiming that she suffered "loss of professional opportunity, loss of professional reputation" and damage to her "career growth and potential." The United States Court of Appeals for the Second Circuit upheld Stewart's claim that her career as a lawyer was harmed when the firm failed to develop her expertise in environmental law.[6]

On the firm level, the drive to specialize—already powerful—is intensifying. Most top-tier service firms today encourage their partners to specialize, and have either created or acquired narrowly defined practice areas. The elite strategy consulting firm Bain & Company, for example, used to pride itself on having only generalists who could move fluidly between industries and issues; more recently, though, Bain's website sports headlines such as "Turnaround specialist . . . appointed head of global airline industry consulting practice" and "Bain & Company appoints new Dubai Partner . . . a specialist in the telecommunications and technology sectors as well as in consulting private equity firms that invest in these industries."

My own former employer, McKinsey & Company, has likewise moved toward an increasing focus on specialization. Mainstream consultants still join the firm as generalists, according to the firm's website, but they typically "specialize in one or more industries during their career," and build expertise at the "intersections of industries and functional knowledge areas." In other words, you might get broad-based exposure when you join, but within some years you'll be the clean-tech expert advising industrial clients on how renewable energy and climate policies affect their industry structure and competitive dynamics. And rather than waiting for homegrown expertise to develop in high-demand areas, McKinsey increasingly brings in experienced hires, such as operations consultants, who join the firm to supplement generalist consulting teams by applying their niche expertise.

Across the globe, firms are acquiring narrow practice areas to round out their specialist offerings. Recently, for instance, in Nigeria, some of the large multinational service firms—such as KPMG, Deloitte, and Accenture—have bought into such seemingly unrelated fields as immigration and visa services, as well as airport protocol. These services, previously handled by small-time players or individuals, augment the accounting firm's offerings for existing clients in lucrative specialist areas.

As a result of all these trends, professionals' collective expertise has become distributed across more and more people and practice groups. Or—phrased slightly more negatively—for compelling competitive reasons, firms have carved themselves up into silos.[7] Yes, this means that the experts within those narrowly defined departments can feed off each other, share information, and enrich each other's expertise. But it also means that getting people to work across those boundaries becomes more and more difficult.

The other driver: Increasingly complex client problems

Specialization in knowledge-based firms is only half the story—and from the client's viewpoint, it's the less compelling half of the story.

Increasingly, clients view their problems as VUCA—meaning "volatile, uncertain, complex, and ambiguous"—a term that is now common in books and articles about management.[8] The concept was introduced by the US military as the Cold War ended, and as Washington surveyed a new multilateral landscape that included potential enemies as diverse as newly formed countries, nonstate militias, and individual terrorists.

Similarly, clients today frequently talk about needing to respond to multiple, diverse constituencies—such as customers, regulators, competitors, employees, shareholders, and local communities—often across many different parts of the globe. As Jennifer Daniels, the chief legal officer of global consumer products giant Colgate-Palmolive, explained, "The reality is that the nature of business has changed sufficiently such that work is more complex, more dispersed, and more global. As a result, we are often not looking for the advice of just one lawyer with one set of expertise. I am looking for the advice of many lawyers across a spectrum of jurisdictions and issues. That puts a real premium on collaboration."[9] And chief legal officers aren't the only ones in the C-suite who are worrying about complexity. An IBM study of more than 1,700 chief executives found that complexity was their number one concern—edging out change management, which had previously topped the list.[10]

In my interviews with clients—the ones on the front line who are facing these complex problems and deciding whether to seek outside advice, and from whom—I discovered that the number-one reason why clients need their external advisers to collaborate with partners in their own firm is to make sure they bring "the full force of the organization to bear on my issues." Clients care little about the firm's internal politics or incentive systems; they just want access to the best advice possible. For example, the chief lawyer for a global bank based in the City of London relayed to me his biggest worry: the "crushing burden" of regulation that had recently come to dominate the financial sector:

> Two of my top law firms also have major practices serving
> the big pharmaceutical and aerospace companies—two
> of the most highly regulated industries on the planet.
> Why don't they send one of those partners to tell me how
> to survive under these regulatory pressures? If they did,
> I'd give them hours to explain how they might help me,
> which almost certainly would lead to more work—indeed,
> the kind of work that really matters to me, where I'm less
> price-sensitive. Otherwise, I'll probably just put the regu-
> latory work out in an RFP and let them bid against each
> other.
>   In the end, I'll get what I need, but it's pathetic that
> I'm the one who has to push them to talk to their own
> colleagues.[11]

Large and complex problems throw the subject into sharp relief, but it's worth pointing out that the same dynamic holds true at the other end of the problem spectrum. An architect friend told me the story of how the owner of a nineteenth-century mill building—recently turned into condos—had engaged her firm to help him repoint the building's brick walls. The architectural firm was large, with international projects; it was unusual for such a high-profile practice to get involved with what might have seemed a project for the local mason. As it turned out, though, the mill building sat on the side of a navigable river, which meant that multiple state and federal agencies had an interest in the project. As did the towns on both sides of the river, as did the local "friends of the river" group, and so on. The property owner figured out, correctly, that my friend's firm had the experience needed to take on most of these challenges—or knew which outside specialists to team up with.

Her story brings together both of the trends described earlier: specialization and problem complexity. Again, both trends argue for collaboration—both within the professional service firm and with other specialists outside the firm.

The solution: Smart collaboration

In my experience as a practitioner and researcher, smart collaboration is an approach that many professionals misinterpret and misapply—at least until they hear it explained from the clients' perspective.

Let's start with one fundamental attitude all clients share: *Clients hate to be cross-sold.* They typically find it self-serving on their adviser's part ("He's just flogging this extra service so that he can get sales credit for it") or condescending ("What? You think I'm too dumb to know I need tax advice? Think again—I already have a whole roster of advisers!"). Unsolicited, decontextualized cross-selling of the "You didn't ask for it, but can I bring along one of my partners from the X department" variety undermines a professional's credibility with clients.

Many professionals are initially relieved to hear that point of view, thinking that it gives them permission to keep focusing on solutions using only their niche expertise. Quite the contrary! Although clients don't want to be cross-sold per se, they increasingly *demand* smart collaboration. As I describe in the following chapters, clients have many reasons for wanting their professional advisers to collaborate with peers in their own firm—and so far, they tell me, most professional firms aren't delivering well enough.

This gap means that fast-moving professional service firms can gain a short-term competitive advantage by delivering efficient and effective collaborative service. But over time, if the trends I've outlined continue to intensify—which I believe they will—then collaboration will become, in the words of one chief executive, "mere table stakes." Given that your competitors are also racing to develop their own collaborative capabilities, pretty soon clients will expect collaboration as a basic, minimum requirement when hiring any professional adviser.

Smart collaboration from multiple perspectives

"What's in it for me?" That's the question many high-powered, accomplished providers of professional services ask—sometimes aloud, sometimes not. To many of them, collaboration looks like a passing fad, or a lifesaver for less talented colleagues who can't survive on their own. Most senior knowledge workers have risen to prominence on the basis of their individual achievement. Why should they change now?

These are good questions, and they sparked and fueled the research program I undertook more than a decade ago. To understand the outcomes of collaboration at the partner level, and also to understand the barriers to doing it effectively, I conducted an in-depth, long-term study of eight different global professional service firms, comprising the fields of law, consulting, engineering, and accounting. An analysis of more than a decade of time-sheet records from these firms gave me a robust, objective accounting of the varying extent and nature of partners' collaboration patterns. Marrying those millions of data points with financial and personnel records allowed my research team to use rigorous statistical techniques for understanding the outcomes of collaboration.

The result: *For the first time, leaders can draw on an empirically based, scientific explanation to convince partners of the benefits of collaboration.* High-performing partners can look at the data as well, and decide whether smart collaboration can help them become even more successful professionally. The answer to that question—as discussed in depth in chapters 3, 4, and 5—is an emphatic *yes*.

The work to understand collaboration continues today. I've amassed a database of more than a thousand partners' answers to questionnaires in which we ask them to write open-ended responses about their experiences of collaboration, including both the benefits and the barriers. In addition, over the last several years, I have conducted more than two hundred in-depth interviews with professionals in more than fifty firms, including C-suite leaders in some of the world's largest and most prestigious global professional firms—all aimed at helping to explain the causes and effects of collaboration.

To further dig into the process and challenges of moving from individualistic to collaborative work, I studied a particular firm in depth for more than two years. I chose that firm because its leaders had initiated a strategic change aimed at moving from a "franchise" model to one based on partner-to-partner collaboration. Multiple rounds of surveys tracked hundreds of partners' reactions to the change over time. Interviews with executives, partners, board members, and clients during that time frame helped me to develop insights about the leadership challenges associated with such initiatives.[12]

More recently, I have sharpened my focus on *solutions*. To that end, I have engaged with more than six thousand partner-level professionals, including participants in executive education courses at Harvard Business School and Harvard Law School, partners at many different kinds of professional firms that have invited me to conduct workshops about collaboration, and firm leaders in small colloquia that I organize specifically to discuss my findings. I've also used my speaking engagements in North America, Latin America, Europe, Africa, and the Asia-Pacific region to build an international perspective, and to make sure that my ideas resonate across cultures.

Further, several firms have engaged me on longer-term projects to work with their leadership team, or directly with some of their key partners, to follow through on the ideas that emerged in their workshops. Again, this work has given me the opportunity to focus on the practical—to try out new solutions, and see which ones work under which conditions.

Finally, I trained my research lens on clients. I systematically interviewed clients across an entire grid of divergent characteristics, so that I'd be certain to hear different points of view. Ultimately, the clients I interviewed represented widely varying roles, from the C-suite and boardroom to the procurement department, across different types of organizations, sizes, sectors, levels of sophistication, and geographies. I wanted to know: Did clients care whether their external advisers collaborated among themselves?

My empirical findings showed that the clients paid handsomely for collaborative projects. And yet many of the professionals I interviewed said, in so many words, "My client won't pay for collaboration." How could I make sense of this discrepancy? If clients do intentionally hire and pay for collaborative efforts, what cues do they use to evaluate their advisers, especially when so much of the work gets done behind the scenes? The ability to iterate between clients' and providers' perspectives has helped me flesh out many of the insights in this book.

To make this book as practical and useful as possible, each chapter contains both descriptive and prescriptive sections: *Here's the problem, and here's what you can do about it.* Sometimes that prescription is integrated into the main text; at other times, it appears in separate sections toward the end of the chapter. Very often, I draw on real-world examples in the prescriptive parts of the book: *Here's what we did, and here's how it helped.*

In chapters 1 and 2, I present the firm's perspective. Chapter 1 focuses on what might be called the "money side." My analyses clearly show that revenues, profits, and client loyalty all go up as effective collaboration—especially involving partners—increases. Moreover, firms with strong internal collaboration don't suffer nearly as much during economic downturns as those that are siloed.[13] There are also a host of defensive reasons why smart firms embrace senior-level collaboration, starting—but by no means ending—with a desire to minimize malpractice suits.

Chapter 2 focuses on what I call the "people side" of a firm: attracting, engaging, and retaining your human capital. Many leaders of professional firms now admit that the war for talent is at least as competitive as the war for clients. Most firms are trying to win by hiring experienced professionals away from competitors or even from clients, but few firms are well equipped to successfully integrate lateral hires. This chapter explains how collaboration draws in high-caliber people and allows them to succeed faster, making them more likely to stay. Collaboration also helps you foster greater productivity and loyalty among your current employees, attract high-potential millennials—another challenge that most firms don't handle well—and build "alumni" loyalty in ways that show up on your bottom line.

Each of the next four chapters adopts the perspective of one of four key constituencies within the typical firm. I encourage you to locate yourself on that spectrum of key players, and see whether my analysis and prescriptions ring true for you. Chapter 3 explores the mindset of what I call *solo specialists*—people who have deep subject matter expertise, but haven't had much reason to reach out and collaborate. Perhaps because they confuse collaboration with cross-selling, they express a stubborn professional pride that denigrates anything except absolute expertise-based work, as in, "I went to grad school to work on complex, sophisticated technical (legal, engineering, etc.) problems. If I wanted to be in sales, I would have done a Dale Carnegie course instead."

They may be excellent at what they do, and they've probably built a reputation based on their individual achievements, but they aren't particularly interested in bringing new topics or experts into their professional lives. Yet, it's in their interest to do so, and this chapter lays out some clear steps to get them started on a more collaborative path that will lead to better outcomes than they could get alone.

Chapter 4 moves up the experience curve to the *seasoned collaborator*—the person who understands the benefits of collaboration, but is frequently frustrated by what she or he considers to be an unsupportive context. And in fact, it's rarely easy. For example, to appropriately tailor large-scale solutions, those domain experts must work closely with colleagues in the local market who have deep contextual knowledge. The combination of large, distributed, and global is tricky enough, but the fact that those local experts have their own client priorities in mind greatly complicates the seasoned collaborator's task.

"This is outrageously hard to do," they tell me. "I'm beating my head against the wall. I need some better techniques." That prescription is a core part of this chapter.

Chapter 5 adopts the perspective of what I call, admiringly, the *contributor*. This person may not be on the fast track to the senior ranks of the firm—perhaps for personal reasons, he's decided to devote his precious time to delivering on metrics that are low risk and more controllable, such as billable hours, so he just churns out the standard work that clients request.

Or perhaps the contributor thinks she lacks the personal characteristics that she associates with big-time rainmakers, like charisma and extroversion, so she sticks closely to the local clients with whom she already has strong relationships—and she ducks whenever a big shot tries to pull her onto a key account. Nevertheless, the contributor is among that invaluable cadre of people who actually *get the work done*, year and year out, and they often can make vital contributions in complex assignments on behalf of high-value clients. With the right metrics, motivations, and training in place, the contributor can be "lured" into these engagements, and be among the strongest facilitators of collaboration.

Chapter 6 explores the psychology of the *ringmaster*: the person who has to get all these fractious, talented, and complementary individuals to pull together in the same direction. (If you're one of the firm's leaders, or if you aspire to be, this chapter speaks directly to you.) You need to create a context within which your great colleagues do the right thing consistently and reliably. This chapter explains how to make that happen.

Briefly, there are three things that ringmasters can do to influence behavior in the direction of collaboration. The first involves *measuring* collaboration. (What, exactly, are we looking for, and who is doing it well?) The second involves getting the compensation piece right: an important (but not *all*-important) component. And the third involves using technology in support of collaboration. In each case, I offer suggestions about both design and implementation. If you're looking for a concise and practical introduction on how to foster smart collaboration—a jumping-off point—chapter 6 should be required reading.

My hope is that many readers will find all four of these role-specific chapters interesting and useful—even the chapters that speak explicitly to the needs of a different constituency from their own. Certainly, a firm's senior leaders benefit from knowing what makes those coming up behind them tick. Equally important, those younger people who aspire to move up the ladder should know why the boss acts the way he or she does—especially on the crucial ground of collaboration.

Chapter 7 explores how the lessons and prescriptions in this book apply to complex organizations well outside the perimeter of professional service firms: Do fundamental truths about collaboration apply more broadly?

My answer—which grows out of an in-depth study of a world-class medical research and health care institute—is *yes*. Although doctors and research scientists are very different from lawyers, architects, management consultants, and executive-search partners in some regards, many parallels are clear: they are all highly trained, specialized experts—often with egos to match. They control critical, portable resources (grants for academics resemble client relationships for partners). They've got reputations they want to protect, whether as principal investigator on a high-profile, nationally funded study or guru adviser to a renowned CEO. The academic tenure track resembles the partnership promotion process at many professional firms.

Not surprisingly, then, you see some similar patterns across all these walks of professional life. Are there obstacles to senior-level collaboration in this rarified context? Yes. Are there personal and institutional advantages to overcoming those obstacles? Again, yes.

Chapter 8 reinforces the third perspective: that of the client. The voice of the client surfaces throughout the book, but it's especially pronounced in this final chapter.

One of the most rewarding aspects of my research in recent years has been synching up the perspectives of the professional service firms in which I've spent most of my time with the views of the clients those firms tend to serve. What do clients see when their service providers arrive in teams—helpful collaboration, or costly churning? The answers may surprise you.

Leaders make collaboration happen

I'll close this introduction by speaking directly to the leader of an ambitious, knowledge-based firm who finds him- or herself reading these pages.

Promoting collaboration to benefit your firm is *your* responsibility. To achieve that end, you have to understand the perspectives of your partners (and future partners), and shape your strategy accordingly. If your high-performing professionals are not collaborating effectively today, it's surely *not* because they're stupid or obstinate; it's often because you are holding them to the kinds of short-term metrics that work against collaboration. Investments in collaboration take time to bear fruit, and you and your leadership team are the only ones who have the authority to demand (and reward) institutional patience.

You—ideally in close collaboration with your senior leadership team—are also the only people with the authority to make the necessary interventions to kick-start a more collaborative approach on the partner level, and then to sustain that approach with subsequent interventions that are well timed and well crafted. Those interventions are described at the appropriate times in the relevant chapters.

Be forewarned, though: when it comes to fostering stronger, more efficient, more reliable collaboration within your organization, there is no "silver bullet." The prescriptions in this book are only the starting point for developing a highly tailored, customized strategy that fits your firm's challenges. My prescriptions are a practical and informed point of departure for shaping a multidisciplinary solution to your complex organizational problem—which is, in fact, the same thing your clients need from you.

The firm may not be burning down, but there's definitely the smell of smoke in the air. Given the lead time that is required to build an organization and a culture to foster collaboration, you have no choice but to start *right now*. Should you choose to go down that road, this book provides you with a map for getting there.

$$\left[\ \ 1\ \ \right]$$

The Business Case
for Collaboration

've worked with many individuals and groups in recent years, focusing on the subject of collaboration. Some of those people and firms are relatively new to collaborative approaches—that's why I'm in the room—and they tend to be a mix of enthusiastic and apprehensive: *Look at the upside! But how on earth do we get there?*

Other firms and their leaders are further along the learning curve, but need to improve. (That's why I'm still in the room.) They tend to be battle-hardened, clear-eyed, and even a little jaundiced: *Thanks, Professor, but we've been at this collaboration game for a while now, and it's not yet clear to us that it's worth the effort.*

Somewhere in the course of these two kinds of discussions, I almost always introduce figure 1-1, which I call "Getting Through the Pain Barrier."

Pointing to the left-hand side of the graph, I address the most obvious pain point: at the outset of collaborative efforts, the costs—both actual and perceived—almost always outweigh the benefits, and the gap can be significant. You need to take a leap

FIGURE 1-1

Getting through the pain barrier

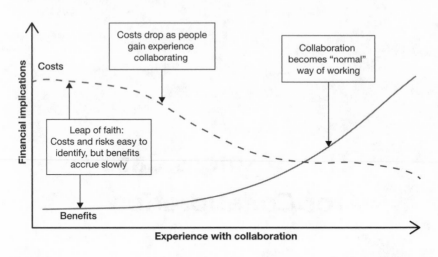

of faith, I tell my audiences. It's easy to point to the challenges of collaboration—as with any new way of doing business—and difficult to see any immediate advantages.

Take the plunge, I tell them, *and hang in there.* The benefits start to accumulate. The trend lines eventually cross, as collaboration becomes the new normal, and their business gets better and better—along all of the metrics that they now track, and also along some new ones.

Introducing the four key outcomes

Let's start with the core premise of this book: collaboration is a significant driver of both financial and people-related benefits for firms. The findings presented here will likely confirm what many professional service firm leaders intuitively already know—but until now couldn't support with hard evidence. If you are one of those leaders, I am confident that you will find here the hard data you need to help convince your partners to drive change within their respective groups or departments.

This chapter homes in on four key outcomes: revenues and profits, client loyalty and retention, innovation, and transparency and risk management. I'll offer a brief preview here, and then return to each of these topics in greater depth, supported by empirical evidence. Let's begin with *revenues and profits*. Simply stated, collaboration across practice groups and geographies is associated with better financial outcomes for firms. For example, delivering sophisticated cross-practice solutions allows a professional service firm to engage with more senior leaders in the client company—becoming the trusted adviser to executives who have not only a greater span of responsibility, but also the authority and budget to hire external advisers to help solve those complex problems.

Multidiscipline client service is significantly more lucrative than more rifle-shot approaches. As additional practice groups serve a client, *each one of them earns more*, on average. In other words, collaborating creates additional value for both the older and newer service providers—and, of course, for their clients.

Looking at longer-term outcomes, we see that collaboration also enhances a professional firm's *client loyalty and retention*. The more partners serve a client, the longer that client remains with the firm, even when an important partner leaves. The relationship is even stronger when those outside multi-expert teams span different departments or offices in their firm, and when they serve multiple contacts within the client organization.

As for *innovation*, collaboration produces more innovative outcomes—that is, solutions that are both novel and useful, and which therefore lead to long-term benefits for clients. Innovation differentiates a service provider from the pack, generating higher profits in the near term and a more sustainable competitive advantage in the long term.

In the realm of *transparency and risk management*, collaboration gives the firm greater oversight of partners' client dealings, thereby reducing the potential for the kinds of misbehaving individuals that professional firms' insurers put into the colorful categories of "body snatchers," "dabblers," and "lone wolves."

All that being said, there are practical limits on collaboration in knowledge-based firms, especially on the business side of the business. These are what I call *boundary conditions*. Collaboration is not a panacea, and there are certainly circumstances—for example, the carrying out of routine, low-cost tasks—in which a collaborative, multidisciplinary approach is not likely to result in the benefits just described. Yet collaboration across other kinds of silos—for example, working together with technology providers, or collaborating across geographic boundaries to take advantage of lower-cost labor in certain locations—may well produce extraordinary results.

Proving it: Collaboration, revenues, and profits

For a professional service firm, the financial benefits of multidisciplinary collaboration are unambiguous.[1] Briefly stated, the more disciplines that are involved in a client engagement, the greater the annual average revenue generated from that client.

Let's return to the simple illustration of this phenomenon first shown in the introduction. Figure 1-2 contrasts the revenue results at three major law firms when one, two, three, four, or five practice areas worked with clients in a given year.

FIGURE 1-2

Strong client ties lead to strong revenue results

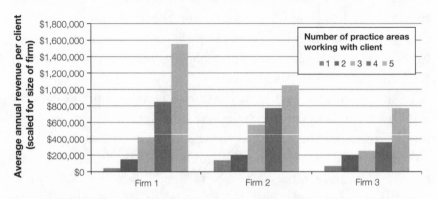

Source: Adapted from H. K. Gardner, "Why It Pays to Collaborate," *American Lawyer*, March 2015.

As you can see for firm 1, average annual revenues triple when two practice groups are involved, rather than one—and that's only the beginning of the upward march of those bars on the graph.[2] As additional practice groups serve a client, the firm can bill a higher amount, and *each group earns more*, on average. That point bears highlighting: *even the incumbent practices earn more when an additional practice joins the mix*. It's absolutely a win-win situation, and this result should allay the fears of professionals who are worried that introducing colleagues will cannibalize their business.

Where does the upside come from? First, having more partners involved with a client gives you more information about that client's needs, priorities, and preferences. Obviously, having more people in the client organization prospecting for work puts you in a better position to generate business. And assuming that your account teams communicate effectively among themselves, you can leverage these insights to spot opportunities that your less-involved competitors might overlook. The data bears out this reality: the more practices involved, the more projects per annum. And the more excellent work you do, the greater your reputation and legitimacy inside the client. As one key account manager explained to me, "Getting more of our people in front of the client more often created a virtuous cycle because we became the top-of-mind adviser. When a new issue came up, we were the go-to team. It simplified life for the client, who didn't need to make a conscious decision or wonder if their colleagues were going to question their choice."[3]

Cross-practice initiatives not only create the ability to generate more work with existing contacts inside the client organization, but they also allow professionals to "move up the food chain" with their client—that is, gain access to more senior executives who have broader responsibilities, larger budgets, and more sophisticated needs. This complex work commands higher margins. "The clients are much more generous on fees," as a partner in another firm commented, "because if it's so big, the deal's got to get done, and they cannot waste time negotiating or nitpicking."

Many clients corroborate this idea. One chief executive recounted for me the story of two different consultants with whom he had worked over time. The first of the two—a more-or-less "pure" marketing specialist—tended to focus exclusively on brand-related issues in his clients' product portfolios. Not surprisingly, his influence never extended beyond the marketing department. The CEO went on to describe one of his current consultants, who had drawn heavily on her cross-specialty experience to recognize that the company's product portfolio affected its offshoring operations, and—in turn—its tax regime. This savvy consultant identified a complex project involving not only marketing, but also operations, strategy, and finance experts. The multidisciplinary project commanded higher fees, and the consultant established a reputation for herself as a go-to person for solving sophisticated challenges.

These kinds of gains tend to be enduring, as well. Especially in an economic downturn, middle managers often find their consulting budgets slashed, but senior executives retain the option of hiring external advisers to help with the projects they deem the most strategic.

For all these reasons and more, cross-practice work is less subject to price-based competition. Whereas clients tend to view an engagement involving single-specialty expertise as a commodity that can be awarded to the lowest bidder, they also generally know that cross-specialty work is complex and harder to pull off. Legal work is a prime example. As the general counsel of one *Fortune* 100 company explained to me, "Despite what they think, most individual lawyers are actually quite replaceable. I mean, I could find a decent tax lawyer in most firms. But when that lawyer teamed up with colleagues from IP, regulatory, and ultimately litigation, I couldn't find a whole-team substitute in another firm."

Figure 1-3, which is based on my in-depth research at one global law firm, provides a slightly different perspective on the same phenomenon. It shows rising revenue per client even as five, six, and seven disciplines become involved. Note that, again, as more practice groups collaborate to serve a client, the average annual revenue from the client (the bars) increases almost exponentially, over and above what each practice would have earned from selling discrete services (the flatter, hypothetical trend line at the bottom of the graph).

FIGURE 1-3

Collaboration versus cross-selling

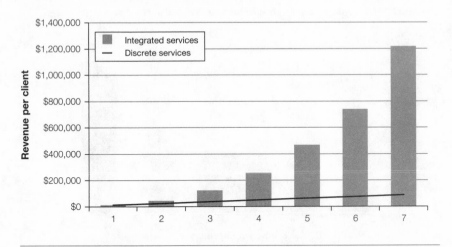

I have observed this pattern time and time again, across a wide array of different professional service firms, including law, consulting, and accounting firms; they may be international or entirely domestic, and range from very small (about a dozen partners) to giant (thousands of professionals). Naturally, the shape of the curve—that is, how much each additional practice adds to the average annual revenue—depends a lot on how narrowly or broadly the firm defines a practice. Nevertheless, providing clients with cross-practice, multi-expert services consistently brings value to the firm.

I also found that client projects involving offices in several countries are significantly more lucrative than single-office engagements. That's because cross-border work is often especially complex and demanding. Think, for example, of issues that arise when multinational companies merge, or when a global company suffers a major cybersecurity breach. Figure 1-4 summarizes the relevant data I've collected on this key point, again in the context of two global professional firms.

Delivering seamless service across national boundaries can be an important differentiator for a firm, which explains why there have been so many international combinations recently—mergers,

FIGURE 1-4

More countries, more revenue

UK- and US-headquartered, international professional service firms

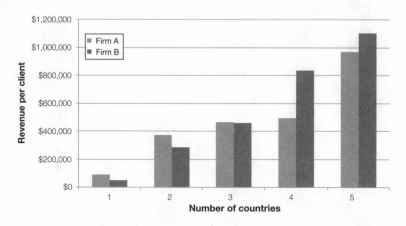

Note: The two firms were of significantly different sizes, although each had a strongly international profile. For the sake of comparison, the graph shows the data after controlling for the size of the firm's overall revenues.

acquisitions, and joint ventures—in the law, accounting, and consulting worlds.[4]

I should state here, however, that the revenue patterns that emerge from these cross-border analyses tend to be "noisier" than they are for cross-practice work. Although cross-border work is more lucrative on average, any given project may defy the trend. Imagine comparing two projects with people involved from four versus six countries—and seeing *lower* revenue in the *broader* project. Why? There may be multiple explanations, ranging from sophisticated strategies to imprudent gambles. A consulting firm with an advanced pricing and work allocation system may be taking advantage of labor cost arbitrage by sending lower-value parts of projects to its offices in less expensive countries, resulting in lower fees for projects that cross more borders. In this instance, collaboration may not boost revenue in the short term, but clients will certainly appreciate the cost advantages and become more likely to send additional projects to firms that help them achieve savings.

In contrast, firms that are early in their learning curve with regard to collaboration may simply be failing to negotiate properly for international work, or they may be suffering from inconsistent quality or reputation in some jurisdictions that prevents them from charging suitable rates there. In such cases, both the firm and its client may still have a lot to learn about providing and using cross-border services.

For professional firms with a domestic focus, cross-geography collaboration—that is, across multiple offices—is similarly beneficial. My analyses show that clients served by multiple offices of a professional service firm generate higher revenues. Obviously, some of those effects are driven by the size of the client—bigger companies with bigger budgets and bigger problems to solve are more likely to need help across multiple locations. But for any given client size cross-office collaboration produces higher returns. And that finding holds whether the offices are a hundred miles apart, as for Philadelphia and Harrisburg, Pennsylvania, or more than two thousand, like Perth and Sydney, Australia.

So far, I've focused on revenues. What about profits? Some skeptical professionals wonder aloud whether multipractice service increases revenues without enhancing profits. One related fear, of course, is that once your firm gets deeply embedded within a client—with huge teams engaged from all across your firm—that client will start using its buying power to demand discounted rates and freebies. Does collaboration translate into doing more work for lower margins?

Initially, this is a real possibility—at least in terms of profit margin percentages. But on average, clients served with multipractice engagements are more profitable in the long run. Here's the typical pattern I've seen across multiple firms: At first, as the account size grows, clients often do exert fee pressure. When firms broaden the scope of their services from one to a few practice groups, discounts rise by several percentage points. Stay the course! Because after that, as the account continues to grow, discounting levels off. At one firm, the pattern of discounts looked like the (slightly disguised) figure 1-5, where the bars represent revenues and the line represents the average negotiated discount. You'll see that the firm lowered its rates by about 1 percent for each additional practice that was added to the client service mix. But once the clients were served very broadly—with seven

FIGURE 1-5

Rate discounts by breadth of service

US-headquartered, international professional service firm

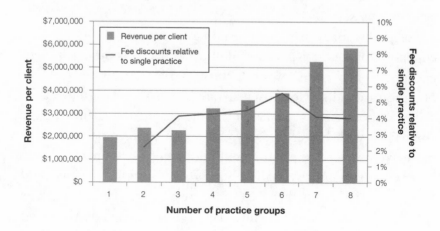

or more practices, presumably deeply embedded in its clients' meatiest problems—the fee pressure dropped back.

Overall, data from both domestic and international law, consulting, and accounting firms shows that the profit margins hold nearly steady (within a few percentage points) as more practices are included in a client's service mix. Do the math: since revenues increase and margins remain about constant, you should earn more profits simply by offering multidisciplinary services to clients. Figure 1-6 shows how this effect works on profits for one US professional service firm.

Naturally the numbers shift, especially depending on which practice anchored the initial relationship. Some firms have what I call a *magnet practice*—the flagship practice that typically engages first with clients, and then draws in other services. For example, in Wall Street law firms, the magnet practice is usually the high-profit M&A group. Not surprisingly, when that practice draws in environmental or employment lawyers who charge lower hourly rates, the margins can be diluted. Don't be fooled by percentages: a slightly lower percentage margin applied to much bigger revenue numbers is still good money.

FIGURE 1-6

More practices, more profits

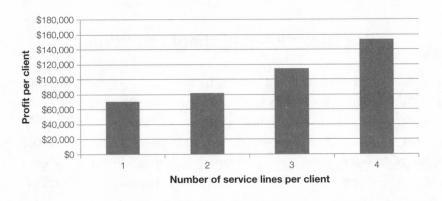

Number of service lines per client

What's more, the slightly lower margins associated with broader client service are almost certainly offset by the lower cost of generating that revenue from existing clients. If firms had a way of capturing the true cost of sales—and most firms don't track this number—they would surely find that it requires less time, effort, and marketing expense and risk to convert an existing client into one that uses the full breadth of services than it does to woo a same-sized, brand-new client away from a competitor.

The bottom line: *Collaboration helps firms grow their profits.*

If you are a professional firm leader, I strongly encourage you to run these analyses with your own data. I am confident that you'll find more or less the same results that I have seen regularly in my work. If you find a different pattern, you should investigate your mix of services and the nature of your internal and external negotiations.

Is collaboration just a way to fleece your clients? Absolutely not. I've shown these graphs to dozens of sophisticated executives, and they realize they need to pay for the value they gain from having their toughest problems addressed. One chief legal officer clarified, "That's what we call strategy! We deliberately wring out the cost from the low-end, single-discipline work because most of it has become commoditized. Then we invest those savings in addressing the high-end work." The CFO of a major multinational summed it up this way: "Margins rise with complexity."

Collaboration and client retention

As mentioned earlier, clients often find it relatively easy to swap individual external advisers with similar replacements from a competitor, whereas finding whole-team substitutes is significantly harder. Over time, a compounding effect emerges: the bigger the team of advisers who have developed a deep understanding of a client (their operations, personnel, technology, processes, finances, risks, and so on), the higher the barriers for a client to consider switching to a new advisory firm.

Intuitively, most firms know the value of these institutionalized clients; I've attended many annual partner retreats where the chairperson's introductory speech referenced their treasured client whom the firm has served continuously since the company's initial public offering in the late 1800s, or some similar story. Surprisingly, though, not nearly as many firms *systematically analyze* their client base to quantify the actual value of collaboration for client longevity, and far fewer take action to address any gaps.

One accounting firm that undertook a massive project to understand this link between collaboration and client loyalty uncovered a surprising truth. The research identified the firm's three hundred biggest clients and found that roughly half were served by a single lead partner, whereas the other half had between two and five different partners who were each responsible for leading client service teams. Next, the research team interviewed each of those clients, asking them, "If your primary service relationship person from our firm were to depart—that is, died, left the firm, or whatever—would you go out to another firm to seek service?"

Look at the results in figure 1-7: of those clients served by a single partner, roughly three-quarters said they'd consider moving their business to a competitor if their relationship partner departed. In contrast, for those served by multiple partners, 90 percent said they'd *remain loyal* to their existing firm.

FIGURE 1-7

More partners, stronger client loyalty

If your relationship partner departed, would you seek another provider?

Single-partner clients | Multipartner clients

28% 72% | 10% 90%

Remain with firm
Seek another provider

Sounds obvious, you say? Then why in most firms are so many clients served by a single partner? Have you looked at the data for your firm? Figure 1-8 shows the recent distribution for the US client base of a major international firm that is ranked in the upper tier of quality by its trade association. If you're following my logic, that graphic should be quite disturbing. In effect, figure 1-7 tells firms how much collaboration promotes client stickiness, and figure 1-8 shows that even well-managed firms aren't taking that message to heart.[5]

From a professional service firm's perspective, the more partners who serve a given client, the more likely that client is to

FIGURE 1-8

Most firms have only one client relationship partner

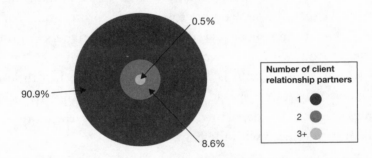

0.5%

90.9%

8.6%

Number of client
relationship partners

1
2
3+

become "institutionalized"—owned, as it were, by the firm rather than controlled by one partner—thus reducing the risk that a departing professional will make off with that client. The effect of large client teams is even stronger if there are more direct contacts between outside and inside professionals, so that no single partner is playing a gatekeeper role and controlling access to client opportunities. Imagine an accounting firm in which the tax partner is getting work from the financial director, the benefits consultants are generating fees directly from the human resource department, and the real estate team has ongoing assignments straight from its own counterparts. Here, even if the partner in the tax practice originated the client relationship and draws on all those other colleagues for his overarching work, he is unlikely to be seen as the sole "owner" of the client, and is therefore not in a position to walk out the door with all the revenues. Stated slightly differently, he'll be less valuable on the external labor market, which may in turn encourage him to keep investing in building collaborative relationships inside his own firm. (The flip side, from the tax partner's perspective, is that because collaboration lowers his external value and chances to jump ship, he'll want to understand what's in it for him. Refer him to chapter 2.)

Of course, even when multiple professionals serve a client, this is no ironclad guarantee that the group can't leave en masse and take the client relationship with them to their next firm. This phenomenon is known as a *lift out* and is increasingly common in professional service firms.[6]

Here's the good news: lift outs are generally constrained to groups working within a single unit. It's far less common for clients who are served by a team of cross-practice professionals to get "stolen" than it is for those served by either sole partners or groups of partners from within the same organizational unit.

To summarize, *breadth is key* when it comes to institutionalizing clients: the more spread out those relationships are across different service lines, departments, or geographies, the more likely the client is to remain with the firm.

Collaboration begets innovation

When clients face a novel issue, they often tackle it with a team. Many read the business press and books on management best practices, and they believe that teams are more innovative than individuals. Not surprisingly, when the task demands it, they expect their advisers to do the same, and collaborate for the sake of generating nonstandard answers.

A growing body of research, including my own doctoral work, supports clients' views that innovation is most likely to happen when specialists team up.[7] For example, a study of 2 million patents and 20 million academic publications across half a century shows that teams are *more productive* than individual scientists, and teams produce innovations that have a *greater impact* in their domain—even in fields like engineering and social science that were historically dominated by freestanding "geniuses."[8] These same authors write, "Surprisingly, even mathematics, long thought the domain of the loner scientist and least dependent of the hard sciences on lab scale and capital-intensive equipment, showed a marked increase in the fraction of work done in teams, from 19 percent to 57 percent."[9] A study of academic legal publications likewise found that teams produced research of far higher quality than that of their solo counterparts; the study's authors posited that the "broadening, diversification, and specialization of legal knowledge" makes a collaborative approach in that field a wise— even necessary—choice.[10]

In my own dissertation research, I found a similar link: consulting and accounting teams that made the best use of their members' different bases of expertise were rated by their clients as performing better along fourteen different dimensions. These teams were also the ones that clients said they'd most likely recommend to others.[11]

And, as noted in the introduction, not every problem requires a new solution. Instead, many problems are more about adapting an existing solution to a client's specific situation. For example, the general counsel for a major manufacturing company noted that his external lawyers advised him, "You need to train every one of your people in a particular compliance area. Roll out a web-based program that all employees will take every year." This gold-plated advice was perfect in the sense of lowering risk and tracking costs. The problem, though, was that only a tiny portion of the client's employees worked in offices—most worked on production lines, without access to computers. What the client needed was more hands-on, classroom learning in the factories and a way to deliver and manually track training in those manufacturing environments. The outside lawyer regrouped with some of his partners who served either utility or hospitality companies (both sectors with similar issues), and also with an unexpected source: professional development experts in his firm's HR function. Together, they managed to transform and tailor his initial solution. The resulting paper-and-pencil "innovation" was more like "back to the future," but it was the nonstandard advice the client needed. This kind of innovation often requires new attitudes, as well as a new configuration of resources, within the firm.

The problem doesn't have to be complex or high-tech to justify a collaborative approach or to call forth a truly novel solution. Consider the following example, which focuses on how the managing director and finance director of a client company judged the merits of the audit firm it had retained. They clearly took for granted the auditor's knowledge of general accounting requirements like the International Financial Reporting Standards (IFRS). As one of them said to me, "Yes, they know IFRS inside and out, and they're expert at applying that to our business. But of *course* they do; that's why we spend all that money to hire them!"

But concealed in this seemingly prosaic context was an opportunity for innovation—a novel solution that ultimately emerged from a junior partner in the auditing firm, who knew his client company well enough to understand that its inventory-tracking system was not as accurate as it needed to be. So rather than reverting to standard procedure—meaning, relying on the existing system—the team went into the warehouse to measure the dust on the boxes to see which inventory was older. High-tech? Hardly. But it was a clever and efficient way to determine where to test and double-check the standard data. Their efforts paid off, uncovering some significant errors that could have cost the company later on.

In this example, the essential collaboration that led to innovation did not take place across disciplinary boundaries, but rather, across both *sectors* (the dust-measuring idea was imported from the retail arena to manufacturing) and *generations*. If the senior partner on the project hadn't been willing to listen to the junior's novel ideas, the project would have been sunk. In short, in serving clients today, it's not enough simply to know how something is usually done; you have to come up with ways that it could be done far better, faster, and cheaper, and ideally in a way that makes the recipient feel special—all of which generally require both specialization and collaboration.[12]

In the introduction, I spotlighted an important challenge faced by most potential clients today: the increasing complexity of the problems they have to solve. As the chief legal officer for one consumer goods company explained, "Almost every significant legal issue I have encountered has been multifaceted in nature. It is rare to have a problem that has only one dimension. Solving these complex issues requires individual lawyers to work together." Likewise, more than half of the CEOs interviewed by IBM in 2012 said that they planned to partner—with other companies, and with professional advisory firms (broadly defined)—in the areas where they most wanted to innovate.[13]

Many of the partners I interview seem to believe the opposite: because their clients are pushing them to deliver better services with increasing pressure on fees, they think they are left with no room for innovation. The increasing power and prevalence of the procurement department in sourcing even complex professional advice especially colors this view.

In that spirit, one consultant approached me after a presentation I'd delivered at his partners' retreat. He said, "I buy what you're saying, but when it comes to my biggest client, I just can't follow your advice about collaboration. Every single matter is decided through an RFP, and my own client is powerless in the face of his procurement department."

But all too often, this is a self-fulfilling prophecy: *There's no room to be creative, so I won't be creative.* By sheer coincidence, I had already lined up a research interview with the global head of procurement for the technology company named by the consultant who had approached me.[14] That interview revealed a very interesting variation on this important theme—a variation that other clients subsequently confirmed: by getting to know their clients' problems extremely well, professional service firms in many cases can refine the terms of the RFP to allow more "breathing room," and therefore more room for innovation.

As an example, the global purchasing head in question told me about one of his company's suppliers that responded to an RFP concerning the move of a particular function offshore. The firm proposed an amended version of the project—one that went well beyond the scope of the original RFP and would draw on multiple specializations within the firm. The client ultimately agreed to this substantial revision in scope. Why? The bidding firm made it clear that its revised proposal constituted a pilot project that—if successful—could be scaled up to have considerable impact across the larger company.

Less dramatically, of course, the bidding firm can accept the relatively narrow confines of the RFP, and—somewhere during the course of the engagement—seek to bring new and relevant capabilities to bear. Remember, it's *not* "Do you want fries with that?" Rather, it's "Here's another dimension of your problem that we can help solve by engaging a team of specialists to innovate on your behalf." Clients still recognize the up-sell, of course, so success hinges on your ability to explain why this case makes multi-expert collaboration the smart choice.

Transparency and risk management through collaboration

Collaboration gives partners greater ability to see their colleagues' work, which lowers the risk of rogue behavior. Although intentional bad behaviors are still relatively rare, they're on the rise. And when they do occur, they can be fatal.

Especially in the legal marketplace, malpractice claims have skyrocketed in recent years. Why? As market pressures increase, some professionals start gaming the system. In an effort to maintain their personal edge and expand their marketability, they begin to promise solutions that they can't deliver. Unfortunately, it's not just the individual who's on the hook in such cases; the firm is also at risk.

In a 2005 study, the American Bar Association came up with a profile of legal malpractice claims over the previous half-decade or so.[15] Almost half of those claims—47.28 percent—were the result of substantive errors by the lawyers involved, rather than failed processes within the firm. The lawyers simply didn't know the law well enough, they didn't apply it well enough, they failed to anticipate the full ramifications of their advice, and so on, and so on.[16] These wrongdoers are what insurers of professional service firms often call a *dabbler*: someone who has a clearly defined area of expertise, but who, when a client brings up a problem outside that area, declines to search out a colleague with the relevant expertise, and instead tries to handle the issue solo.

In the ensuing decade since that study, the problems faced by lawyers and other professionals have only increased in scope and complexity. The chances that an individual professional—even a talented one—can simply bluff his or her way through a complex case have gone down, and the associated risks have gone up. And the phenomenon isn't limited to law firms. "Mistakes have supplanted client misconduct and conflicts," a contact at a professional firm's insurer told me recently, "and the failure to collaborate is a key part of those claims."[17]

Increasingly, as the financial pressure on partners grows, professional firms have had to contend with two other kinds of risk takers, whom insurers also have colorful names to describe. The first is the *lone wolf*, someone who keeps a client account exclusively under his own control. When no peers are allowed access to the account records or personnel, the risk of unauthorized activities increases dramatically. That's the reason, for example, that both Europe's banking authorities and the US Securities and Exchange Commission have recommended that banks require their traders to take two-week holidays, during which their colleagues would take over their books and ensure that everything was as it should be.[18] Ongoing collaboration, spread over time and across multiple team members, would enhance transparency even more.

Finally, *body snatchers* are those partners who attempt to supervise extensive amounts of work conducted by juniors in another department, rather than involve a partner from the subordinates' area of the firm. Often they are motivated by financial metrics that allow them to use lower-cost resources outside their own unit, or perhaps their own resources are constrained. The risk, though, is that they have neither the expertise to conduct appropriate quality control nor the authority over the junior staff to handle issues through formal processes, such as performance reviews. Most human resource officers in professional service firms also recognize that mistreatment of subordinates—for example, overwork or unrealistic demands—is more likely to occur when partners and their juniors are in different departments. By encouraging teams of partner-level peers to collaborate, firms can help to prevent these sorts of errors and abuse.

Nothing can entirely eliminate these risks, of course. But having more informed eyes on the account—one natural by-product of collaboration—can certainly mitigate them.

Are clients *really* willing to pay?

Let's be clear: these benefits flow only if clients are delighted by the value their teams provide. Partners often say to me, "But my client won't pay for collaboration." They point with frustration to clients' growing use of e-billing software that flags activity codes such as "teamwork" or "meeting" or even "internal discussion" on the advisers' bills so that the client can negotiate whether to pay for them.[19]

Ben Heineman, who worked for years as Jack Welch's chief lawyer at GE, has written multiple articles questioning why in-house legal departments should be convinced to buy multiple services from the same external firm. In essence—as he wrote in one of those articles, entitled "Big Isn't Always Best"—the benefits of pursuing collaboration for its own sake aren't immediately clear.[20] No client is willing to pay for inefficient advisers who hand off work among themselves. Clients expect their professional teams to use adequate project management discipline to control quality and avoid billing for unnecessary work, poor work, and rework.

At a more sophisticated level, clients also increasingly recognize that their advisory firms benefit from collaboration, and expect them to "invest" in the relationship. As one general counsel told me,

> I may want to get deeply involved in a matter and ask that there be regular calls that include the whole outside legal team. Some firms are happy to do this. Other wrestle with it and will try to talk me out of it from a monetary or efficiency perspective, saying that it will be costly to have their whole team on the call. I will sometimes push back and say that some of the purpose of the team call is to educate the outside legal team about our business. If a firm wants to have a deep relationship with our business, their people need to know and understand what we do and how we do it.
>
> The more a firm's lawyers know our business, the more we are going to want to hire them. So we have to come to some kind of accord where everybody can participate. But, some of that training should be on the law firm's dime and some of that participation on our dime. If you have that conversation, most firms are willing to find an appropriate middle ground where we are both investing in deepening our relationship and achieving great results.

One of the first hurdles you need to overcome, if you hope to achieve the benefits outlined in this chapter, is gaining your client's commitment to performing collaborative work. Then—as the preceding client commentaries strongly suggest—you have to figure out who should pay for the learning curve that makes such work possible.

Where collaboration may *not* help

Early in the chapter, I acknowledged that many kinds of professional engagements don't benefit much from the collaboration I advocate in this book.

Embracing collaboration typically implies that your firm is trying to move up the value chain. But to the extent that your firm is involved in routine, low-cost tasks—and is likely to remain in that niche—cross-practice collaboration may not make much sense for you. Performing the audit for John's Hardware Store, for example, is not an exercise that's likely to benefit from the involvement of multiple specialists.

Can you, and should you, leave John's Hardware Store behind? Ultimately this is a strategic question, encompassing many issues beyond collaboration per se. Certainly, some contexts warrant placing bets on small, high-potential companies. In places like Silicon Valley, for example, it may well make sense to perform single-office, single-discipline work like reviewing employment contracts or leases, hoping that you'll then land the juicy IPO work down the road. Other times, low-margin work is needed to gain entry or sustain a relationship with large clients. Some people argue that routine audit work in many accounting firms acts in precisely this way—not exactly a loss leader, but the bare-bones work that establishes critical relationships with a client's executives and board that will lead to higher-margin work across other disciplines.

If you decide to pursue single-discipline work, then you need to be innovative and flexible in your approach. It probably requires a different kind of collaboration: for example, your core professionals may need to collaborate with a resource center in a low-cost geography. By the time I worked at McKinsey in the late 1990s, the firm had already set up a knowledge center in India to handle routine or straightforward research tasks; it took well over a decade, but many of today's law firms are following suit. Recently, for example, the elite London-headquartered law firm Allen & Overy set up a center in Northern Ireland staffed by local lawyers to perform tasks related to the firm's M&A work, and the firm's leaders said they hoped to save £10 million over five years.[21] Even small firms are getting into the act, expecting to wring out their costs and price their services more competitively. A raft of legal process outsourcing (LPO) companies have sprung up, providing services such as document review, legal research and writing, and patent reviews that used to be bread-and-butter work for law firms. Your partners must embrace collaboration with these external providers, which requires many of the skills, attitudes, and approaches discussed in subsequent chapters.

And to the extent that you do embrace a migration strategy—that is, using collaboration to move up the value chain—keep in mind that this is likely to create both winners and losers in your firm. Some partners will be threatened by the mandate to move up the value chain. Part of your job as a leader is to help those partners find their place in a new world, and upcoming chapters give some guidance for doing that.

On to the collaborators themselves

In this chapter, I have focused on what many leaders of knowledge-based firms think of first when they mentally run through their firms' challenges: making the firm run better and—by extension—making a profit. Savvy leaders know, though, that they're competing not only to gain a bigger share of the clients' spend and attention, but also to attract and retain the marketplace's most valuable talent. Can collaboration help with this battle, too?

Chapter 2 dives into the topic of people-related outcomes of collaboration.

$$\left[\ 2\ \right]$$

The People Case for Collaboration

Today's knowledge-based firms are increasingly fighting a war not only for clients and profits—as detailed in the previous chapter—but also for talent.

Senior partners everywhere recognize that this war has multiple origins. In many places, increased partner mobility has fostered the emergence of a free-agent mentality. Encouraged by growing legions of headhunters, knowledge workers today have a keen sense of their value in the marketplace, and face far fewer cultural taboos about jumping ship for a more lucrative offer. In some of the hottest markets, it is not unusual for professionals with an in-demand specialty to receive three or more calls *every week* from recruiters or competitors.

In many professional fields—including law, accounting, engineering, and consulting—the entrance of international firms into previously domestic markets has fueled competition for top-end partners. For example, when US firms began their push into London, stories abounded of City lawyers doubling or even tripling their income by joining the first wave of partners to sign up with those newcomers. But despite spending huge sums of money and vast amounts of partners' time and energy recruiting these stars, many firms struggle to properly integrate their lateral hires. My research helps to explain how this failure stems in large part from collaboration problems—and also points to some clear remedies.

But even firms that are not yet facing these kinds of international incursions may experience another kind of pressure that arises strictly from within the organization. Leaders have to be constantly vigilant about their firm's health—broadly defined, to include both financial health and high morale—or risk losing their hottest talent to spin-offs.

Of course, it's partly about recruiting the right people. But just as important, it's about helping them be productive and engaged in their positions. David Maister, the preeminent professional services guru of the last quarter-century or so, observed a number of years ago that there is a "close connection between morale, commitment, and productivity in professional service firms."[1] Research in the intervening decades—much of it focusing on the psychological forces that tend to predominate in the workplace—has confirmed that observation.

Today we have a pretty robust understanding of the complex relationships between collaboration, partners' motivation and attitudes toward their firms, and, ultimately, their retention levels. My own research and survey work, based on a wide range of firms around the world, builds on and extends these findings. As we did with the financial benefits covered in chapter 1, here we look at a complementary data set—hard evidence that makes it clear that collaboration can make an important and unique contribution to building the people resource at knowledge-based firms.

This chapter lays out the case for collaboration as a winning strategy for integrating laterally hired experienced talent and making them more productive, attracting and retaining the best talent (especially millennials), keeping your talent motivated and engaged while they're with you, and even maintaining them as "friends of the firm" when they leave.

Hiring and integrating laterals

One of the biggest challenges in knowledge firms today is recruiting laterals into the firm—and then finding a way to hang on to them and make them productive.[2] Collaboration is essential to this transition, but it has to happen *quickly*: if laterally hired partners are to be successful at their new firm, they have to be sufficiently integrated with incumbent partners and clients *within the first eighteen months*, and preferably sooner. Specifically, two things must both happen in that short time: laterals need to have the opportunity to work on at least a couple of the firm's incumbent client accounts (pitches, if not actual projects), and they need to get help from at least a couple of long-term partners on client work they generate (either with clients they imported, or with new ones). If only one of these scenarios happens, lateral hires are at a higher risk of leaving; if neither happens, they're likely to be gone by their three-year anniversary, as illustrated in figure 2-1.

And note that our analyses are what researchers call a *conservative test*, meaning that we report only the findings that are statistically significant across multiple firms. Partners in two firms

FIGURE 2-1

Collaboration and lateral hires: Two paths

Illustration of empirical research findings based on four domestic and international firms

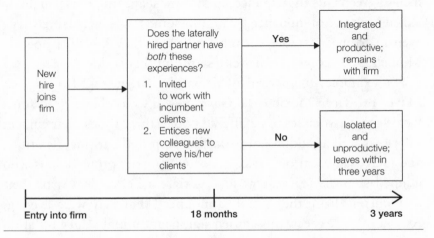

outside my data set—one law and one accounting firm—have told me that analyses of their own data reveal that the critical window for achieving collaboration is as short as *six months* after a lateral partner starts to work! Clearly, firms need a well-designed plan, flawless execution, and clear accountability processes if they expect to help laterals achieve two-way collaboration in such a short time after joining the organization. We'll get to the elements of such a plan—the "how-to" points—shortly.

The upside and downside of lateral hiring

Why are laterals such a hot commodity? Talented problem solvers with specialized expertise are essential for helping the most desirable clients tackle their most difficult issues. This demand leads to some dislocations in the marketplace. For better or worse, lots of firms today are trying to build up whatever practice group is hot at the moment. Take cybersecurity: across most professional sectors, clients are deeply troubled by either the threat or the actual experience of having their data and systems compromised. It's an issue that reaches all the way up to the board level, and experts who can credibly advise on these risks open the doors to senior players at client firms. The result? Every professional firm in this particular game wants to have the best cybersecurity experts in its stable, rather than in someone else's.

Layered on top of this is the breakdown of the former gentlemen's agreements that divided up the landscape into what might be called "spheres of influence." This phenomenon is increasingly true even in formerly stable, localized markets like Phoenix, Bogota, Munich, and scores of other cities around the world.

For example, the arrival of firms like Greenberg Traurig and Mayer Brown in Mexico and Garrigues in Colombia caused some local senior associates to be offered two to three times their current salary (as well as additional perks like preferred parking, flex time, and increased vacation days). Reportedly, many professionals who jumped ship didn't even try to negotiate a better deal with their then current firm; they simply announced that they were leaving. As you might expect, this caused significant initial salary inflation in these two markets, and it forced local firms not only to embrace more sophisticated and institutionalized talent processes, but also to better articulate the general value proposition of working at a local firm. Those strategies may not be enough: most firms in these jurisdictions feel that there is a "new normal" when it comes to salaries and that more poaching—and especially lift outs—will continue to occur.

Even in the elite consulting firms, mobility has increased dramatically. It used to be that the cultural walls at places like McKinsey, Bain, and BCG were so high, and the moats so deep, that movement among peer firms was highly unusual. These days, those walls and moats are far less forbidding. Around 2010, for example, a partner left one of those elite firms to move to a direct competitor. As his exit neared, however, he discovered that his firm's partnership agreement didn't even cover the possibility of such a lateral move; a protracted conflict ensued about his right to cash out shares and other key financial issues. Since then, however, the cultural taboos appear to have weakened, with more such moves in the past few years than at any time previously.

For all these reasons and more, laterals are hot. The problem is that, in and of itself, the strategy of accumulating stars and hoping for the best simply doesn't work very well.

After spending vast sums to build and buy stables of thoroughbreds, extend their geographic reach, and practice breadth, today's knowledge-based firms have reached a sobering conclusion: all that talent can't be harnessed for competitive advantage or profit enhancement *unless they find a way to get partners to collaborate*. To maximize the worth of those expensive individuals, firms must integrate their partners' diverse and distributed knowledge in a way that clients value. But research shows that firms are generally quite poor at integrating laterals in a way that taps their full value.

For example, the Wharton School's Matthew Bidwell—in a study of lateral hiring aptly named "Paying More to Get Less"—looked at six years of personnel data from the US investment-banking branch of a financial services corporation. He found that, despite external hires generally having more education and experience than internal hires, external hires performed significantly worse for the first two years of their employment than workers who were promoted to the same job from within the organization. Furthermore, he discovered that lateral hires were far more likely than internal workers to leave their job—either because they quit or were fired. At the same time, Bidwell concluded, external hires cost the firm 18 percent more in salaries than did their internally promoted colleagues.[3]

Most firms recognize that it takes several years to bring an experienced hire up to speed—even to reach the level of performance they displayed in their old firm, let alone to become still more productive.[4] Yet in the legal sector, for example, the chance of a laterally hired partner staying more than three years is generally no better than a coin toss.[5] One study of leading law firms in London yielded some truly abysmal statistics: fully 20 percent of lateral hires were no longer with their firms one year after joining, and 50 percent had left within five years. The reported average cost of each of these failed hires was something north of $150,000, but most experts in the field suggest that the actual cost of those failed hires—consider, for example, the opportunity costs of partners' time spent interviewing and onboarding them—to be double that figure.[6]

Another problem is the bad assessment of, and an overemphasis on, a candidate's existing book of business. Many firms use a lateral partner questionnaire to gauge the size and value of such a portfolio—and most of them know that they have to discount that book by some percentage. The problem is, *what* percentage? Again, experts—both recruiting professionals and senior leaders who have been burnt in the hiring game—advise that a realistic discount rate applied to a portfolio might be as high as 60 percent![7] So what are you really buying?

Even successes don't come quickly. Compelling data demonstrates that professionals who switch firms are likely to fall off quite significantly in terms of performance, and that it takes them three to five years to climb back to their former level of productivity.[8]

The risks of lateral hiring extend far beyond payroll hits. Obviously, the arrival of a new player on the scene creates a potential threat to the existing partners or would-be partners. Imagine the reaction of the rock-star senior associate coming up through the ranks with expertise A who fully expects to make partner— and then learns that the firm has decided it's more expedient to hire an outsider with expertise A and an existing book of business. That internal rock star can be forgiven for concluding that his or her chances of promotion just plummeted. And is that internal star going to be in a collaborative frame of mind, vis-à-vis the newcomer? Not likely!

In addition, lateral hiring can cause tremendous upheavals in the compensation system, given that the acquiring organization generally needs to pay much more for an individual brought in from the outside in order to compensate them for the risk of changing employers. In US law firms, for example, the pressures associated with lateral hiring are often what lies behind the enormous disparity in compensation between partners within the same firm: although the median spread between the highest- and lowest-paid partners inside a US firm is ten to one (already quite a gap), that ratio swelled as high as a staggering twenty-three to one in one firm where lateral hiring was rampant.

Finally, the biggest risk might be the watering down—or worse—of an organization's culture.[9] Sometimes the addition of employees with different perspectives can be hugely beneficial for firms by opening up new ways of thinking, which in turn open up new opportunities.[10] But unless you're deliberately seeking and hiring candidates with a specific, diverse set of characteristics, you're leaving the evolution of your culture to chance by hiring people who come from firms with cultures radically different from your own. One boutique consulting firm, for instance, added five partners to its existing fifteen during a boom year, but within a year the firm's leader and most of its partners were worrying about emerging fissures and infighting within the formerly harmonious group.

What's the answer? Some industry leaders, such as the law firm of Wachtell, Lipton, Rosen & Katz, have nearly prohibited lateral hiring in an effort to husband their resources and preserve their unique culture (although even that venerable firm has made a few notable exceptions, such as hiring ninety-year-old Robert Morgenthau, whom the *New York Times* has described as "a legendary former prosecutor with a Rolodex as extensive as the Dead Sea Scrolls").[11] Executive search firm Egon Zehnder has a limited ban: it hires from other leading professional service firms, but not from the other executive search consultancies that are its direct competitors. At one point, for instance, forty out of Egon Zehnder's 270 client-facing staff were McKinsey alumni.[12]

Assuming that your firm concludes that the potential upsides to hiring laterals outweigh the downsides, there are a number of steps you can take to better your odds with laterals. They fall into three categories: *analyzing data and preparing the firm*, *assessing the candidate*, and *posthire mentoring and accountability* (see the summary in figure 2-2). Let's consider each in turn.

Analyzing data and preparing the firm

First things first: you need a robust, data-based analysis that forms the business case for each lateral hire. Many firms kid themselves that they've already got such a system in place, but most of the plans

FIGURE 2-2

Three-stage process for hiring and integrating laterals

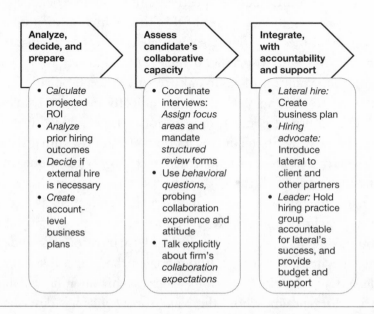

I've reviewed were more about arguments than analyses—which is not surprising, given that they were written by time-pressed partners who hadn't been supplied the relevant data. Instead, engage your financial and business development experts to collect and dissect both internal and market data to calculate anticipated returns on investment (ROI) for each proposed candidate. More specifically, analysts should work with partners in both the proposing practice group and adjacent ones to understand a range of *realistic* scenarios, and then calculate how sensitive the initial projected ROI is to these differing assumptions.

Whether to hire and how many to hire should be based not only on these financial models, but also on strategic factors, such as expanding business opportunities, new offices in specific geographic markets, partner turnover, and newly developed (or growing) practice or sector-focused groups. For each of these factors, you need to analyze current capacity and utilization to reveal whether the emerging market needs can be covered by an existing internal resource. Set the bar high to convince yourself that a lateral is the *only* option.

As the COO of a US-based consulting firm phrased it:

> In at least 80 percent of the cases where a partner requests a lateral hire, our analysis of staffing and utilization data shows that we have spare capacity somewhere in the firm to do exactly that role. Occasionally it requires a slight retooling of a senior associate's skills, but that's a much more certain investment than seeking an external candidate.
>
> When I push the requesting partner, he or she usually thinks that a lateral hire will either be quicker than retooling, or they want to have the individual sitting in their own office for the convenience of communication.
>
> We have now implemented a more formal process for requesting a lateral. In the course of writing up the required business case, the partner often solves his own problem: by conferring with colleagues and gathering data about the request, he often uncovers the necessary expert already in-house. Now our requests are based strictly on specialized expertise that truly doesn't exist here, or on strategic issues

where the firm wants to grow—and the latter are typically instigated by members of the Executive Committee.

So bottom-up requests have fallen enormously, and we haven't suffered at all. Quite the opposite.[13]

Also scrutinize the organization's readiness to absorb a new partner. Is the practice group appropriately leveraged? If you hire a lateral partner, will she have adequate associate support for her business? Has that office or practice just hired a cohort of other laterals who are taking up all the onboarding attention and energy? Your ability to answer these questions ties directly to your ability to help a newly hired partner succeed.

I also encourage firms to run the numbers in another way: Which practice groups, or even individual partners, have successfully built a team through lateral hiring? Gather and review your lateral hiring data from the last five years or so, with a specific focus on (a) who pushed for or sponsored the request, and (b) how well each of those laterals fared, once hired. You may well find a strong correlation between certain partners' or practices' attempts and success rates, in which case you should reward them by giving their future requests greater legitimacy. In contrast, your analysis might reveal pockets of "churn and burn," which strongly suggests that the offending groups fail to strategically consider their hiring requests, use the wrong hiring criteria, or lack the proper ways to integrate laterals once they arrive—a subject that we'll return to shortly.

If you do decide—based on convincing evidence and a sound strategic plan—that a lateral hire is the best option, then you should require a business plan toward that end, as described by the COO cited earlier. The plan should include specific client objectives, along with a named individual who accepts accountability by agreeing to specific deadlines for initiating and completing the actions.

Assessing the candidate for "collaborative capacity"

No doubt your firm already has well-established policies for assessing the merits of a potential hire. So if they're actually getting the results you want, then don't short-circuit the procedures that have proven themselves over time. Use them—but also consider augmenting them with additional techniques that can help you collect evidence about a candidate's *collaborative capacity*.

For example, multiple interviews mitigate the risk of bias from a single opinion. Some firms put interviewees through dozens of interviews with staff members and partners, in multiple geographies and offices. Egon Zehnder provides an interesting example: "Recruits undergo anywhere from 25 to 40 interviews at a minimum of seven different offices on two different continents. If two or more of the interviews result in doubts being expressed about the potential candidate, no offer is made."[14]

Merely setting up multiple unstructured interviews is basically a waste of time, however, because they may or may not unearth critical issues; partners outside the candidate's area of expertise will only walk away with vague impressions of cultural "fit." Instead, making multiple interviews productive requires significant coordination within the firm, both before interviews—in order to figure out which situations and competencies each interviewer will focus on—and afterward, to cover gaps and probe possible weaknesses. For example, in one consultancy, as interviewers meet with a particular candidate, they feed back their points of view and make suggestions about issues that can be probed in subsequent interviews. Eventually, these interview notes should be mined to reveal competency gaps where the successful candidate needs to improve, setting the stage for an integration and training plan for the prospective employee.

In the interview process itself, the current best practice is to use behavioral questions, rather than hypothetical ones. Candidates are asked to describe particular situations they have faced, how they handled them, their personal emotional response, and perhaps what they learned from the experience. For example: "Can you provide me with an example of when you made a bad decision?" Follow-on questions might include: "How did you feel? Did you take steps to rectify it? Did you take the hit or try to minimize the fallout?" Interviewers keep digging based on the candidate's emotional response to each question.

The objective is to break the candidate out of predictable and standard responses, thereby enabling the interviewer to gain a situational context for the candidate's emotional response. This will elicit more insight into candidates' problem-solving approaches and emotional intelligence—skills that are essential for client service. The theory is that the best predictor of future behavior is past behavior, in similar circumstances that were either recent or reflected long-standing behavior patterns.

Some interviewers employ a variation on this theme, engaging potential lateral hires in a discussion about how he or she would recommend responding to an unfolding, real-life scenario at the firm. "To assess their problem-solving acumen," one veteran consultant said to me, "I share a real situation that I'm trying to solve. I probe them for their approach, possible solutions, contingencies, risks, and so on to determine how sophisticated their abilities are."

Obviously, this kind of interviewing is new for many partners. It requires training and practice, which many will resist. But consider this: many of the probing, listening, analyzing, and empathy skills that are essential for interviewing are the *same ones that skilled advisers use with clients* to uncover and understand complex business issues. So the partners who become excellent spotters of collaborative candidates are the ones who are better equipped to discover client opportunities where those candidates' expertise could be useful.

How can you directly assess a candidate's actual collaborative capabilities? My advice is to get the issue on the table well in advance of the interview. If you're using a search firm, make sure those recruiters are extremely well briefed on your demands for collaboration, and are prepared to prescreen candidates for this quality. Candidates should know that they will be closely questioned about their teamwork experiences, as both leaders and followers, and that they shouldn't bother to apply unless they have a strong track record with demonstrable outcomes. Anyone who backs away from these kinds of statements is well weeded out.

Once the candidate is in the chair, and after the kinds of behavioral questions described above have been explored, tackle collaboration directly. Outline the firm's expectations for collaboration with as many specific, successful examples as possible. Be clear about how collaboration will be measured and rewarded, both financially and otherwise. Candidates need to know how much the firm cares about origination versus execution, and exactly how those activities are tracked. Explain the extent to which the firm values and rewards nonbillable activities like mentoring, marketing, firm management, recruiting, pro bono work, and so on. Again, clarity helps to eliminate noncollaborative candidates through self-selection, which is a very efficient way to weed.

Remember, the goal is to find candidates who can not only produce revenue, but do so by drawing on others' capabilities and contributing their own expertise whenever possible. To put it more bluntly: if you want your partners to collaborate, then stop hiring jerks.

Posthire mentoring and accountability

To reiterate my basic point in this section: collaboration is essential to ensuring that lateral hires can become successful and productive. So how, exactly, does collaboration help? Collaborating brings lateral hires up to speed with firm practices, allows them to get to know their colleagues, and, most important, builds trust between lateral hires, their colleagues, and new clients. The trick, of course, is making sure that your firm is set up to foster this kind of lateral-incumbent collaboration.

Most firms already have a nominal "buddy system" for incoming hires, but far too few of those programs actually work. Take these specific steps to create the highest chance of successfully integrating a lateral hire:

- Work with laterals immediately upon their entry to the firm to develop a strategic client service plan that identifies specific opportunities for them to involve incumbent partners. Leaders should facilitate those introductions and make it clear to incumbents that they are expected to participate. Incumbents may be inclined to distrust the newcomer ("She came in here with that other firm's clients; I'll be damned if I'm going to share my clients with her"). That resistance has to be rooted out and worn down.

- Assign a peer mentor for the new hire who will help her learn the cultural norms—the kinds of issues that HR staff would not address, such as people who serve as "honest brokers" in the firm to help connect partners for client or other work. Ideally, this mentor will be someone the new hire connected with during the recruiting process so that they have already established a level of interpersonal trust.

- Gain commitment from a few specific people in the hiring group (practice, office, or ideally, both) who are responsible for introducing the newcomer to several predetermined accounts or other kinds of strategic contacts, as outlined in the prehire business plan. Require them to report on progress—to you, or at least to their practice leader (whose feet you then hold to the fire), not to a functionary in HR. Again, the key here is *specificity* and *accountability*, rather than a vague hope that partners will do the right thing in the midst of all their other pressing concerns.

- Provide a budget for laterals to visit colleagues (even for exploratory conversations) and set the expectation that they will use the full budget (appropriately) within the first six to eight months. Then follow up.

- Hold formal internal road shows for newcomers to present their client work to offices, practice groups, and sectors. Make sure the leader of that group has spoken with the new hire ahead of time, so that he or she can (1) suggest specific people or account opportunities that the lateral can reference during the presentation, and (2) ensure that the highest-potential collaborators attend the road show.

- Invite lateral partners to mentor strong associates. Nothing helps someone learn a subject better than having to teach it.

- Involve the lateral hire in the mechanics of the firm. For example, once the newcomer has settled into the firm—say, after about two years—assign him/her a committee role or another leadership position.

- Make it clear to hiring groups that their ability to hire future laterals will depend on how successfully they integrate each newcomer. You might not be able to see immediate financial results, but you should be able to track activity: How many partners have used the newcomer's expertise to develop joint pitches, to create new IP such as white papers or conference presentations, or to visit clients? When partners do create these opportunities, be sure to celebrate them across the firm. Recognition for good behavior not only encourages more partners to engage in it, but also helps spread the newcomer's reputation as a collaborative, value-adding asset within the firm.

In today's competitive marketplace, your firm's ability to attract, integrate, and ultimately retain lateral hires is a critical competence. Done right, it allows you to boost collaboration across your firm. Of course, "right" requires strong leadership, sustained efforts, and strong commitment from your partners at all levels to collaborate with the newcomers. But the payoff will be worth it— and the alternative is pretty dire.

Attracting and retaining millennials

Now let's look at the impact of collaboration on attracting and retaining "millennials"—people born roughly between the early 1980s and the mid-1990s. Although they currently make up about a quarter of the total workforce, in just over a decade millennials will exceed 75 percent of the global workforce.[15] Any lurking skepticism among the older generations in your firm notwithstanding, it's true: people in this age cohort will eventually take over your firm. Most likely, they will do so with skill and passion, if given the chance.

The first reason for worrying about attracting millennials is purely numbers-driven. Accounting firms, for example, are now facing real talent shortages, because it's increasingly hard to attract high-quality talent into the accounting profession. Having fewer candidates available means that there's a battle among accounting firms to get high-caliber people in at the ground level.

The same can be said about law firms. Fewer and fewer people are applying to law schools. And although the elite law schools are still getting roughly the same number of applicants, the quality of those applicants appears to be dropping. Some data also suggest that many of those scoring highest on the LSATs (US law school entrance exams) don't even apply to law school.[16]

In short, for some of the most venerable professions, there is a real shortage of excellent future talent. This has both near-term and long-term implications. In many professional service firms, leverage is key: firms make their money by charging out junior associates at sufficiently high hourly rates so that profits can flow up to the partners.[17] So you need worker bees for leverage today, to be sure. But even more, you need them to be your partners in a decade. If you're not getting them, that's hugely problematic.

Even if you recruit millennials successfully, however, retaining them presents another kind of challenge—and it's one that collaboration can help meet. On one panel discussion I led recently, a panelist said something striking. "Working with millennials is a really different experience," she observed. "I recently had a young associate chase me down the hall saying, 'Hey—why did you cut this paragraph out of the client document? I thought it was a really good paragraph.'" The associate pushed hard, in the hallway—asking for justification, and challenging the partner in ways that had never happened before, in all her decades of practice. In response to this anecdote, I noticed, many audience members were nodding in recognition.

As this example shows, "collaboration" means something different to millennials. They expect to be more involved in all aspects of the work. They demand to be continually challenged, and to be able to challenge their hierarchical superiors. They expect to get exposure to both important assignments and to top decision makers early in their careers.

In particular, millennials want to work for leaders who empower them, according to a massive research study involving 16,637 millennials in forty-three countries.[18] In fact, for millennials in

North America, Western Europe, and Africa, "empowerment" was the most important attribute they sought in their leaders. What exactly does this mean? The definition of empowerment varies from person to person, but the relevant research suggests that most millennials want to be able to make independent decisions and choose their own paths.

There's yet another cultural factor at work here. The "cult of the CEO" has declined dramatically in recent years, and people today—especially young people—believe in entrepreneurship as a sort of personal value. As they see it, teams are the way that people get to be more creative, to tap into innovation and be entrepreneurial.

Millennials also value a good work-life balance. Again, the ideal balance varies from person to person, but many millennials seek flexible hours and enough leisure time in their personal lives. Well over half of millennials prioritize being able to spend time with their families, and nearly 50 percent said that they would be willing to sacrifice a well-paid and prestigious job to improve their work-life balance.[19]

This does not mean, however, that millennials expect simple nine-to-five workdays. In fact, many want fast-track careers with constant promotions, and are open to working harder—for longer hours and under more stress—to increase their chances for career success. This is important for firms to understand: millennials often seek out flexibility as a way of achieving their desired work-life balance, rather than simply working fewer hours. As one associate noted in our interviews, it is more about decision than balance—that is, being able to make the personal choice about what to sacrifice in a given situation, such as pursuing a professional opportunity instead of taking a long-planned vacation.

Taken together, the implications of these findings are clear. If your partners insist on operating in a siloed, anticollaborative way, they're probably going to lose some of their most valuable young associates quickly.

So let me suggest two ways that a firm can proactively attract, retain, and lead millennials.[20] Both of these approaches present a double benefit. First, they address millennials' preferences for involvement, challenge, empowerment, and flexibility, as just described. Second, they enhance the collaboration skills of this younger generation of professionals, so that they're both technically prepared and psychologically inclined to engage in collaboration when they make partner.

The first is what I describe as a *coordinated work assignment system with "free-market" backup.* Why are both centralization and decentralization important? First, having a coordinator who assigns projects to associates addresses millennials' fears of lacking development opportunities, which is especially important early in an associate's career, when he or she may be nervous about building a professional network within the firm. Meanwhile, the free-market corollary provides continuity and choices along the way. If a partner and associate find a mutually beneficial working relationship, they can carry on. But juniors can also satisfy their entrepreneurial bent by seeking new relationships.

The law firm of Ropes & Gray addresses this issue particularly well. They have a system in which associates fill out weekly reports about their work—what they are currently working on as well as how much time they have for new work. Associates are able to request specific types of work, which coordinators try to find for them; they are also asked to assess how many new matters they want to take on. Both aspects of this approach enhance millennials' feeling of autonomy and being able to maintain a work-life balance. It also offers associates their desired development opportunities, by allowing them to request and pursue work in certain practice areas of their choice.

A supplementary free-market backup system will further help to address associates' preferences for flexibility and influence. Giving associates the opportunity to maintain relationships by working repeatedly with certain partners helps to strengthen their networks and reputation. As one associate noted: "When you get to choose which partners you work with and what to work on to some extent, you feel more engaged." Engaged associates with strong internal networks are more likely to stay longer and be more productive. Over the longer term, these relationships become the foundation for partners to develop a pipeline of strong contributors for their clients, which is a core component of a highly collaborative firm.

The second approach I advocate in this context is an effective *pro bono program*, which can address several key concerns of millennial associates. First, it can satisfy the desire on the part of young people for challenging work. By carefully doling out pro bono opportunities, a firm can ensure that associates work on issues that give them increased responsibility and experience in areas that excite and challenge them.

Second, because there is no pressure from a paying client, pro bono cases are an opportunity to give associates more independence—fostering their sense of autonomy and underscoring the fact that they have the flexibility needed to maintain a work-life balance. In addition, by allowing associates to explore areas beyond their practice group, pro bono work can counteract a common millennial fear of getting pigeonholed, while at the same time building up a knowledge base that will enhance their ability to collaborate on cross-discipline projects. Finally, a firm can use an associate's performance on a pro bono case to assess and improve his or her people and project management abilities—both important underlying competencies for effective collaboration.

Are there less sweeping steps that a firm—particularly a smaller one—can take to address the concerns of millennials? Yes. These might include, for example:

- **Giving better feedback.** Millennials crave a sense of knowing how they're doing. Train professionals at all levels how to give effective feedback—specific, clear, and understandable—as well as how to receive it and how to act on it productively.

- **Developing a culture in which managers—partners, senior associates, staff members—feel not just empowered but obliged to give informal feedback.** Goldman Sachs is credited with the saying, "Feedback on the run is better than none." Even if the feedback feels rushed or incomplete, it's better than allowing someone to repeat errors unknowingly.

- **Focusing on flexibility.** Firms hoping to appeal to millennials' desires for a better work-life balance might consider ways in which they can offer increased scheduling flexibility—for example, expanding telecommuting options. Again, millennials don't necessarily believe they should be allowed to work fewer hours, but they want more control over the hours they do (and don't) work. Skills for this kind of virtual working make cross-geography collaboration smoother as well.

Making today's ranks more productive and more loyal

In this section, let's focus first on why fostering collaboration among today's players, at all levels, is good for the firm. Again, "good for the firm" is less about feel-good outcomes—although there's nothing wrong with those—and more about positive financial and strategic impacts. I'll highlight three such outcomes: commitment and belonging, goal alignment, and what I call "meaning and mastery."[21]

Commitment and belonging

Decades of psychology and sociology research show that the higher the number of formal or informal connections between individuals and their colleagues, the more those individuals are committed to both their job and their employer.[22] The point is worth emphasizing: employees who work more in teams develop a stronger psychological attachment to the organization, with the result that they tend to see the firm as an important part of themselves.

Have you noticed how some of your colleagues say things like, "We are looking to grow in the X market" or "We take it seriously when a partner says Y"? In organizational behavior research, those sorts of "we" statements are a strong predictor of not only a person's desire to stay employed in an organization, but also his or her willingness to engage in critical firm-building activities like mentoring, recruiting, and management tasks.

My own survey and archival research confirms that many knowledge professionals' motivation, sense of belonging, and ultimately retention rates increase as a result of their collaborative experiences.[23] Many partners who had participated in collaborative client engagements reported that the most important benefit for them was the opportunity to meet new colleagues or deepen existing relationships. For example, one respondent wrote about "the camaraderie that comes with working as a group." Conversely, another welcomed collaboration because otherwise "being a partner can feel quite lonely sometimes."

Partners also mentioned how collaboration helped them feel supported in their work. For example, one wrote, "A problem shared is a problem halved—it is reassuring to have the right expertise on hand. I feel more supported and less anxious about the responsibility I carry." Still another answered, "I'm more engaged as part of a team."

That respondent was speaking to specific circumstances, but our empirical analyses show that it's fair to extrapolate to a bigger picture. We have compelling statistical evidence across firms that people who collaborate more—that is, participate in substantive client work with a greater number of colleagues—not only stay longer at their firms, but are more financially productive while they're there.

And committed, collaborative partners almost certainly generate positive trickle-down effects, too. When partners are better at collaboration, they are more likely to involve more junior partners and senior associates in substantive client work—not delegation of the "do this discrete task and return it when you're done" variety, but rather, engaging smart minds to help solve complex problems. It's not just taking their ideas as background for top-to-top discussions, but exposing those juniors directly to real-life clients. Juniors on those sorts of teams not only get increased opportunities to learn and demonstrate new capabilities, but also receive greater mentoring. Each of these aspects, in turn, enhances the retention of both high-performing associates and young partners.

Goal alignment

The more contacts a person has within an organization—such as the kinds of relationships that emerge from working on deal teams or joint pitches—the more strongly that person will believe in and accept the organization's values and goals. Senior leaders often bemoan their partners' references to "my" clients instead of "our" clients. Collaboration could be the remedy: collaborative experiences motivate people to move beyond seeing themselves as a "franchise," and instead view themselves as part of an interdependent team.

Knowledge-firm partners often volunteer this perspective when responding to my survey questions about their personal experiences of collaboration. One wrote, for example, that he valued teamwork with fellow partners because it produced "the feeling that colleagues and I are working towards a common goal, namely the success and prosperity of the firm as a whole."

Another observed that by "working together as a team, your sense of pride and accomplishment is much higher." Collaboration across internal boundaries—such as practice groups, business units, or offices—breaks down the oft-decried (but too rarely countered) "silo mentality."

Meaning and mastery

Another way that collaboration among partners can increase motivation and productivity is by giving people a broader perspective on clients' problems and a deeper understanding of how their specialty contributes to a bigger solution. Psychological research has convincingly demonstrated that when employees feel that their work has meaning and is important to their organization—and by extension, to clients—then they exert more effort and become more committed, both to the team and to the organization.[24]

In a study that sought to identify the key differences between high- and low-performing teams, the Gallup organization asked 1.4 million employees from fifty thousand teams questions about everything from mission and purpose to pay and career opportunities. Next they picked out the statements that high-performing teams agreed on, but others did not. At the top of the list: "At work, I have the opportunity to do what I do best every day." Teams whose employees "strongly agreed" with this statement were 44 percent more likely to earn high customer satisfaction scores, 50 percent more likely to have low employee turnover, and

38 percent more likely to be productive.[25] Deloitte tested Gallup's findings by having a sampling of their own teams fill out a six-item survey. Again, the employees from the highest-performing teams all agreed with a modified version of the same statement: "I have the chance to use my strengths every day."[26]

In response to my surveys, partners frequently mentioned their ability to learn from their peers during collaborative work. Broadly, the type of learning people talk about falls into two categories: content and process. Respondents reported gaining "knowledge about what other parts of the firm are up to, as well as market opportunities"; reaching a "broader understanding of what our client's business is, and which individuals to target for a particular business proposition"; and "learning more about nuances of other colleagues' business lines."

Beyond content knowledge, partners also mentioned developing their professional capabilities—for example, enhanced skills in processes such as problem solving, preparing for client pitches, and communication—through collaboration.

How to foster employee productivity and loyalty

The preceding examples may have implied that collaboration automatically generated these benefits, but in fact, it's only *excellent collaboration* that ensures them. If partners simply call together a team and divvy up the work assuming that "the sum equals the total of the parts," the benefits are far from assured. Worse, ineffective and uncoordinated group work wastes time and demotivates people.

You can increase the odds that your partners are equipped and willing to lead their collaborative efforts in ways that generate the maximum returns. How?

- **Create a firmwide approach for effective project launches.** McKinsey, for example, has a format in which a leader is expected to kick off every new project by briefing the team on the client and the project objectives, and then clearly discussing how each person's piece fits into the bigger picture. Teams also spend some time getting to know each other's work styles, strengths, and development areas. This step—which can take less than half an hour if the members of the team are already familiar with each other—is essential for aligning members' goals, helping them know where to turn with questions (which avoids the leader's becoming the sole-source bottleneck), and allowing them to see how their specialty contributes to a bigger solution. Develop a template, train partners and senior managers how to use it, and then give the system teeth: withhold their expense code until they actually conduct the project launch.

- **Facilitate personal within-team interactions.** People won't build relationships or feel the benefit of peer support unless they have the opportunity to interact during collaboration. Provide a travel budget that allows members some face-to-face time—ideally, early in the project, when they need to establish trust. Throughout and at the end of the project, a modest celebration fund will encourage teams to focus on their wins. These interactions enhance members' sense of pride and accomplishment, boost firm morale, and build the "glue" that is the essence of a collaborative culture.

- **Embed explicit learning processes.** Taking a cue from elite military units, the best team leaders use the time right before the celebration event to conduct a short after-action review (AAR) to boost team members' learning from both mistakes and successes.[27] AAR is a form of group reflection; participants review what was intended, what actually happened, why it happened, and what was learned. Critically, the intent is to learn rather than blame, and to prompt the sort of reflection that makes learning possible.[28] As a firm leader, you should model this behavior, and hold your partners accountable for doing it, too.

- **Provide a technology platform for sharing information.** It should be easy for collaborators to see each other's work in progress and to share knowledge about the project. This transparency helps foster a sense of common purpose by giving participants a deeper understanding of the issue and how various pieces intersect; it also aids learning as participants get exposure to others' ways of thinking—not simply their end results (more on this topic in chapter 6).

Building alumni loyalty

Your firm can't and won't retain everybody. (The odds and the economics are against it.) But a collaborative approach is likely to engender their ongoing loyalty even after they have moved on—and this loyalty can be of real value to your firm.

How does collaboration play a role in this? Simply stated, somebody who feels tightly tied into the firm is going to behave as a friend of the firm after they've left. McKinsey—my former employer—never releases its numbers, but long-standing industry lore has it that the firm derives a large majority of its revenue through its strong relationships with its alumni. McKinsey also touts its alumni network, including a database of more than twenty-seven thousand former consultants, as a major benefit for potential recruits.[29] Here's how the firm's website puts it:

ALUMNI—A COMMUNITY FOR LIFE

As profoundly stimulating as it is at McKinsey, people do leave. We're OK with that.

In fact, we're proud of what they achieve as global leaders. Around a quarter of our alumni have started their own entrepreneurial ventures, and more than 400 are CEOs of organizations with revenues north of $1 billion.

We think it's great that there's a lot of McKinsey in places other than McKinsey. *Because of the collaborative, supportive nature of the culture, people here make friends for life.*

Our alumni number nearly 30,000 and work in virtually every business, public, and social sector in 120 countries. Through formal events and informal networking, former McKinsey consultants make and sustain professional relationships. For those alumni who are interested, we regularly communicate via e-mail, bi-monthly webcasts, LinkedIn, and surveys through the McKinsey alumni website. This dynamic network is a lasting benefit of a McKinsey career.[30]

The accounting firm of PwC counts more than a hundred thousand former employees in its alumni network, and the firm reaps many benefits from staying connected with them. First, its communities of practice—which include alumni—help the firm identify new trends and connect with potential clients. Second, PwC has created a new class of what might be called "semi-alumni"—that is, people who no longer work full time with the firm, but return to work for short stints during especially busy periods.

The prescriptive point here is to make sure that people feel enough affinity with the firm while they're with you that after they leave, they remain eager to share expertise, contacts, and other resources. Collaboration helps instill this perspective: if they have been part of a strong, collaborative team, then that kind of identification can be enduring. However, it probably lasts only if a few other essential factors are in place:

- **Clarify expectations.** If you have an up-or-out promotion system, make it clear from the moment you start recruiting that most people don't make partner.[31]

- **Keep people informed with honest feedback about their progression.** When it becomes evident that they're not on track, give them a choice (if possible): "Up your game to these specific standards by showing improvement in these specific ways, or start looking for another place." Feedback should never be a surprise.

- **Keep communications positive but realistic.** McKinsey has a clear mantra that even people who don't succeed at the firm are still "winners," but that they need to find a place where they can leverage their skills better or thrive in a different environment.

- **Give people time to search for the next opportunity, and help them find positions that fit their skills.** Firms find it mutually beneficial to place leavers with existing or desired clients, but the sophisticated ones know that having employees leave on good terms is the most important aspect.

- **Allow the person who's leaving to control the message.** At McKinsey, most people left for "an exciting new opportunity." Except to a few close friends, perhaps, it was never clear whether leaving had been their choice or whether they were managed out. And it didn't matter, because by the time they left, they really did have a great place to land.

Those five steps are critical for helping to translate the positive experience people had while collaborating as your employees into lasting relationships after they leave your firm. Chances are also good that if your firm's culture and talent management systems are robust enough to support this sort of alumni-building program, they will also help to foster collaboration before people consider leaving.

Moving to the other side of the table

Here's a key takeaway from this chapter: collaboration doesn't just make people *feel* as if they are in the right place. In fact, it's a self-fulfilling prophecy. Collaboration makes the "fit" better, makes the hard work more efficient and effective, and thereby makes the firm more successful.

The many specifics in this chapter—the how to's—may lead the reader to believe that embracing collaboration is little more than a thinly disguised strategy for getting more work out of people. Far from it! Collaboration can be inspirational, motivational, and even joyful. A management consultant recently told me about his experience pitching new business. He had teamed up with a fellow partner, and the two of them made it their mission to go after some very high-profile potential clients in faraway parts of Australia. He said that he had the courage and fortitude to do this only because he had teamed up with somebody—together they felt braver, and had a much higher risk tolerance. "It certainly didn't always work," he said, smiling at the recollection, "but even when it didn't, she and I always ended up at the pub, laughing it off over a couple of beers. Whereas if I had suffered that same rejection on my own, I *for sure* wouldn't have gone to the next pitch."

This is a good preamble to the chapters that follow. The chapters thus far have adopted the firm perspective: Why should the firm worry about and invest in collaboration? The next four chapters look at the same question from the other side of the table: Why should key individuals within the firm bet on, and invest in, a collaborative approach?

We start in chapter 3 with what I call *solo experts*: those individuals who have already demonstrated their worth, are reasonably confident in their ability to sell as many hours as they want based on their own expertise, and need to be persuaded that collaboration will open new opportunities for them.

Collaboration and the Solo Specialist

C hapters 3 through 5 focus on individual cohorts of collaborators—or potential collaborators—within the firm. This chapter's subject is what I call the *solo specialist*. This professional, usually in the middle or upper ranks of a knowledge firm, has made a reputation for himself based on demonstrated expertise in a particular niche. He has a solid client roster that depends on him for his particular skills and he is the go-to person within the firm for client service in that specialty.

Let's suppose that this description fits *you*. Let's further suppose that you're pretty much satisfied with the status quo, and that you're not inclined to disrupt your well-oiled machinery by introducing collaborators. Of course you delegate to underlings, because you appreciate the value of their leverage, but you don't involve peers from other disciplines unless the client problem truly demands their specialized knowledge. In other words, when pushed, you can and will collaborate, but you don't see the point in doing so proactively.

In this chapter, I am out to change your mind. I argue that to keep growing and prospering, you need to bring colleagues into contact with your clients. In the long run, you're going to need them to do the same for you. As the saying goes: *What got you here won't get you there*.[1]

Alternatively, let's suppose that you're a senior leader in your firm, and when you see the phrase *solo specialist*, you know exactly whom I'm talking about. You have a number of them in your ranks—thank goodness. They are reliable revenue generators, and they continuously help buff your firm's reputation in a very competitive marketplace. They have a solid franchise in that marketplace, and they work it well. Put a little more baldly, they control large chunks of your firm's key client relationships. Should you risk upsetting your solo specialists, and disrupting their proven formula, by encouraging them to collaborate? Do you, as a firm leader, have a longer-term obligation to broaden and deepen relationships with the clients in question?

As we will see, the answer to these key questions is clearly yes.

Can the solo specialist benefit financially from collaboration?

Let's begin with the punch line. My research clearly shows that *rainmakers who collaborate—that is, who share the work that they originate—end up with significantly bigger books of business than those who hoard work.*

To illustrate how collaboration enhances a professional's ability to generate business, let's compare the very different paths taken by two professional firm partners—real-life people, by the way— who had a lot of superficial similarities: same-aged men who had worked for the same amount of time in the same practice area at the same firm, had graduated the same year from law school, and billed about the same number of hours per year. Take a look at the two unequal-sized spider webs depicted in figure 3-1.[2] Each dot on the diagram represents a partner in their firm, and the lines between them indicate that they've spent at least fifteen hours that year working together on a specific client project (not merely working on separate projects for that client).

FIGURE 3-1

Collaboration and business development

Two (nearly) identical professionals: Same practice, graduation year, time with firm, annual hours billed

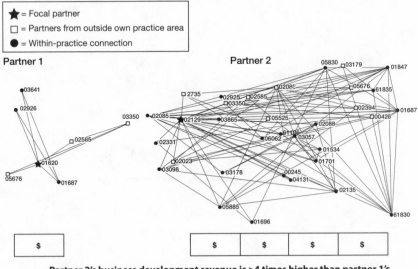

Partner 2's business development revenue is >4 times higher than partner 1's

What's going on here? They billed nearly the same number of hours in a given year, but—as the diagram shows—they spent those hours very differently. Partner 1 brought six other partners into client work he generated, half of whom were from outside his own practice area, as indicated by the square dots in the intersections. (A round dot indicates a within-practice nexus.) Partner 2, by contrast, involved more than thirty other partners in his client work, two-thirds of whom were from outside his practice. Clearly, partner 2's cross-practice approach paid off: total revenue that year from his clients was more than four times higher than the revenue that partner 1 generated from his client base.

Figure 3-2 carries the analysis forward over time. In this case, we're comparing two accounting firm partners who, again, are very similar according to key demographic and professional measures. The big difference is that partner A (top) starts in 2011 with a larger network, and then continues to increase the number of partners that he works with. As shown, revenues from clients where he's the lead partner increase

FIGURE 3-2

Impact of collaboration and network size on revenue over time

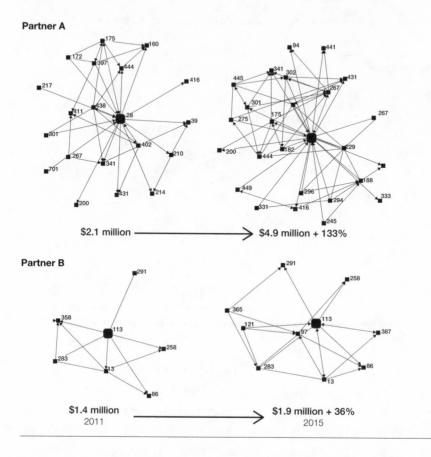

by 133 percent over the next four years. In contrast, partner B's network is smaller to begin with and grows only marginally; as a result, the revenues associated with the clients where he's the lead partner increase only 36 percent between 2011 and 2015. These fairly simple figures can't tell us whether collaboration led to the increased revenue or was a result of it. But that correlation is worth investigating.

My research examining these kinds of outcomes over a decade shows a clear causal pattern. Solo specialists who systematically involve other partners in their work benefit by significantly growing their books of business in ensuing years, even after controlling for the size of the solo specialist's book in the starting year. In other words: no matter how much work the partner generates this year, if she refers some of that work to other partners, especially partners outside her own practice group, then her origination amount will *increase significantly the next year,* and more so than that of her peers who hoard their work. Again, this pattern holds, even after controlling for other factors that are likely to affect individual billings, such as one's office, practice group, organizational tenure, and previous year's billings. I've now replicated these findings using data from multiple professional service firms that vary in terms of field, size, geographic scope, and compensation system.

If you're in a sophisticated firm that assesses your performance in terms of profitability, collaboration helps there, too. Figure 3-3 summarizes research on this issue, in this case drawing on the operating results supplied to me by a US domestic professional service firm. As you can see, net revenue—let's call it "profit" for simplicity's sake—clearly increases based on the number of additional practices or services offered to a client by the lead client partner (or team of lead partners).

What about the impact of the number of other people involved? On average, a strong correlation exists between net revenue and

FIGURE 3-3

The value of including more practice areas

Total profits generated by lead client partners based on service breadth

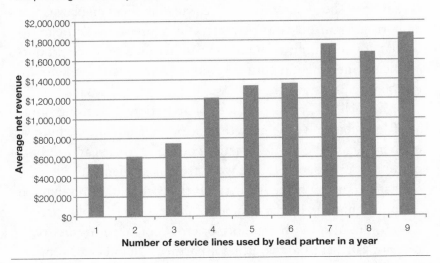

FIGURE 3-4

Total profits generated by lead client partners based on the size of their network

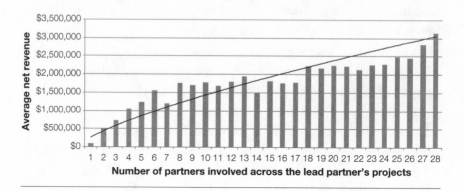

the size of a lead partner's network (which I'll define here as the number of partner-level collaborators involved across the lead partner's projects in a given year). Figure 3-4 summarizes the results of my study of this question. Again, the results are not perfectly correlated, but the trend line is powerful.

Finer-grained analyses can distinguish the impact of building business with existing versus new clients. The biggest effects on subsequent-year revenue come from cross-practice collaboration in the context of a solo specialist's *existing* clients: in other words, the more she involves partners from other practices this year, the more money she generates from her current clients next year (see the bottom right box on the matrix in figure 3-5). You can also see that collaborating with partners in her own practice produces significant incremental future revenue from existing clients (top right, figure 3-5).

For *new* clients, cross-practice collaboration is a strong predictor of long-term revenue growth (bottom left quadrant), but even collaborating with your in-practice colleagues this year will boost your ability to generate future work from new clients (top left).

What's going on here? It turns out that origination revenues are determined not just by the number of partners that a solo specialist involves, but also by the number of cross-practice *projects* sold in one year. Further analysis, using a partner's "number of projects"

FIGURE 3-5

Effect of collaboration on subsequent-year business development revenue

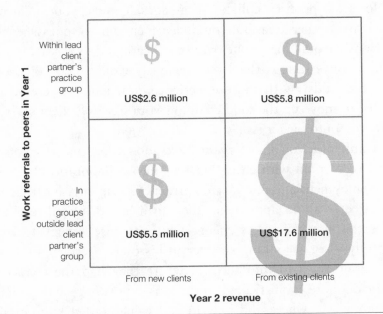

Within lead client partner's practice group

US$2.6 million

US$5.8 million

In practice groups outside lead client partner's group

US$5.5 million

US$17.6 million

Work referrals to peers in Year 1

From new clients

From existing clients

Year 2 revenue

instead of "number of collaborators" as the independent variable in year 1, shows that this factor, too, significantly predicts the specialist's origination revenues for the following year. In other words, solo specialists benefit not just from selling a few huge projects that involve dozens of colleagues—such as major M&A deals, or the kinds of postmerger integration projects that are the domain of the very top-end rainmakers—but also from building up their practice by selling a greater number of smaller, multipractice projects.

There are a couple of explanations. The simplest is obvious: delegation creates opportunities for leverage. The more work you can hand off, the more time you can spend prospecting for new work. And of course, by building a smart team, you're creating a scouting unit that can better understand the client's needs and seek out novel opportunities. A second explanation may be a little less obvious, but even more important: by collaborating, you're *learning*. As you come to understand other practices and how they add value to clients, you gain the ability to have broader strategic conversations. You not only learn the jargon and assumptions of other domains, but you also gain a whole new set of lenses through which to examine your clients' problems.

No, cross-practice collaboration doesn't make you an instant expert in another area. But you *do* learn enough to spot issues that previously would have gone over your head, and to at least initiate certain conversations that you previously would have considered out of bounds. With more experience, you gain the confidence needed to move up the food chain, as your existing client starts to draw you onto bigger issues.

Meanwhile, you make *them* look good too. One tax consultant I've worked with eased her way into collaboration by using her employment and real estate partners to help advise her client's tax director about approaches their firm had delivered to clients in related industries. The client—who was wise enough to listen carefully—began looking smarter in his own meetings, and over time drew the trio into settings where they had the chance to advise on more sophisticated work. This exposure gave them more insights about where and how to add value, and they continued growing the scope of expertise and practices involved.

Perhaps it goes without saying, but revenues from this client have soared.

The real and perceived obstacles to collaboration

The data presented earlier begs an obvious question: If collaboration holds the potential for such huge gains, then why do so many partners resist it?

The surveys I conducted with thousands of professionals across a wide range of firms point to a number of answers.[3] First, these gains take some time to materialize: it's not as if a partner's daily rate jumps the first time he or she completes a complex transaction. Second, there are barriers and risks involved. So when successful solo specialists run their personal cost-benefit analyses, even if only loosely or intuitively, they may well decide that collaboration is unlikely to pay off—at least not in the short term, in which they're largely driven by the pressures to boost their own chargeable hours and books of business. It's the tyranny of success: for the solo specialist, high expectations never go down. They stay high, or get higher.

Can you change that cost-benefit analysis? Yes, by lowering the impediments to collaboration and reducing its inherent risks. Let's look at each of the six barriers revealed by my survey research. Although the relative importance of each one shifted from firm to firm, they tended to show up in almost every context I studied. First I'll draw on the comments of people who have actually wrestled with them. Once I outline the barriers, I'll return to offer advice for how to overcome each one.

Competence trust

Simply stated, from the solo specialist's point of view, *competence trust* means *Can I trust that the partner I bring into my client relationship won't screw up that relationship?* Even if you're not anxious about a colleague's purely technical competence, you might worry about his messing up in more nebulous ways—for example, not responding quickly enough to your client.

The farther someone's expertise is from your own, the harder it is to accurately judge that person's competence—and the harder it is for you to trust him or her. When knowledge professionals from different practices work together, they may initially have to bridge dissimilar "thought worlds"—for example, new jargon, differing assumptions, or unfamiliar approaches.[4] That kind of bridging requires both a leap of faith and, in many cases, shared experiences and the passage of time.

Concerns about technical expertise often show up in firms that have grown through recent mergers—which, these days, is an increasingly common phenomenon. Collaboration faces a structural hurdle: partners often doubt that everyone who got scooped up into the combined firm would have passed the test if they'd been interviewed individually.

International expansion also can fuel trust concerns, because cross-cultural misunderstandings or stereotypes can feed into the story line: *People from [fill in the city, region, or country] are not as hardworking as our domestic partners, or not as well trained, or not likely to work on weekends, or won't interrupt their family holiday to return a client call*—or just about any other generalization that feeds a nervous partner's anxiety about cross-border collaboration.

When talking about collaboration with solo specialists, I often hear these sorts of worries about professionalism, responsiveness, and other client-handling protocols. Research undertaken by Harvard's Center on the Legal Profession confirms that lawyers *ought* to worry about this issue: chief legal officers reported that they are likely to reduce work given not only to the specific lawyer who underperformed, but that a majority of those penalties (54 percent) encompassed the entire team and/or department of the underperforming individual.[5] This negative halo effect can last for years.

In other words, if I bring you in and you screw up, I'm very likely to take a hit due to your incompetence.

Interpersonal trust

Is there a risk that the aggressively competitive partner will undermine my relationship in order to get work of his own? Or that the new lateral hotshot will set out to steal my client?

Even people who don't believe that their colleagues would deliberately sabotage them can harbor worries about losing control, not getting enough credit, and so on. My research suggests that these fears arise more in firms with extensive lateral hiring. Although a partner will be applauded for bringing his book of business to a new firm, this prowess cuts both ways: when his new colleagues consider his deftness at making off with critical, transportable assets—which, after all, he has done pretty recently—they may think twice about introducing him to their key clients. Even in firms that grow organically, the concerns are surprisingly common.

This mistrust appears to stem from two issues. First, as soon as the firm grows beyond a certain size—150 is often cited as the "natural limit" to a strongly interdependent community—the interpersonal bonds that inherently strengthen trust begin to erode.[6] Second, regardless of a firm's size, today's commercial pressures often produce greater competitiveness between partners.

Interestingly, almost every time I present these results at a firm's partner retreat, someone in the room pushes back, refusing to believe that their own partners felt that way. But trust me: they do. An intense debate—almost a food fight!—erupted during one such meeting, when I shared some of their colleagues' (anonymous) survey responses. These included quotes like:

> "Collaboration is only for partners who are more interested in exerting power over others than in serving the clients."

> "Partners are only 'collaborating' for personal gain, willing to steamroll anyone in their path."

> "I can't depend on anyone. It's every man for himself. They won't have my back."

This is clearly not fertile ground for collaboration.

Confidence and capability to dig into the client's broader issues

The biggest complaint I hear from the client side is that external advisers fail to understand their business. Most clients I interview tell me that few of their outside advisers even venture to *ask* about their most pressing concerns, outside the narrow domain of the task at hand.

Many solo specialists admit to being hesitant about introducing topics in which they are not thoroughly versed. In their survey responses, they tend to write things like, "I don't know how to approach client issues where I'm not the clear expert," or "I won't venture conversations outside my core knowledge. Which is what it takes to collaborate." This anxiety is understandable. Even far more experienced business developers admit that they're reluctant to walk into a client meeting with a one-question agenda: "What's keeping you up at night?"

But that's an excellent question, and the hesitation to ask it means that many partners miss the chance to find ways that their colleagues from other practice groups could truly add value. Instead, they're stuck trying to pitch work to clients who don't need (more of) that type of service, and are therefore unreceptive.

In addition, professionals often hesitate to introduce their colleagues into a client account because they're worried about either admitting their weakness or becoming a mere gatekeeper. If that's your barrier, you need to rethink your position. Clients repeatedly tell me that they fully expect their advisers to draw on others. As one C-suite client said: "I am deeply suspicious of people who purport to know everything. The best people are those who know what they don't know and who know how to get help when they need it. I want lawyers who, when they don't know the answer, diligently apply themselves toward finding people who do know it, and then proceed to work with them in productive ways."

If you are a solo specialist trapped inside your expertise silo, hold on: help is coming.

Lack of knowledge about your own firm's offerings

It's not enough for a professional to uncover opportunities to serve a client on broader, cross-practice issues. That professional also needs to know how his or her own firm's offerings map onto that need. But as firms grow, staying current on valid inside offerings becomes increasingly difficult.

One partner admitted to me, "I lack knowledge about what my firm can credibly do—or not do." That deficiency often prohibits professionals from building a cross-practice offering clients would value.

One firm ran a contest at its annual meeting to uncover partners' knowledge of the firm, asking questions like, "True or false: We have a thriving health care practice in each region." Most partners failed: they knew less about their own organization's offerings than the public could have found online with just a few clicks.

Inefficiency of the collaboration process

Many professionals are simply not used to working in teams, which means that their reluctance to collaborate is not merely a question of motivation, but also a practical one involving basic how-to's. The costs appear at two stages: startup and ongoing coordination.

For example, one survey respondent wrote, "The size and geographical spread of our firm sometimes makes finding the right person logistically challenging."

Even after finding competent, available contributors and convincing them to sign up, some professionals shy away from the efforts required to successfully lead a team. As one lawyer wrote, "I went to law school so that I could tackle sophisticated legal issues. If I wanted to manage teams, I would have gotten an MBA." Others commented: "Working on my own is a quicker alternative" and "The involvement of too many people can sometimes result in duplication and lack of decision making."

Some respondents highlighted the challenges of integrating diverse expertise, such as "dealing with different styles and approaches to executing business." Others worried about the lack of agreed-upon standards across disciplinary boundaries, such as "not knowing what specifically another business line recognizes as quality work." And finally, people worried about whether collaborators can adjust quickly enough, and effectively enough, to the client culture. "Our clients are really different," one person wrote, "so we have to adapt to their expectations about response times, terminology, even formatting. It might sound trivial, but when you try to deliver a joined-up approach, there are real tussles about who's right."

But as you know, it's the *client* who's right. Clients aren't interested in internal tussles, and certainly won't pay you to work out two solutions on their nickel. No wonder you're worried about inefficiency.

Politics of collaboration and messiness of managing peers' work

Beyond mere coordination costs, many partners are concerned about the arduous, politically delicate process of trying to lead peers who are unaccustomed to following others. Of course, the truth is that few professionals truly work "solo"—but most are accustomed to delegating to junior staff in their own group, whose skills are similar (but inferior) to their own and whose advancement depends on pleasing the partner. Many professionals are far less accustomed to coordinating with peers across departments, which tends to be significantly harder.

On this score, some of my respondents wrote of a "disconnect on expectations." Fair enough—and that disconnect may not become clear until the collaborative process is well under way. Finally, we should always remember that people—even the most successful solo specialists—are human, and don't want to risk getting their feelings hurt. One professional I surveyed wrote of the "fear of bothering/getting shut down . . . some people are not very approachable, and everyone is busy so the environment is not always conducive to collaborating."

Ways for solo specialists to kick-start collaboration

Taken together, these six barriers seem fairly formidable. Can the would-be collaborator overcome them?

The answer is yes. In every firm that I've worked with, across a wide range of fields, geographies, and cultures, at least a reasonable proportion of the firm's professionals have figured out how to collaborate effectively in order to develop, grow, and retain highly valuable clients. One of their most important strategies is pure perseverance, because—as you might expect—collaboration does tend to flourish with experience. Once they build their collaborative network and develop a cadre of experts whose competence and character they trust, both the risks and the coordination costs of collaboration decrease. As they learn the jargon, technical approaches, and assumptions of others, they begin to work with peers more efficiently.

Recall the "pain barrier" figure from chapter 1, showing that over time, the costs fall and the benefits rise—but *only if you stick with collaboration long enough.*

There are additional strategies that can help professionals reap more benefits from collaboration sooner, by directly tackling the six barriers just described. At the risk of sounding repetitive, I'll walk through these six barriers again, in the same order, suggesting ways that solo specialists can head off, successfully tackle, and overcome them.

Build competence trust

What do you do when you want to collaborate and have an identified opening on your team, but you're not sure who in your firm is competent to fill that slot? "Easy," you might say. "You turn to the obvious suspect: the most senior partner, the grey-haired guru with the sterling reputation."

Case closed? Not really, because sometimes resorting to the most obvious and appealing solution creates more problems than it solves. First, your resident gurus are almost always overloaded. They may devote just enough time to address the specific issue from their base of expertise, but they're unlikely to go much further—say, in coaching you on how to contextualize the advice to convince clients, or brainstorming competitor reactions, or pitching in on follow-up work.

Second, the more junior professionals—the ones who are hungry for work and client opportunities—rarely get the chance to make their full contribution. One partner, irritated by the way that his firm responded to requests for proposals from major clients, told me, "It's just favoritism, and it benefits only a few 'fair-haired boys.' The partners who control the work have an unbelievably strong reluctance to share it outside this tight club." Certainly it's inefficient for both these overburdened bottlenecks and the underutilized high-potentials. Economists scratch their heads when they come across a market that won't clear, and this is one of them: many firms suffer from both excess demand (for input from experts) and excess supply (of people wanting to contribute).

So what's the solution to the competence-trust problem? Figure out who plays a brokering role in the firm—not necessarily the formal leaders, but partners who have a large network and are willing to be honest with you about others' strengths and weaknesses. Ask them to refer you to partners who are likely to fit well with your client's needs. This means not only their expertise, but also their work and communication styles, and any other factors that might help you judge their potential "fit" with your client.

Over time, build a team whose expertise you can count on. One low-risk way of testing others' capabilities is by working with them on a third partner's project. Obviously, this strategy hinges on your developing an effective network. So next time a colleague rings to ask for your input on a client, rather than weighing the opportunity costs (i.e., the time you could have spent developing your own clients), reframe the situation as your chance to develop contacts that you might tap in the future. Join, help, and learn.

Foster interpersonal trust

One firm I work with has a psychotherapist on retainer. He spends a day or more each week with partners, helping them work through personal and interpersonal issues that arise in the course of their work. He tells me that trust issues rank among the partners' most common challenges—and yet, some people do find ways to place their trust in their colleagues: "Some people are more wary, paranoid, expecting relationships to go badly based on their own life script from childhood, marriage, or wherever. Others are optimistic and will take chances on other people, thinking it'll get lived out in a positive way."

His experience has taught him that all but the most psychologically vulnerable partners can learn to develop trust, but that many people may need repeated, safe interactions before they get comfortable with each other. The problem is especially acute for lateral hires, because not only do they not know whom to turn to, but others may avoid them as potentially disloyal (and therefore dangerous) colleagues. One of the safest ways to figure out whom to trust is to use referrals. Just as "honest brokers" inside the firm can help you find someone with the right expertise, they should also be able to recommend people whose character meets your standards. When asking around about who has the expertise to fill a gap on your client team, be sure to ask the critical (albeit awkward) questions about their character.

Another thing to keep in mind: quality attracts like quality. If you act with integrity—sharing credit where it's due; giving people constructive and honest feedback, rather than talking about their mistakes behind their backs; and bending over backward to be transparent about your client relationships—you're much more likely to be a magnet for other trustworthy partners. And don't forget that today's associates are tomorrow's partners. Treating them with dignity and fairness is more than a moral issue; it's smart business, if you want to develop a reputation as a trustworthy partner who attracts high-quality collaborators.

Develop confidence and capability to dig into the client's broader issues

How do you get smart enough to ask your clients that key question: *What's keeping you up at night?*

My first observation here is that you can't fake it. You need to develop a genuine interest in the client's business—not just in the kinds of technical issues you may be focused on, but the "big picture." What are the company's leaders proud of? Where's their most intense competition coming from, and why? What are the biggest risks to their business and their career?

One way of developing this big picture is to look on their coffee tables. What do they read on a regular basis? Subscribe to and read those publications to get an insider view of the client company's competitive context.

Loke-Khoon Tan is a partner and head of the intellectual property (IP) practice group at the law firm of Baker & McKenzie.[7] He has, together with his partners, built a highly successful legal practice advising some of the world's best-known luxury goods companies. His initial focus was IP issues in Asia, but several years ago, with backing from his firm, he founded a luxury and fashion "subpractice" within the firm. He subscribes to *Women's Wear Daily* to keep his finger on the pulse of the industry, and jokes about the odd looks that he sometimes gets from his postman. He spends his free time reading unlikely journals, he explains, to make himself smarter:

> I feel obliged to pick up as much industry knowledge as possible. Today we can point to multiple successes that happened because we understand the industry—deeply.
>
> But I also read the trade press to pick up little items that might be top-of-mind for my client, like gossip, trendsetters, big events. I find that dropping one or two of them into a client conversation gives me some credibility and also helps to deepen the relationship.

Seek out the best salespeople in any organization, and you'll find that most of them have their own version of this technique. When I was a sales rep at Procter & Gamble, back in the 1990s, many of my more seasoned colleagues were avid readers of *Progressive Grocer, Supermarket News*, and similar magazines.

This isn't all that hard, and it's not all that unusual. So I'm astonished when, as often happens, I ask a partner what his or her client's bonus depends on, and the answer is, "I'm not really sure." Yikes! If you are determined to help your clients succeed, personally and professionally—and you are, right?—you need to understand their personal and corporate metrics. If a client's boss is holding his or her feet to the fire on the issue of cost containment, for example, then your pitches for lots of new work in your established model are likely to be unrealistic and annoying.

On the flip side, you can turn around a strained client relationship by uncovering and engaging in their deepest, darkest concerns. A consultant from a global firm recounted this story about "EnergyCo"—one of the world's major oil and gas companies:

> It was a time when EnergyCo had turned off all their consulting spend, but that didn't matter for us. With the help of an outside consultant, we learned how to hold conversations focused on the issues that mattered most to them. Despite the drought, we maintained a dialogue—we told

that we wanted to invest in the relationship and to learn with them. Together we zeroed in on a huge issue for the industry: how to handle late-life assets in areas of diminishing reserves.

Over time we got to know the COO. He would have never given us the time of day. A real bruiser. But we eventually got an initial meeting with him and it went well, met a number of his people. Why did it work? Because the rigor we'd implemented into our thinking about that account gave me, and the wider team, confidence to see those people and talk about their issues in a much more credible way.

When we first met him, we didn't go with PowerPoint slides. He hates consultants, sees us as adding no value. Instead, we got him engaged in a conversation about operational issues. We brought along one chart, which showed an example of what we'd done for a competitor in the North Sea. He actually pulled his chair around to our side of the desk to look at it.

I bumped into him at a reception a couple months later, and he spoke to me like a long-lost friend. Very warm, open. Turns out, a very significant RFP came in the other day in that area we've been focused on. And the RFP only went to us and one other small boutique—none of the firms that we'd regularly compete against.[8]

Also remember that there is safety and comfort in numbers. At the end of chapter 2, I recounted the story of the two consultants who shored each other up on a cold-calling trip across Australia. They were prepared to be rejected—as indeed they were, more often than not. They were also prepared to be wrong, and to offer opinions that might not come from a full data set of knowledge, which in turn meant that they were prepared to be vulnerable. Why? In part because they were working toward a common cause.

Further, pick something you're truly passionate about. Loke-Khoon Tan, introduced earlier, got involved in the luxury and fashion industry because he was interested in it personally. His

after-hours hobbies focused on branding. In his work as an IP lawyer, he was regularly exposed to the industry, and made lots of
contacts within it. He found those contacts to be intriguing and creative people—in part because he shared their interests. "Marrying
my hobby and my work happens naturally with clients like [big
name fashion house]," he explains. "Developing knowledge about
them, and bringing that knowledge to work, is both fascinating for
me and enables me to contribute to the firm. I do it because I *want*
to do it."[9]

Finally, you have to keep the faith that over time, with practice,
you'll get better at these conversations. Honest—you will. In the
meantime, as one experienced lawyer said, "You've gotta be willing to put yourself out there, be prepared for it to go badly, and
then have a laugh if it does. If you've got an honest curiosity about
their business, clients will most often respect that you're trying to
learn, even if you're a bit clunky at first."

Do you still find yourself paralyzed at this prospect? If so, consider turning to a professional coach or licensed psychotherapist to
address the underlying reasons. You may think I'm joking, but I'm
not. You would be surprised how prevalent this practice is among
your client executives—and, most likely, among your competitors.

Learn about your own firm's offerings

How fast is your firm changing? The faster the pace of change,
the more likely it is that your understanding of the organization
is lagging behind reality. Again, this is something that you can fix
on your own, although having interested partners in this exercise
certainly helps.

Use every chance you can—from firm retreats to casual conversations around the office—to ask your fellow partners what they're
working on. Again, authenticity matters: you need to be truly curious, rather than just pumping them for information. Recognize
that some people (you, perhaps?) might hesitate to engage in what
they see as self-promotion, and need to have their knowledge
drawn out of them. One executive coach who participates in my

research panel points out that in the United States, for example, some women and ethnic minorities may be cautious about being perceived as "pushy" and therefore underplay their strengths unless directly asked.[10] You can unearth some relatively hidden gems by assuring them that you're genuinely interested and that their sharing will help you both—as well as your potentially mutual clients.

Tell colleagues about the hot-button issues in your sector, and ask whether they've seen similar things in the industry where they focus. Clients might really value some input that you think is tangential. For example, the chief legal officer of a major financial institution recently shared with me his biggest desire from his outside lawyers: "What keeps me up at night is the huge regulatory burden. I know that these firms also serve big pharma, aerospace, and some other massively regulated industries, but they've never once offered to send someone along from those sectors to talk to me about what it's like to work in such an environment. If they did, I'd give them hours."

When's the last time you perused your own firm's website? It's probably filled with insights about your colleagues' latest deals, client wins, sector expertise, and thought leadership. Another excellent but underused resource is your professional development staff: ask them what training materials have been created for new joiners. They may have created brief videos that encapsulate the highlights of core practice groups as part of their onboarding materials, but more senior partners could use this video library as a fantastic refresher. Try downloading the set onto your phone and watching one each time you're sitting on an airport runway. If the materials are good and you're an attentive student, you'll soon be up to speed.

Create a more efficient collaboration process

Some would-be collaborators are put off by the perception that everything gets harder with a bigger, broadly based team—and that these difficulties far outweigh the benefits. What countermeasures can you take?

First, *get the right resources on the team.* Think carefully about what "right" means, which may involve something other than rounding up the usual suspects. Making the effort to get real experts on the team—rather than defaulting to those who are familiar but less adept—will ultimately pay off. Ideally, think beyond pure content expertise: the perfect contributor for a cross-specialty project is one who also has sufficient cultural intelligence to operate on a challenging, sometimes confusing team. Take your time, if possible: getting the right person slowly is usually way better than getting the wrong person quickly.

Second, *launch the project effectively.* Professionals often fail to hold appropriate project-planning discussions to align expectations, partly because they personally value professional autonomy and are extra cautious about encroaching on others' autonomy. In my experience, it's better to overdo this (slightly) and be told to back off than to underdo it and have the project flounder.

Third, and concurrent with the launch, *develop a clear purpose for the team.* Then communicate it well and frequently enough so that people understand it, buy into it, and keep buying into it. It is also essential that team members know "who knows what," so that they can quickly turn to the right expert with queries or suggestions.

It's tempting to believe that professionals who have worked together in the past already know each other's relevant knowledge and strengths. My research shows, though, that even familiar teams often make erroneous assumptions about others' knowledge. The discrepancy between members' beliefs about others' knowledge— what I call "expertise dissensus"—tends to create conflict and lower performance, but it can be overcome by an effective team launch and a clear statement of purpose, regularly invoked. When partners know how they and others fit into the bigger picture, they can hold each other mutually accountable for both timely and high-quality deliverables. A small investment in up-front planning and communication can improve team output by as much as 30 percent.[11]

Fourth, *get contributors up to speed fast.* After you've spent so much time learning the client's preferences, make sure team members are briefed. Also make sure they're clear on practical issues like billing guidelines. These aren't glamorous tasks, but they provide critical support for the glamour moments.

Artfully handle the politics of collaboration

Finally, and perhaps most important, you have to focus on leading your high-powered peers effectively.

Politics are hard enough at the outset when you're negotiating experts' roles on your team; they become even messier once you begin working together. Leading peers who are unaccustomed to following others can be an arduous, time-consuming, sometimes thankless process. I wrote earlier about the mindset of professionals who are in the habit of delegating to tractable juniors (who don't talk back, for the most part). These kinds of solo specialists may cringe at the reality of leading teams of colleagues who are experts in their own domains and have their own sources of power and prestige.

Even when the partner who's officially responsible for the client is nominally in charge of the engagement, collaborators need to agree on how to allocate responsibilities and resolve conflicts. Coordination is tricky, because a project is often a considerably higher priority for the professional who sold the work than for the ones who are "merely" contributing. Professionals often shy away from broaching difficult conversations with their partners, in part because—as noted—they personally value professional autonomy, and are extra cautious about encroaching on the autonomy of others. Oddly, this fastidiousness rarely extends to the client: "I'm happy to go toe-to-toe with a client when I think they're wrong or unreasonable," one partner told me, "but I'd hesitate to do that with a peer."

Here's the rub: this apprehension about contradicting or overruling a colleague may well stand between you and an effective collaboration. At the end of the day, you have to deliver excellent service. As one somewhat frustrated collaborator put it: "You need to have an honest conversation. If a client tells me that they don't like a particular partner—I'm talking raw feedback from a client— what's the point of appointing or continuing with someone who can't be effective? But that often does happen: we allow the partner to stay on the account because we don't want to offend him, or we ease him off without giving him the straight story."

Collaborative leaders must be role models, prepared to provide timely and direct feedback, and to intervene immediately to defuse team conflicts. They have to be forceful and decisive—and at the same time, they must reflect periodically on their own inclinations to drive toward a solution, versus keeping their minds open to novel approaches that fully leverage members' knowledge of local conditions and requirements.

Messy? Yes. Easy? No. Important? Yes.

From the firm's perspective

At the outset of this chapter, I suggested that readers who are senior leaders at knowledge-based firms have a special responsibility vis-à-vis the solo specialists within their ranks—that it's in the firm's interest to encourage them to collaborate, even at the risk of annoying them and disrupting their proven success formulas. You have a longer-term obligation to broaden and deepen institutional relationships with the clients whom those solo specialists currently serve.

One way to get there is to invent and implement a set of robust client succession and coverage plans that expand key client relationships beyond the solo specialists who currently control them.

Let's dig deeper. Most professional service firms pride themselves on their "entrepreneurial" culture. This translates into encouraging professionals to build their own businesses—both by developing relationships to win new work, and by growing those nascent accounts into giant ones. Almost by definition, this autonomy translates into difficulty for those firms that seek to play a more active role in centrally managing those accounts over time. As a result, they tend to leave the originating partner in charge of the account for as long as he's willing to lead it.

But there's a problem of fairly recent vintage. This entrepreneurial, live-and-let-live tradition took root at a time when most partners—whether following the rules in their partnership agreement or just reflecting the dominant societal norms—retired when they reached their midfifties. At that time, too, firms were small enough so that the apprenticeship model still reigned: the master rainmakers brought up their protégés in a way that made client succession a somewhat predetermined, natural event.

Several recent trends have put this laissez-faire approach under increasing pressure. First, many firms have eliminated age-based mandatory retirement.[12] Second, the financial crisis that started in 2008 forced many knowledge professionals—like many in the larger economy—to dip deeply into their savings, which means that they have been compelled to work longer than planned. The upshot is that many firms find that their partners are hanging on to their clients until the bitter end, often in wind-down mode rather than build-up mode.

What's the practical result of this aging in place? In many cases, a gap opens up between a firm and its clients. Of course, this phenomenon is bigger than the solo-specialist cohort. In fact, the senior leaders of many professional firms are older than their client counterparts. The leadership of many *Fortune* 100 and NASDAQ companies—the chief executives and general counsels, for example—is already transitioning to younger boomers and Generation X-ers. For example, about 20 percent of *Fortune* 100 and 30 percent of NASDAQ general counsels are Gen X members, compared with fewer than 5 percent of the leaders of the top US law firms.[13] This growing age gap makes it harder and harder for many firms to connect with their client counterparts. Aging relationships become more fragile, as younger executives find that they connect better with—and therefore want to award more business to—professionals in their own peer group.

But the aging-in-place solo specialists who tightly control their client relationships pose a special management challenge. For one thing, they create a structural blockage in the system: aspiring Gen X-ers underneath them are more likely to jump to competitor firms than wait for their chance. When they leave, they take their knowledge with them—including some of the firm's best intelligence about how the solo specialist's accounts might be made accessible to the larger firm.

Of course, there are blunt-instrument solutions, such as mandatory-retirement-age policies. Although such plans have fallen out of favor in recent years—because people are staying healthier longer, and these plans are increasingly seen as ageist and unacceptable—some firms still require partners to retire as early as in their fifties. But the solution to one problem often creates others. Pushing an older partner out tends to be painful for all concerned. All too often, the change is (or feels) abrupt, and the departing partner generally receives very little support from the firm. Some partners are lucky enough to be offered a role as consultants, but most have to navigate their new lives on their own.

Beyond the psychological stresses that their partners undergo, firms, too, are put under stress by forced departures. Leaders are increasingly aware of the huge experience and knowledge bases that disappear when an experienced partner—and especially a solo specialist—walks out the door. A leader in one international consulting firm that had no systematic method in place to transition clients when partners did retire recounted this example:

> One partner in our Zurich office had some very important relationships with our Swiss clients. He kept insisting he was going to retire at sixty, but everyone dragged their heels on transitioning his clients—maybe they didn't believe he'd give up such a lucrative practice. In fact, he retired when he said he would—and it really left us holding the bag. We lost a lot of those clients in Zurich.

What is to be done? One response is a carefully considered transition plan for potential retirees, which focuses as much on what they are transitioning *to* as on what they are transitioning *from*.

Let's look at two examples of firms using broader transition programs that successfully respond to the succession challenge. The first is the global law firm White & Case, which instituted an innovative program to proactively address its partners' transitions.[14] Starting ten years before a partner reaches typical retirement age, the firm begins a series of formal conversations with *every* partner to discuss his or her professional expectations for the coming years. This dialogue not only prompts the necessary self-reflection, but also allows the individual to start taking steps toward reaching his or her objectives.

For example, many skilled lawyers imagine themselves serving as nonexecutive directors on corporate boards—but few understand how much planning this move requires. Experienced leaders can inform and coach them. Furthermore, knowledge of the partner's intentions helps White & Case plan for how to transition client work smoothly, effectively, and proactively.

One inventive step that White & Case has taken is the creation of a Client Council, where a group of senior partners act as an advisory board for lead client partners. The lead partners develop a detailed client plan and are then accountable to the council for how they are delivering against the plan.

According to White & Case's chairman, Hugh Verrier, "The Client Council is not just authorizing the lead partners to build and broaden the team serving the clients. It acts also as a mechanism to monitor and help. The members give the benefit of experience, thoughts, advice. And, to give the process some teeth, the council also gives input on compensation for the lead partners."

If the council notices succession issues within the key client program, it intervenes to guide the transition. It actually has the power to change the lead partners, although this option has rarely been used. Instead, the council works with the lead client partners to encourage them to promote a proactive, smooth succession. Although still in its formative stages, the program has so far been successful by combining advice and accountability.

Our second case study involves another law firm that I will call Jones & Jones, which has a similar transition program that begins much earlier in the participants' careers.[15] Starting just five years after an individual makes partner, Jones offers access to a coaching program that helps each lawyer to think about his or her career in more holistic terms. Every five years thereafter, each partner has a "refresh meeting" with the coach, up to the point when they jointly conclude that retirement is within the coming ten years; then coaching meetings happen more frequently.

A leader in that firm described how starting the program early in each partner's career eliminates any stigma associated with it. It's considered a normal, healthy part of partnership, rather than a process designed to manage out underperforming older lawyers. The leader also noted that, although the coach's sessions with partners are confidential, the firm benefits significantly from having lawyers who are more reflective and conscious about their career moves.

Often, the lawyers themselves will approach leaders to discuss their aspirations—say, for a leadership role in the firm, or a desire to temporarily cut back on hours, or to obtain a prominent role in a local nonprofit organization.

"The program was designed as a transition program," commented Jones's managing partner, "but the self-awareness and transparency generated through it benefit the firm throughout a partner's career." You can see how a carefully structured transition plan comes to bear on the challenges posed by the solo specialist.

You should also give clients considerable input into the transition planning. As one client remarked, "Nothing is more irritating than having some bloke show up and say, 'Hi, I'm your new key account manager' as if I'll automatically warm up to him and trust him with my biggest issues. Normally the new lead partner is someone who's already been serving on the team, but as the client I ought to have a say in which of the current people I think is best suited. More than one firm has lost business by surprising me in that way."

Beyond these kinds of transition plans, firms deal with the challenges of the solo specialist by implementing a system of *laddering*—that is, matching up your professionals at each rank with client counterparts of a roughly similar age or experience level.[16] Laddering presents multiple benefits. First, it puts in place an organic client-succession structure: when the top dog finally moves on, you have the great luxury of a tried-and-true replacement. Your firm looks smart, and your client stays happy with the relationship. Second, a functioning ladder is a source of important business intelligence. The top dog at the client company may not choose to open up with your top dog about sensitive issues, but that exchange may very well happen at the subordinate level.

Perhaps this surprises you. Shouldn't the lead partner of the relationship be most in tune with the client, and therefore most likely to get the straight story? No. My study of about seventy-five client service teams in a global professional firm revealed a surprising truth. For each team, we asked the same set of questions of each team member, of the partner responsible for the account team, and of the main client (for instance, the head of the audit committee for accounting teams or division chief executive for the consulting teams). The questions related to how the client perceived the team's work: were they satisfied with the work, would they recommend the firm to others, and so on.

Not surprisingly, the lead partners had a lot of faith in their understanding of clients' beliefs, saying things like, "I'm frequently in touch with the client, and I'm pretty sure they'd raise any issues with me directly." When I interviewed those clients, however, they revealed that they sometimes felt awkward giving tough feedback straight to the relationship partner. Instead, they often channeled their concerns directly to the on-the-ground team—which, as it turned out, was also faster.

This study ultimately exposed an unexpected reality: in contrast to the lead partner's often inflated view of the team's performance, the team members' perception of their own performance was much closer to what the clients reported. The lesson for leaders? Even if you succeed in laddering, which allows your team members to align closely with their client counterparts, you need to make sure that *internal* communication flows freely so that the junior members' insights quickly reach the partners who need that knowledge.

Short-term pain, long-term gain

As we've seen, both solo specialists and their firms can benefit enormously from an increase in collaboration.

No, it's not easy. For the partner who is new to the collaborative approach, it often requires shouldering short-term pain to make long-term gains. How? By building a set of reliable collaborators across practices and offices, partners can avoid time-consuming background research about who knows what and how responsive they will be.

Coordination costs also fall as partners learn the jargon, technical approaches, and assumptions of other practices, which allows them to work together more efficiently. Unlike the first time two partners work together—the juncture when they need to figure out how to share intangible outcomes like recognition for a great outcome, or airtime at a client pitch—professionals who understand their colleagues' moves, including their credit-sharing norms, can work together with less tension and fewer startup costs.

Again, over time, the benefits begin to compound and grow more rapidly, as the exponential effects of a growing and glowing reputation kick in. Ideally, you hear the client saying, *We wouldn't go to anybody other than that team for answers to our toughest problems.*

Meanwhile, the firm's senior leaders have their role to play. How do you encourage the solo specialist to keep being his or her productive self—and at the same time, set the stage for greater successes in the future, both for the firm and for the individual? Fostering collaboration is one powerful answer.

In chapter 4, we explore the special case of what I call the *seasoned collaborator*. Actions talk louder than words: the seasoned collaborator *is* interested in collaboration, understands its value, and therefore wants to do it better. But even when collaboration is smart, it's not easy. The next chapter has words of advice for these valuable partners.

$$\left[\ 4 \ \right]$$

The Seasoned Collaborator

This chapter speaks to the professionals I call *seasoned collaborators*, an invaluable cadre of partners who are sometimes referred to—with near reverence—as rainmakers. I tend to avoid that term, mainly because it's overused, but I certainly don't minimize the value of rainmaking. If you're a senior leader in a knowledge firm, you know who these individuals are, and you treasure them.

By definition, seasoned collaborators don't need to be convinced to collaborate. They understand that referring work to colleagues—and in the process, developing a loyal team capable of delivering extraordinary client service—is the surest way to build a robust portfolio. Now they want to take it up a notch or two, which may mean involving higher-ups in the organization, including the C-suite or even the board. Or it may mean more strategic interaction with the client, using collaboration to proactively drive the agenda, rather than pulling together a team merely when the client brings up an opportunity. These are ambitious goals, and they aren't easy to achieve.

The bigger the account, the more stressful leading that account becomes, even for the seasoned collaborator. This should come as no surprise. And the more sophisticated the client, the more likely it is that the advisers with the specialized technical expertise needed to address the complex issues are distributed throughout the firm, and possibly around the globe. But to appropriately tailor large-scale solutions, those domain experts must work closely with colleagues in a local market who have deep contextual knowledge. The combination of large, distributed, and global is tricky enough—and on top of that, those local experts tend to have their own client priorities, which often clash with those of the seasoned collaborator. And on top of *that*, times have changed. Given the rapid consolidation in most professional areas and the increasingly fluid movement of professionals between firms, the cultural mores of collegiality and cooperation that might have historically governed relationships within the firm are no longer as powerful—or may be absent altogether.

So if collaboration is difficult, stressful, clash-inducing, and countercultural—a seemingly daunting list—why should the seasoned collaborator want to take it up a notch? One answer we've seen already: *What got you here won't keep you there.* On the more positive side, highly experienced collaborators derive a number of intangible benefits from collaboration, which I discuss in the next section.

Celebrating the intangibles

The seasoned collaborators I address in this chapter have gotten well past that nerve-wracking stage when it wasn't clear whether collaboration would ultimately pay off. Now that the benefits are outweighing the startup costs and they're reaping the return on their investment, they can focus on some of the less tangible rewards that come from collaborating. Yes, money remains important—not only for its purchasing power, but also as a status indicator. But most seasoned collaborators conform to the general patterns traced by successful people in all walks of life: the older and richer they get, the more likely they are to seek meaning. And collaboration helps there, too.

Again, money still talks. And the competitive juices that helped them succeed in the first place are still flowing. (That's a good thing, because in most professional fields today, not even the most successful rainmaker can afford to be complacent.) But I'd also point to four intangible benefits that, taken separately and certainly taken together, further motivate the high-level collaborator.

The first is the *intellectual challenge of complex work*. Most professionals crave intellectual stimulation; it's part of the reason they spent years in graduate school preparing for a knowledge-based career. Collaborating across disciplinary boundaries gives them that challenge in a very potent form. It allows them to move up the food chain through their clients, advising people whose problems are increasingly complex and interesting. As one partner said, "If I'm doing work just in my specialty, then I'm almost certainly talking to clients with a narrow scope and more limited responsibility. Once I move into more sophisticated work, I move up toward the C-suite, and that's when the conversations get interesting."

A second intangible benefit is *power*. When a CEO is in crisis and picks up the phone to seek your advice, it's a heady experience. Whether it's advising the world's business elites, winning a huge grant as the principal investigator in a research lab, or directing hundreds of professionals on a worldwide account team—all are sources of heightened power and prestige, and in most cases, they are the result of a collaborative effort.

The third on my list of intangibles might be summarized as "staying young." Rainmaking sets you apart—in both a good sense and a bad one. The firm greatly appreciates your financial and reputational contributions, and justifiably celebrates you for them. Your very success distinguishes you. At the same time, the more rarified the air you breathe, the less likely you are to get your nose rubbed in new (and sometimes rude) realities. Being set apart can mean being isolated.

In the 1990s, when GE's CEO Jack Welch was already a celebrated business statesman, he made a surprising move: he found a twenty-five-year-old computer whiz within the company to serve as his technology mentor.[1] (He also insisted that his C-level colleagues do the same.) When people later wondered aloud how this relatively senior executive could make a powerful case for widespread digitization at GE—which he did—Welch had a ready answer: a young colleague had showed him the ropes. Of course, youth is only one of the broadening dimensions that one can encounter on a collaborative team; I use it here as a stand-in for team diversity.

I also pointed out in chapter 2 that it's often the "worker bees" on a team who are most in tune with clients. Seasoned collaborators "stay young" by building smart junior people into their network—younger colleagues who may be better positioned to pick up on weak-signal client problems.

Not surprisingly, perhaps, this list of intangibles ends with the concept of *legacy*. As the leader of one major law firm told me, "Some lawyers are more partner-like than others. Just as entrepreneurs want to leave a solid business behind for their children, these partners are motivated to pass on a strong client relationship to the next generation."

Social science research has determined that for many successful people, building a legacy—that is, leveraging your achievements and values in a way that helps others succeed after you're gone—is a prime source of enduring happiness.[2] By helping to institutionalize the client relationship across multiple partners, seasoned collaborators build their legacy.

To summarize, the tangible and intangible benefits of collaboration are considerable—but they come at a price, and they present hurdles that need to be overcome. I have identified three such team-related hurdles:

- Building the right team

- Developing the necessary leadership for that team

- Managing a multicultural, distributed team

Let's look at each in turn.

Building a committed, accountable team

As a seasoned collaborator, you know that you can't function without colleagues who are willing to drop their "own" clients when your higher-priority client needs them. In other words, you need a team that is both committed to the project and accountable for its results. As one collaborator phrased it to me: "When you need a partner in X jurisdiction with specific expertise for a particular project, if you're friends, they'll do anything for you. But it doesn't always happen. When you don't get that buy-in, and when you don't have that relationship, it becomes impossible to finish the jigsaw, and to put that final piece in. Getting people to commit time to your client that isn't as important to them as it is to you can be *tough*."

Ideally, of course, partners on your team should act as internal champions for the client within their local office, region, and practice group. They need to be willing and empowered to deal with operational client issues such as staffing, billing, and quality assurance as well as more strategic issues like handling local business conflicts.

I think I hear the sound of eyeballs rolling skyward. Yes, building this team is difficult. It's also crucial. One major professional firm conducted a strategy review of its account management processes, which concluded, "The biggest challenge for the lead client partners has been to incentivize their wider team partners to take on responsibility for managing and growing client relationships beyond their own silos."

As one partner told me candidly, when talking about partners in his fast-growing firm, "People no longer feel the same personal accountability to each other that makes them interrupt their own agenda to help on another partner's client. I feel like I need to negotiate or incentivize, whereas before, people would just do the right thing for each other."

So what is the seasoned collaborator who's trying to do *more* collaborative work—and more effectively—supposed to do?

The first step is understanding what the specific barriers are for those experts whom you want to entice onto the team. After you've targeted the experts whose contribution you need, start by figuring out (1) what holds each of them back and (2) what would personally motivate them. Be creative about what strings to pull for each partner.

Obstacle: Partners' overflowing plates

In some cases, a potential partner may decline to participate in your project because he or she is already swamped with other high-profile client work. At this point, *consider an alternative*. Do you really need this specific guru—or would another, perhaps slightly more junior, partner be a reasonable alternative?

If you absolutely need the guru, you may have to resort to a combination of relationships, flattery, and descriptions of the upside potential, in terms of revenue and even greater reputation-boosting work. And when you talk about the proposed project, highlight the strategic benefit that the person's involvement would bring. Again, people like to know that you understand them, and value them.

Keep in mind that even if you "land" your guru, you're probably going to get only limited attention from him or her. When people are already putting in thousands of billable hours a year, the chances are high that they won't be able to make a substantial investment in a new client. Most likely, they'll go to the pitch, and then not do the vital follow-on work.

You therefore need to *backstop this person* with a highly capable associate or other professional who can keep the project moving after the guru gets called to put out the next fire. In addition, you probably need to *take some calculated risks* by involving players on your team who—because they are relatively unproven—may be less obvious choices. Even though you might have to invest some energy in getting these partners fully up to speed, this is generally a good investment, because hungry junior partners are more likely to commit time and energy to your broader client effort. Look for the ambitious people who haven't yet "arrived"—people who need to get this kind of work into their portfolio.

Over time, developing a pipeline of capable contributors makes you less dependent on overly busy partners who might become bottlenecks. And it starts you down the path of building that legacy benefit.

One partner at a major global law firm experienced a considerable win when she went out on a limb like this. She had struggled to build a committed team to provide the expanding set of services her client's general counsel was willing to buy from her. As she told me: "Senior people simply weren't willing to sign on, even though the client had been deemed a global priority account. Even asking the practice heads and office managing partners failed to turn up partners who were keen to invest their precious time in building out new work for my notably demanding client. So finally, I used my own network to uncover a recently promoted partner who was keen to dive in."

After just one year, this junior partner had made huge strides with the account, earning the client's trust and further expanding the set of services being provided.

Involving less-tested colleagues on your team may initially feel risky, and as noted earlier will likely take some investment to make sure they're thoroughly briefed and ready to contribute. For your own comfort, you'll want to check in more frequently than you might with a "safe pair of hands." But through these leadership actions, you'll develop a cadre of talented young professionals whom others will see as trustworthy—which will keep opening new doors for them, and keep cementing their positive feelings toward you.

Remember that this sort of forward thinking is far more than altruism. As Jack Welch would certainly testify, the chances are high that you'll learn a lot from your more junior colleagues. This is especially true when they start bringing home unique perspectives from their client interactions at different levels. And demographics that might seem unusual for you or your firm may fit the client perfectly. "There are a whole lot of optics around age at Google," one professional who works regularly with the internet giant told me. "I can't put a sixty-year-old white male on the team. They'd prefer an ambitious thirty-five-year-old woman."

In many cases, optics aren't just optics, especially when seen through the client's eyes. They are very real obstacles that can trip you up.

Obstacle: Key accounts with lower rates

Here's an unwelcome truth: differences in labor rates across different countries, combined with tougher terms and standards demanded by key clients, can pose barriers to getting new members on a client team. As one partner told me, "One problem internally is selling a client to other partners in other offices when they realize that they need to work at a discounted rate. If they have local clients that are not discounted, then this key account is not the priority for them."

Short of rejiggering your firm's fee structure (an important topic covered in chapter 6), here are a few steps individual partners can take:

- **Be fair and generous on fees.** If partners in your firm negotiate fees or rates, bend over backward to be fair to colleagues you invite onto your team. Even if your client is more important than theirs to the firm, don't expect them to drop everything to handle your matter, or to work without fair compensation.

- **Be creative about what strings to pull for each partner.** This grows out of the previous point. Motivating someone is often a combination of several approaches: emphasizing the revenue opportunity and reputational benefits of working for the client in the short and long term; persuading the individual partner's local leaders—such as her practice group leader or regional managing partner—about the upside of having the partner devote her attention to the key account, so that they recognize her efforts on behalf of the firm when bonus time rolls around; and perhaps using some additional forms of credit sharing or other mechanisms to at least cover the startup costs for a partner who initially trades her higher-rate work for the promise of a more steady income stream in the future.

Obstacle: Onerous quality control

After you attract team members who are willing to contribute, you need to make sure they are capable of delivering the highest levels of service. As one accounting partner put it:

> Everyone is keen to do good work and do a great job. How do I make sure that happens? The client doesn't want me involved because of cost concerns, but I need to oversee quality.
>
> For now, I try to stay more involved without billing time to [the job]. But that is a bit exhausting. I have other

billable work that I have to do. You're judged on what you bring in terms of revenue and collections. They'll say, "It's great that you're sending work around to other people," but the truth is, the leaders are looking at my day-to-day P&L.

What can you do to ensure quality control without logging volunteer hours that you don't have? The most important tactic is to *clarify objectives well in advance*. This may sound like Management 101, but it has distinct nuances in this context. This process of communication should include not only the goals for the specific project, but also a thorough briefing on the client's culture, values, and service expectations. In a mature professional firm, the account leader may be able to rely on his or her business support professionals to create a client dossier that informs account newcomers about the client's business operations and strategic objectives, the major projects their firm has recently handled, and the current key relationships and how they are interconnected. If you don't have the luxury of support—or maybe even if you do—consider assigning the briefing task to senior associates on the team. This responsibility forces them to become deeply familiar with the account, and it raises their profile with other partners who join the team.

Assuring high quality is especially hard when it comes to those peripheral members who contribute infrequently. Unfortunately, that frequency is determined not only by partner availability, but also by the workflow from the client. Typically, that workflow is lumpy. One partner recounted his particularly challenging circumstances to me:

> We have five hundred lawyers in forty-nine offices doing work for my client. Some do only twenty minutes every so often, or take on a few-thousand-dollar project now and then. So of course, those lawyers don't have the context or the insider knowledge. As client leader, I can't stay on top of each of the individual projects. Yes, mistakes happen and we try to catch them through our supervision. But the real issue is that they don't give us enough work in each area to get people up to speed.

Of course, the best way to develop capable, trustworthy partners is to start long before they become prospective partners. I know this isn't helpful advice for the seasoned collaborator who needs to put out a fire *today*—that is, who's facing a near-term staffing challenge—but I'll go ahead and put in a pitch here for formal development programs for professionals at all levels. Your particular firm's structure may or may not permit you to be a champion of such programs—but if you can, be that champion. Feed the pipeline, and at the same time, burnish your own reputation as someone who helps create opportunities for others.

Obstacle: Partners' desire to retain control over local clients

"Control" means all kinds of things in this context: exerting influence over the relationship or over the community of involved players, preserving autonomy, keeping proprietary information secure, and so on.

Autonomy deserves some special attention here. Certainly, ego enters into the picture. One partner said, "I'm not used to playing second fiddle, and I'm not sure I want to." Many firms attract professionals by touting their entrepreneurial culture—and then act surprised when the partners want to be their own bosses, which to them means serving as the primary decision maker and chief contact for an account.

But concerns about autonomy take other faces, as well. A potential partner may be reluctant to give up time on his local clients because he fears losing control over his workflow, and thereby becoming dependent on others to "fill his plate" with work from their key accounts.

This situation is especially tricky when conflicts of interest arise between clients handled by different partners in your firm, and you as the account leader need a colleague to give up his local client in order to serve the key account that you lead. Here's a typical problem faced by a client leader in one international law firm (the details are fabricated to protect the identity of the real-life clients, but the situation is real):

> Not long ago we were asked by one of our firm's core clients, Boeing, to take on a piece of litigation in Brazil. But some partners in our São Paulo office are actively working for Embraer [a Brazilian aerospace company], which is a Boeing competitor and not one of our firm's designated strategic accounts. Their local client brings us about a million dollars of work per year; Boeing historically hasn't been important for us there, but generates tens of millions globally.
>
> The best talent was already involved in Embraer. I don't want to be served with second-class litigators just because that office prioritizes some local account. I didn't need to involve our chairman, but it came close. It showed me that in our partners' minds, many local offices are not part of the global firm.

In most professional firms, decisions about conflicts are handled by a committee—but even if the decision comes out in favor of the client you're responsible for, then you're left trying to convince a grumpy, demotivated partner to contribute his best to the team. What's the right response? You need to help these partners develop a road map for how their relationship will evolve within the client and the wider account team. Give them a vision for how they will become embedded in the client team, and assure them that you'll provide opportunities for them to get in front of key executives to build their own relationships and reputations.

We also need to deal with the reality that giving up a client means losing more than mere revenue. How so? Many professional-client relationships have deep roots that cross the line into friendship. This is not a bad thing, per se, but it can make certain kinds of calculations murky. Most people have a complex set of reasons for their support of one approach and their resistance to another—motivations that they might not fully understand themselves, and which friendship greatly complicates. I was on the phone with

Gerard, an experienced partner in an international consultancy, discussing why his colleague Richard had turned down the chance to take a leading role on a project for Gerard's client. I asked, "Do you think it's a financial or political motivation?"

Gerard's response:

> It's financial, partly, because if he has a client safely in his pocket, and that relationship makes him up to $1 million per year, then it's a safe bet. I was offering Richard a client with even more upside, but you need to provide best service, otherwise they won't give the work. So there's a bit of risk and uncertainty, and it's always easier to defend the status quo rather than go with hope.
>
> But it was also probably the psychological issue: Why should I take on a client that is "someone else's," when I could work for my "own" client? Richard had a close relationship with the chief operating officer there; they'd practically grown up together since Richard was a cub consultant and that guy was managing a small business unit. It's an emotional attachment, even though not everyone would admit it.

Even the most experienced account team leaders find it extremely hard to counter these kinds of objections, unless they have the strong backing of their firm's leaders. That backing has to be forceful enough to create a clear cultural mandate, such that other partners understand that giving up local clients to service higher-profile, higher-revenue clients is clearly expected.

But that's not enough. Even if you have that kind of backing, you still need to attract the highest-quality professionals onto your team as *willing contributors*. If they come on board merely in response to a top-down mandate, it is highly unlikely that you'll see the sort of devoted service you want to provide to your clients. Here are some steps that may help you attract a motivated team:

- **Ask current team members to vouch for you.** They can let others know that you're an efficient leader who is generous about sharing credit, and who isn't a micromanager.[3]

- **Manage with respect.** Don't waste others' time by repeatedly changing objectives, and don't create fire drills with fake deadlines. Most partners know better than to treat their peers like this, but they fail to recognize that their reputation for abusing associates' time is also a turnoff for partners who hear about it.

- **Get to know people in all sorts of settings.** Networking opportunities arise at many venues, such as at partner retreats or firm events. You need to be seen as someone who will reciprocate, be responsive to others' clients, and be a good ambassador for the firm. If you've shared a meal, a laugh, or a victory on the sports field, trust is much easier to build.

- **Communicate openly—even when it's bad news.** Ask questions. Seek advice freely, and offer it tactfully when you see a need. Most people don't like to give negative feedback to their peers, and you're probably no exception. But partners who join you on client work shouldn't have to guess whether their contributions are up to par. If you give people constructive, honest, and timely comments, you'll maximize their ability to learn from your project, which is one of the key benefits individuals gain from collaboration. You'll also build a team of capable, loyal people who can handle complicated projects, which will give you the confidence to pitch such work to clients. Regular communications help to foster a greater level of accountability among the wider client team partners. The best relationship partners hold regular team calls and in-person meetings, post blogs on the intranet about client opportunities and "wins," seek input from others on their client strategy, hold lots of one-on-one meetings to help individual partners navigate the client's business, and brainstorm issues and opportunities.

- **Turn the people around you into better collaborators.** If they *do* screw up, resist the impulse to chew them out. Also resist the far more typical impulse to grit your teeth in the moment, but then grumble about them behind their backs. Again, give people constructive, honest, and timely comments.

- **Share credit and recognition generously.** Finally, you absolutely need to publicly recognize the contributions of your team members. People know what they've done well, and they know that you know it, too. Try never taking credit for anything, and see what happens. My prediction: people will start insisting that you accept at least *some* of the credit.

Developing a high-functioning leadership team

Let's assume that you have overcome the obstacles described earlier and have successfully assembled a committed, accountable team. The second of the three hurdles—which the would-be collaborator usually clears more or less in tandem with the larger team-building effort—is developing a high-functioning leadership team for the account. In some cases, rallying a set of committed, accountable members may turn out to be the easy part. The harder task may be establishing effective coordination and communication among the *leaders* of that team.

The late J. Richard Hackman, former chair of Harvard University's social psychology department, and Ruth Wageman, also a prolific scholar of teamwork, have conducted extensive studies of executive teams in both corporate and nonprofit organizations.[4] Their work identifies characteristics that explain some of the difficulties these top teams face:

> For all members of such teams, the team role is the second—and lower-priority—job. Typically ill-composed, these teams suffer from amorphous purposes that result in a default task strategy of mere information-sharing. Interpersonal dynamics within the team often reflect the tendency of members to seek greater status and recognition, as well as to personally lead rather than to share

leadership. These motives, moreover, are reinforced by reward systems that measure and celebrate individual leadership accomplishments.

In my experience, these counterproductive dynamics are equally applicable to leadership teams that are responsible for key accounts. In fact, I would argue that these dynamics are often *exacerbated* in professional service firms. In that context, partners are often expected to treat each other as pure equals, to the extent that even the "leader" title doesn't really give anyone much confidence in his right to tell his peers what to do.

Fortunately, there are steps that you as a team leader can take to help overcome these leadership shortcomings.

Create a clearly bounded group with an explicit, shared purpose

Start by defining what the leadership *team* needs to accomplish, which is more than the sum of its individual contributions. For example, the leaders collectively might decide to target a certain level of revenue or profitability growth, or aim for new types of work that require cross-practice efforts. Because pursuit of these objectives probably requires trade-offs of time, attention, and resources from both the client service team *and* the client, such decisions belong to the leadership team.

Once it's clear what goals the team aims for, then determine which of the possible candidates have both the capabilities and the desire to contribute to the leadership team. Too often, account team leaders are designated by default: the rainmakers with the biggest books. But the best leadership teams are deliberately designed to include members with both the skill and the will to lead. Each is necessary; neither is sufficient by itself.

Meanwhile, keep an eye on those who *don't* wind up in the inner circle. High producers who are not on the formal leadership team may be secretly relieved to have fewer administrative burdens, but their egos will need to be managed so that they still feel like valued contributors in other ways.

Agree on a clear set of leadership team roles and responsibilities

Many professionals avoid a candid discussion of responsibilities, either because they don't see the value or because they are sensitive about stepping on a peer's toes. But both concerns are misguided: without role clarity, the leadership team is likely to have higher rework and more dropped balls, and making assumptions about another's duties and accountability is less, not more, respectful.

Because the way you divide responsibilities directly affects your client interactions, your choices might well be constrained or otherwise influenced by client preferences. For example, some clients demand a regional and practice group client team structure that mirrors their own team, such as a local account leader in each main market. In contrast, other clients are prescriptive only on outcomes—as in, "Make sure we're fully informed, and always know who's accountable for what." When clients insist on a single point of accountability, otherwise known as the "one throat to choke" model, then the account leadership team obviously needs to reflect this client priority. Don't, however, allow the need for a single point of accountability to squelch the opportunity to create a client-service leadership team; it merely affects the way you allocate roles on the team.

Finally, make sure that each leadership-team member understands that his or her role is both to guide the whole account and to lead the efforts of the subteams—for example, of their region or department. Just as a main task for your client's CEO is keeping each divisional or functional leader focused on both delivering their own business unit's objectives and ensuring the success of the whole organization, your job as a member of the account leadership team is to help each member see both his individual and collective responsibilities. Research shows that members who perceive their roles in this fashion are considerably more likely to develop shared criteria for decisions that maximize collective outcomes, and they are more willing to make choices that trade local for enterprisewide benefits.

Articulate explicit, shared team standards and ways of working that minimize politics

Transparent communication among team leaders—which includes a well-defined, agreed-upon code of conduct—is essential. Each member has a role to play in helping the team feel as if even the toughest, most awkward situations are discussable.

Often, the items that need to be considered are those that create tensions between an individual leader's "own" constituency and those of the broader team. For example, Alejandro, Teresa, and Robert (not their real names) were coleaders of a major client team at a US accounting firm. They'd followed the first two principles outlined earlier closely. They were armed with an agreed-upon strategy to grow their team's profits by 11 percent in a year, and a clear understanding of how each of them would contribute in their own respective departments of audit, tax, and risk advisory.

Despite early progress toward their target, both Teresa and Robert grew worried that Alejandro was using his time with the client's board ineffectively, by focusing too narrowly on audit results. They thought he should instead be using his influence to cement their firm's reputation for more strategic advisory work, and they were frustrated that he hadn't opened up more C-suite doors for their groups. Their own department heads were expecting them to demonstrate the ability to penetrate more senior levels at their clients, and this should have been a great opportunity.

As their frustrations started to boil over, both leaders opted out of more and more team phone calls rather than address the issues directly; because of Alejandro's seniority in the firm, both Teresa and Robert feared risking a confrontation with him.

An external facilitator helped the team identify underlying dynamics and hold a nonthreatening conversation about them. It turns out that Alejandro was equally frustrated with the situation, feeling as if his coleaders were failing to take enough initiative in the account. The team developed clear guidelines for how to bring up such issues going forward, and reserved a regular spot on the agenda for the topic, "How does this new initiative affect your group and your personal priorities?"

This example is consistent with research on top management teams in major companies, which has found that outstanding teams are significantly more likely to place members' individual concerns on the table, and to engage in open discussions about the trade-offs and synergies between members' different sets of departmental responsibilities and those of the account team as a whole.

Coach each other

Create the expectation of—and not just a tolerance for—active, constructive, and timely feedback among account team leaders.

As a team member, you can start this process by requesting critiques from your peers on specific events, such as a pitch meeting you all attended. Ask for a concrete suggestion, such as "What was the one thing you saw me do that was most effective, and tell me one way that I could do better next time." It's best to warn people in advance that you're going to ask them, so that during the event they can devote some thought to the topic.

Line up support for the leadership team

Together, the coleaders should identify the main areas in which they could use additional help, and then think broadly about where to source it.

In chapter 3, I referred to the puzzling phenomenon in which professional service firms exemplify what economists would call a "market that fails to clear." This means there exist both *excess demand* (overburdened leaders who need help juggling numerous responsibilities) and *excess supply* (professionals who want greater responsibility so that they can grow and demonstrate skills). Delegating work to up-and-coming professionals is clearly an important piece of the puzzle, and account team leaders should actively manage the pipeline of future leaders to ensure that they are all optimally challenged.

This step requires frequent, albeit often brief, conversations among leaders to ensure that they are not overburdening any given associate and are spreading the work effectively. But coleaders should also consider how they can tap into business support professionals or other back-office staff in addition to client-facing professionals. These employees often have great insights to offer but are typically underutilized for important tasks; giving them meaningful work as part of a client-facing team is truly a win-win.

Managing a multicultural, distributed team

We are well into the implementation phase here, so hurdle number three—the unique challenges inherent in managing a team that is both multicultural and geographically distributed—has most likely already surfaced in one form or another.

Even if your team isn't global in a geographic sense, it probably operates from multiple far-flung locations and draws on a wide range of experience bases. Managing these kinds of large collaborations tends to incur significant coordination costs, like projects delayed due to incompatible schedules, cultural or linguistic misunderstandings on cross-border work, or missed deadlines caused by technology failures. Cross-border matters are especially challenging, because each involves coordinating professionals with different assumptions and ways of working. On top of those complexities, layer on the difficulty of running a *virtual* team—whose members might never all assemble in the same room at one time.

Let's look at a mini case study. A French lawyer consulting to an international, Paris-headquartered client felt pressured by his co–account leaders in the United States and Asia to drive for faster growth.

"I understand that I need to be very active," he commented to me, "but in the French culture, we cannot be quite so aggressive as elsewhere. For Paris clients, you need to be pushy without *seeming* to be pushy. It's a delicate balance that outsiders don't grasp."

In his view, the best way to accomplish his objectives was to build relationships over time and for the long term:

> I need to see them very regularly. I like to have one-to-
> one meetings, spend time outside the office, take them to

> lunch. That's where you get the information. By contrast, my counterparts from other parts of the world expect to fly in here, go along with me to a client meeting, and walk out with a mandate. Frankly, that's more likely to lose work than win it.

But my conversations with his counterparts revealed their mounting frustration with the pace in Paris:

> We in New York are stymied until he sorts things out and decides to make the move. How much foie gras does it take before we can just ask for the work?

One of the things that makes working at a distance so complicated is that it affects both the way we *feel* and the way we *think*—and any viable solutions have to address both.[5]

So let's take a short detour into human psychology. On the one hand, working with distant colleagues provides numerous triggers—physical distance, time zones, culture, language, reliance on technology, and so on—for something social psychologists refer to as *social categorization*, or what might be called the "us and them" reaction. Thinking of our colleagues in terms of categories, rather than as individuals, isn't inherently a bad thing; in fact, it's a critical cognitive shortcut that helps us to simplify our ever more complex environment. The problem arises when we also place ourselves in one of those categories, which generally causes us to view those in the same group (our ingroup) more positively, and those in other groups (our outgroups) more negatively.

This is especially problematic in distributed collaborative work, as the "otherness" of our distant colleagues is reinforced daily and along multiple dimensions. Speaking via video conference with a colleague in a different location—a person who speaks with an accent, exhibits different cultural values, and is available for only two hours of your normal workday—can make that person feel worlds away.

And there's more. Beyond affecting how we feel about our far-flung colleagues, working at a distance inevitably affects the information we have about them. Evolution has given us the ability to notice, interpret, incorporate, and leverage a vast amount of data as we try to make sense of our daily experiences. We gather that information assiduously, and we use it. We depend on it, in fundamental ways.

Consider how much you know about your colleagues who are geographically close. You understand their relative positions in the office power hierarchy, you are aware of other projects that might be competing for their time and mindshare, and you probably know something about their underlying motivations—what makes them tick. All of this helps you to understand their actions. And as much as we might want to deny it, factors we might consider irrelevant—personal lives, moods, or even the weather—play a role. (Does having your commute time tripled due to bad weather, or being sleep-deprived due to a sick child, have an effect on your day? Of course. Do your office mates understand that, and cut you the appropriate slack? Very often they do.) Unfortunately, barriers in the form of distance, time, culture, language, and technology all block the flow of such information, creating what George Mason University professor Catherine Cramton has dubbed the "mutual knowledge problem."

In short, when interacting with distant colleagues, we lack a large percentage of the information we usually rely on to collaborate effectively. And to make matters worse, the two problems just described tend to reinforce each other. We don't share as much information with our outgroups, and the less information we have about our distant colleagues, the more we see them as "them."

Even when the team is distributed across offices or around the world, however, we can take concrete steps to equip ourselves and our teams for delivering exceptional service. I'll point to two steps: focusing on commonalities and making information symmetrical.[6]

Focus on commonalities

The problem with "us and them" thinking is that it leads us to home in on our differences and undervalue our similarities. The good news is that it's relatively easy to reverse this focus. Highlighting the things we have in common with our distant colleagues is the best way to reduce the problem—and foremost among these commonalities should be your shared objectives.

Remind your team of its goal. Have an open conversation around the question, "Why are we working across geographies?" Discussing why you have chosen to collaborate with colleagues at another location—for example, to better serve global clients, or to provide a more complete solution to an important local client—helps ensure that these goals are shared by everyone.

Recognize your interdependence in reaching your objectives. Couple the question above with this one: "Why does my success depend on my distant colleagues?" Reinforce this day-to-day by looking for opportunities to remind your team members of their reliance on other locations.

If you don't have a ready answer to either question, you should rethink whether the benefits of a global team outweigh the costs. But if you do have an answer, that discussion will focus team members on common objectives and interdependence, turning "us and them" into "we."

Make information symmetrical

Focusing on commonalities, however, will get you only so far, because nearly every interaction serves up reminders of the differences between offices. Unfortunately, there is no silver bullet. But remedies do exist—if you're willing to invest in small, ongoing actions to get bigger, long-term benefits.

Schedule brief, frequent meetings to share task-related information on a regular basis, rather than "as needed," because we rarely know for certain when the knowledge we possess is needed by our distant colleagues. Beyond the obvious benefit of coordinating the actual work, regular communications help keep team members engaged and committed to the client team.

Take time to share personal updates as well. Yes, it's tempting to dismiss such communication as irrelevant or a waste of time—especially when under pressure—but it is in fact *vital*. Keep in mind that global virtual work runs counter to millions of years of evolution. Tackling the symmetrical knowledge problem requires activities that often feel forced or artificial, like scheduling time for "spontaneous" inter-action, or investing in technologies to create virtual water coolers. These shared experiences increase the feeling of "we," and the result-ing trust and familiarity are vital when a true crisis erupts.

Give (and take) a virtual tour to provide context. The more you and your distant teammates know about each other's environment, the better you will be able to make sense of one another's behavior. At the start of a project, offer each person involved the opportu-nity to share a bit of their context. This shouldn't take the form of name, rank, and serial number, but rather, can be a succinct sketch of the elements in your environment that are most likely to affect your ability to collaborate effectively. Jordan, a partner in the Sydney office of a large accounting firm, shared a helpful approach:

> I started to work on a matter with a partner in New
> York and knew we'd be having a number of late-night or
> early-morning videoconferences. So I took five minutes to
> give him a rundown of my workspaces. I focused on things
> that were most likely to interrupt future calls: my anxious
> client who's just taken on a new role, my occasionally over-
> eager assistant, and—when working from my home office—
> my dog. The interruptions were much easier to deal with
> when they came up, simply because he was expecting them.

You know best what works in your case. Is it a quick pan of your office with a webcam? A verbal walk-through of whatever context really defines you? The objective is to help your distant colleagues understand your work environment, and thereby build mutual knowledge and trust.

Effective global collaborations boil down to a simple truth: we must invest time and effort to foster the things that come naturally when we work face-to-face. That investment is both necessary and productive. And it's essential to take those steps early and pro-actively when you still enjoy a bit of breathing room, so that you have the benefit of a well-functioning team when the pressure heats up—as I discuss next.

Anticipating and handling
performance pressure

Done right, collaboration is a powerful competitive tool—especially when wielded by seasoned collaborators. So what can go wrong?

In today's hypercompetitive marketplace, professional firms and their leaders face unprecedented pressure to deliver superior results. Every professional would like to think she does her best work when the stakes are highest—for example, in important multijurisdiction or major cross-practice client work. Paradoxically, though, the pressure on account teams to perform exceedingly well often drives them to suboptimal outcomes. This pressure—to deliver exceptional results in critical situations—sometimes leads us to focus on avoiding failure, rather than seeking true excellence, and this anxiety in turn leads to subpar results.[7]

"We were seriously feeling the heat," as one high-ranking partner in a Big Four accounting firm admitted. "It was a make-or-break project for us. We threw our best and brightest against the problem, but the more we rallied our team, the worse it got. I still don't know what went wrong."

Performance pressure can be a double-edged sword. Although it motivates people to ramp up their efforts, they may also inadvertently react in ways that are ultimately counterproductive. In particular, they may pull back and retreat to their respective comfort zones. But this retreat typically results in two unintended consequences.

First, *collaboration suffers*. Because many professionals have type A personalities, under stress they tend to become even more task-oriented, impatient, driven, and controlling. For them, taking time to communicate effectively—for example, to explain issues to a nonnative speaker who approaches his work somewhat differently—feels like a waste. But this reaction can kick off a downward spiral, in which meetings are cancelled and communications get curtailed. Coordinating and delegating across language and cultural barriers without the opportunity for a face-to-face meeting begins to feel more and more risky, especially for professionals who have traditionally been rewarded for individual achievement and personal reputations. The question becomes, why *not* retreat to my comfort zone?

Performance pressure also narrows people's perspectives, such that they have more trouble than usual understanding others' points of view, which further damages the kind of communication that is essential for cross-disciplinary or cross-cultural work. A diminished appreciation for cultural differences, and even for practical realities like time zones, generates trust-damaging conflicts that undermine the team's ability to deliver seamless service.

Second, under performance pressure, *innovation suffers*, because we reject many of the novel inputs that seem riskier. Ideas with outcomes that cannot be guaranteed get passed over in favor of the "tried and true."

Cross-border projects are especially challenging in this regard. Approaches that have proven optimal in one country may be inappropriate in the international context—or may appear to be too risky to try. We're aware, intellectually, that our client is expecting innovative results on their sophisticated cross-border work; but the pressures of coordinating a multicultural team can subtly influence us to seek simplified approaches that end up appearing less novel or less tailored than expected.

Obviously, these outcomes are the *exact opposite* of what we are aiming for when we undertake projects for our most demanding and sophisticated clients. But most of them happen so gradually, and so naturally, that they are hard to identify in the moment, especially when our teams are focused exclusively on results without regard to interpersonal dynamics.

The unintended consequences are especially likely to sneak up on seasoned collaborators, many of whom are seriously stressed by their firms' changing priorities. Lead partners who have always been trusted to drive performance through their client relationships are anxious about their firm's increased use of financially driven performance metrics and other central controls. Even the most experienced partners face intense pressure to perform better than ever or face severe consequences—such as the loss of compensation, higher scrutiny and monitoring, or lower status, sometimes in the form of being removed from prestigious committees or even losing their role as account leader.

Unfortunately, there are no easy answers. But four steps can help you manage your own and your team's reaction to performance pressure:

- **Identify your natural tendencies, and compensate where necessary.** Under pressure, people instinctively revert to their most comfortable leadership style—which for most type A professionals is not ideal for encouraging collaboration and innovation.[8] Resisting this shift is incredibly difficult, so instead find coleaders or project managers who can complement your style or at least help you keep perspective.

- **Anticipate especially high-pressure situations.** On high-stakes projects, equip the team with additional resources, such as more time, on-call subject matter experts, or administrative support. Decide with the team how you'll handle dysfunctional team dynamics when (not if) they arise.[9] Encourage team members to get their personal lives in order before the heat turns up: warn loved ones of the impending project, organize backup child care or help with other personal responsibilities, and rest up.

- **Use all your resources.** Typically, pressured teams rely too much on high-status, formal leaders—like you—because following the boss feels safe. Counter that tendency by monitoring participation during meetings: Are junior members contributing? Are ideas from staff listened to? If participation and decision making become too narrowly based, you're failing to leverage potentially great ideas and handicapping your ability to stay focused on the big picture, where you're needed most.

- **Involve the client.** It feels counterintuitive, but exposing novel ideas early to your client (with appropriate caveats, of course) is *less risky* than waiting to do a "big reveal" at the end. In-process client participation not only builds their commitment to the jointly developed solution, but also helps keep you focused on optimal, not merely acceptable, solutions.

In closing, here's some good news: done right, you can actually harness performance pressure for some very positive effects. Well-led teams under pressure are more motivated, work harder and longer, and take advantage of a high-stakes project as an opportunity to shine. You're still the successful seasoned collaborator you've always been, and whom the firm treasures—and now, through smart collaboration, you're having more impact than ever before.

Next: Singing to the undersung

The seasoned collaborators whom I've talked to in the course of my research already know a great deal about how to work successfully with a wide range of colleagues. They've shared their wisdom and experience, as well as their open questions. This chapter has captured some of those lessons, and addressed some of those questions.

But there are plenty of other fertile grounds, valuable perspectives, and open questions. For example, in every chapter so far, I have made passing references to a cohort within the firm that is traditionally undersung: a group I'll call the *contributors*.

In chapter 5, I lay out the ways that this group, too, can benefit from collaboration—and show them and their firms' leaders how to capitalize on their potential.

Collaboration and
the Contributor

A s discussed in chapter 4, a seasoned collaborator's ability to hand off work depends on finding one or more trust-worthy colleagues who are willing to join the team. But this can be a problem. Sometimes nobody takes the bait.

Why this reluctance? The answers vary, depending on whom is asked. This chapter explores the professional world of what I call the *contributor*. It focuses on the pros, cons, and how-to's of collaboration for people who are typically a member of the team, rather than the leader. Stated differently, the seasoned collaborator *sends* work, and the contributor *receives* work.[1] The lead client service partner creates collaborative opportunities and the contrib-utor helps deliver on those opportunities.

The contributor category contains a couple different kinds of professionals, which I group together because they tend to have similar views of collaboration-related challenges and opportuni-ties. The first kind of contributor is the "up-and-comers." These are young specialists who instinctively understand the value of collaboration. They are ambitious, and want to be where the action is. They get the idea that client problems are increasingly complicated, and that complicated problems increasingly need the kinds of solutions that only sophisticated teams can provide. They understand that these problems are inherently more interesting than less complicated ones—more stimulating, from a professional standpoint—and that clients will pay more to have them solved. They may even have a sense of the longitudinal arguments in favor of collaboration: today's freestanding specialist is increasingly at risk of becoming commoditized, and therefore replaceable.

Another kind of contributor somewhat resembles the solo specialists described in chapter 3, albeit on a less senior level. These are highly skilled individuals who must navigate the tension between spending their time and effort on developing their own clients versus contributing to work that other partners have generated. As one young lawyer bluntly stated it to me, "Every minute I spend helping [my fellow partners] build their business is time I could have invested in building my own franchise. In this business, nobody gets an Oscar for a supporting role."

Similarly, professionals in an in-house strategy or accounting function—or researchers in a think tank or similarly positioned young knowledge professionals—must decide how much energy they want to devote to meeting the goals for which they are individually accountable, versus working as part of a team to accomplish collective projects. Not surprisingly, some are inclined to keep their heads down and grind out work within their own practices.

All these contributors help the firm succeed, day in and day out. If you are a firm leader or a seasoned collaborator, you know who these contributors are, and you know that at their best, they're invaluable.[2]

Contributors themselves have probably found a fairly steady, low-risk rhythm. So why strike out in a new direction? In some cases, their lives have changed in ways that make them more available. (Perhaps the youngest kid has headed off to boarding school or college.) In other cases, they—like the up-and-comers—are deciding that they want the opportunity to work on more cutting-edge challenges, spend the day with more interesting people, get the special psychological reward of playing on a high-functioning team, and potentially make more money. Perhaps they've gotten a taste of collaboration, and want more. Or maybe they're worried that the path they've taken so far—for example, hitching their wagon to a star rainmaker who keeps the work flowing—is increasingly risky. Stars move between firms more than ever, and don't always take their loyal teams along.

For all kinds of contributors, collaboration is a promising way ahead. This chapter explains why, and lays out some strategies for getting those benefits sooner. A time lag between the initial embrace of collaboration and the flow of resulting benefits is inevitable—but both contributors themselves and their firm leaders can take steps to make collaboration easier and more rewarding, and thereby speed up the payoff.

The benefits of collaborating on others' projects

No matter which type of contributor you are, you already have a pretty good thing going. Sure, there are risks to sticking with the tried and true. But there are also risks associated with changing your proven formula. The rewards of building "someone else's client" might not be obvious—the effects are often hard to trace, and the short-term impact on a professional's payout depends a great deal on the specifics of the firm's compensation policy. So again, the question becomes, Why should you rock your own boat?

I propose four answers to that question.

Service work leads to successful business development

Long ago, professional services guru David Maister came up with a typology of the sector that has become almost universal parlance: *finders*, *minders*, and *grinders*. One of his main points was that all three of these groups are important, and successful knowledge-based firms build and maintain a pyramid that keeps them in balance.

True enough. But it's also possible to move between groups. Simply stated, working as someone else's grinder equips the contributor to become a finder—and to get increasingly good at that new role.

I've surveyed partners across dozens of knowledge-based firms about the reasons they don't collaborate more in their client work. One of the top reasons they cite is that they lack the capabilities and confidence to pursue cross-practice matters.[3] But this is a self-fulfilling prophecy: if you don't practice something, you don't get better. Working on cross-practice projects significantly predicts a partner's rainmaking in subsequent years. In fact, when I examined the thousands of partners in my database, I found that, on average, collaborators grew their book of business with existing clients by tens of thousands of dollars just by having worked on a couple of extra multipractice projects in the prior year.[4]

Interviews with both partners and clients suggest that these results occur because working on multidisciplinary projects helps contributors learn how to sell more-sophisticated work to their own clients. By participating on cross-discipline teams, contributors learn about other domains, giving them a stronger ability to identify broader issues facing their own clients and the confidence to open up conversations about them. As one collaborating contributor put it: "After I had worked with a few tax experts and started to really understand what they do, I realized that there were offshoots from my own area of expertise where my client could benefit from tax advice. I knew just enough to open up those conversations with my client, and then I brought in the expert once the client was intrigued."

But collaboration provides learning beyond subject-matter knowledge. Contributors also develop the internal relationships that allow them to sell more complex projects to new clients with the confidence that their partners will help them deliver high-quality work.

Up to a point, the more cross-practice engagements a collaborating contributor works on in one year, the more success he or she is likely to have the next year selling work to new clients. This effect does taper off, however. Preliminary results suggest that contributors who spend more than about three-quarters of their time servicing others' clients may fall into a "service partner trap" where they fail to spend enough time prospecting new clients. Most firms expect contributors above a certain seniority level to generate at least some revenue, which is why this trap is potentially dangerous.

Colleagues refer work to you

Even if you have little responsibility for client development, collaboration is beneficial because it builds your reputation in the right circles. As a contributor, you already realize the benefit of receiving work referrals, but you might not appreciate just how much collaboration feeds into that process.

How so? When you work with a colleague on a project, you build that colleague's faith in your integrity and competency, thereby helping to overcome many of the trust-related barriers discussed in prior chapters. The more partners you work with, the more people who will feel comfortable sending you business.[5] "I got to know the quality of Susan's work when we were both working a deal for Matthew's client," one partner told me. "She impressed me with her sharp insights, so when my own client was facing some restructuring issues, she was the obvious one for me to ring up."

This quote probably resonates with collaborative partners who've both received and offered work referrals. I suspect, though, that the contributor who is not accustomed to collaborating may still need convincing. If that describes you, consider this point: my analyses across multiple firms confirm that collaboration enhances one's reputation with direct collaborators, who are willing to refer work to that partner for the first time ever after working together. On average, *every six additional collaborators will lead to one new referral from those collaborators in the next year.* In one mid-sized accounting firm, for example, that referral was worth tens of thousands of dollars in incremental billed revenue for the contributor turned business developer.

No, even the most appreciative lead partners can't send you more work if their clients don't need your expertise—but even in those cases, they are very likely to spread word of your expertise to colleagues who do need it. In other words, collaboration enhances a professional's reputation beyond her direct collaborators. The more colleagues a professional collaborates with, the more first-time referrals she will receive from others who have learned about her through word of mouth. At one firm, for example, it took working with just two extra partners to generate a work referral from a brand-new contact—who, presumably, had learned about the partner's expertise through word-of-mouth recommendations. And because getting work referred from others is more efficient than prospecting for new work on your own, these referrals are highly valuable in helping you reach your revenue targets.

My analyses show, conclusively, that *the more a partner collaborates on client work that others generate, the more his or her own revenues will grow in subsequent years*, regardless of office, practice group, organizational tenure, or present-year revenues. To put it in concrete terms, for each additional partner collaborated with in year 1, the originating collaborator is able to bill about 0.5 percent more in year 2. For example, for the average lawyer in the *American Lawyer* Global 100 who increases his collaboration network by just one extra partner per month, that translates into incremental billings of $22,000—even before accounting for the associated increase in hourly rates, which are discussed in the next section.

True, that sum alone might not be substantial enough to change a professional's behavior. But consider figure 5-1.

This graph, based on one firm's actual data, shows how the effects of collaboration compound over time for two different partners—let's call them Jen and Kim.[6] Imagine they start with the same number of work referrals—in this case, five. In the first year, Jen (represented by the top, thick lines) works hard to build her collaboration network both by accepting referrals sent to her and by sending some work to others. By the end of year 1, she has reached the firm's top quartile in terms of the number of partners she's worked with. Also, the number of work referrals she receives from both new contacts (thick solid line) and prior collaborators (thick dashed line) has risen significantly; the effects continue to swell over time, as Jen's teammates spread her reputation.

FIGURE 5-1

Impact of collaboration on work referrals over time

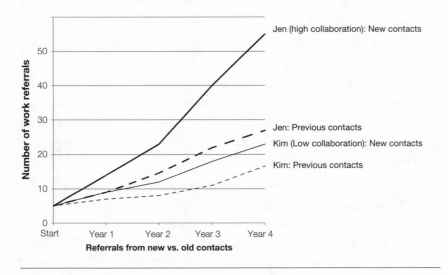

On the other hand, Kim (represented by the figure's thin lines) starts building her network more slowly; by the end of year 1, the number of referrals she gets from both prior and new contacts is still in the bottom quartile. As a result, her reputation continues to spread much more slowly over these four years. By the end of this period, Jen is receiving more than twice as many referrals as Kim. Granted, this illustration is based on the *average* effects of collaboration across many partners in a firm—some will probably gain a bit more and some a bit less from collaboration. But overall, understanding that the effects of collaboration definitely compound over time—in part the result of the significant growth in the professional's reputation—might well prompt a partner to invest in their collaborative future.

Collaboration drives your reputation and rates

Professional services are notoriously opaque—that is, hard for clients to judge their value, even after a service has been performed—either because they are so deeply intertwined with many other client actions and decisions, or because the results appear only after a considerable time lag, or both. Despite the uptick in clients' use of metrics to parse and analyze their "spend" on knowledge-based services, that nagging uncertainty remains. The practical result is that many clients still make their hiring decisions largely on the basis of a professional's reputation, gleaned from word-of-mouth recommendations. The implications for you, as a contributor who is contemplating collaboration? Working on other people's projects can spread and burnish your reputation in clients' eyes, and increase the demand for your services.

Obviously, you won't be surprised by the assertion that a strong marketplace reputation allows you to charge more. But what *may* surprise you is the clear effect of collaboration on these rates. Across the many firms I studied, the more cross-disciplinary projects that the partners worked on, and the more complex each project was, the more their hourly rates increased in following years. These analyses all statistically controlled for other ways of explaining variations in rates, such as a partner's practice, office, seniority, gender, and other variables. The simple fact remains: cross-practice collaboration experience is a very robust determinant of your ability to raise your rates faster than your colleagues who do more siloed work.

So, for example, the average noncollaborating lawyer who billed $500 an hour in 2008 would now bill about $600 an hour. But if that same lawyer had done a significant amount of complex, cross-practice work in the interim, his or her rate would now be well over $750.[7] Even if you're not the kind of professional who bills by the hour or day, you should realize that in this context, money is a proxy for reputation. In other words, it's an easy way to quantify the link between your collaboration experience and its market value.

Why does that happen? Clients recognize your ability to provide strategic direction, rather than just pure technical expertise. They're willing to reward you for delivering value when they're considering their most sophisticated issues.

Even in the short term, collaboration helps boost rates. In one firm, for example, professionals who have worked on a project originated by a partner in a different practice typically charge rates 8 to 10 percent higher than for in-practice work. Part of this discrepancy comes from clients' inclination not to push back on smaller components of the bill—that is, in cases where the out-of-practice partner billed relatively few hours. But senior people on the client side tell me that they're willing to pay for specialist expertise when it clearly enhances the outcome.

The evidence is compelling: the greater the proportion of your billed hours spent working outside your practice, the higher your rates will be relative to average colleagues.

Collaboration can help you weather the next storm

Collaboration insulates professionals from the worst financial effects of an economic downturn. This argument is only a big deal when it's a big deal—and at those times, it's a *very* big deal.

For example, in one firm, partners who collaborated with at least ten other partners each year in the three years prior to the 2008 recession maintained their revenues in 2008–2009, whereas the revenues of those who were isolated practically fell off a cliff. What's more, collaborative partners' revenues climbed much more quickly afterward.

There are two explanations for this phenomenon. The first is a version of portfolio theory, drawn from Finance 101. Just as a competent financial adviser will warn you not to put all your retirement savings into a single kind of investment, smart partners in the knowledge industry spread their bets over a range of different clients. By the law of averages, some of those clients inevitably fare better than others during a recession. At the same time, the most collaborative partners are apt to be involved in multiple sectors, some of which are likely to be countercyclical. Finally, different practice groups fare differently in different phases of the economic cycle. Contributors who had the benefit of strong relationships with their bankruptcy- and restructuring-oriented colleagues had plenty of work flowing their way in 2009.

The second explanation is psychologically based. We humans are tribal, at heart, and when food gets scarce, we "take care of our own"—the phrase that one partner used to explain his recession-era behavior to me. And as he further explained, he didn't consider the whole partnership to be his tribe. Instead, he was referring to the small cohort of tightly knit partners who were sharing work before the downturn really started to bite down.

Of course, very few partners began collaborating in order to protect themselves from calamity. If they'd seen the downturn coming, they'd have hedged stocks, made a killing, and retired when the economy turned. So think of this sort of protection as a nice by-product of collaboration—that insurance policy that turns out to be a very wise investment. It's not a big enough reason to change behavior, in and of itself; but it's a nice benefit, nonetheless.

Strategies for collaborating as a contributor

Collaboration can feel like a risky gambit: as we've seen on both the individual and firm level, it requires up-front investment, but yield rewards only over time. However, the would-be collaborative contributor can adopt strategies to reduce his or her costs, increase benefits, and shorten the payback period for collaboration.

Let me suggest two overall strategies: cultivating relationships with appropriate partners, and developing your own skill set in ways that will make you more valuable to potential collaborators.

Cultivate relationships with high-profile partners

You need to work on collaborative projects with partners who are in charge of prestigious client accounts. The higher the profile and status of their network, the more influence those partners have on the perceptions of people both inside and outside the firm. So how do you get yourself on the radar of partners who can benefit from your expertise and help you build your capabilities and your revenues?

First, *target specific clients and their relationship partner.* Chris, a partner in the New York office of a global law firm, uses this tactic. From discussions with colleagues or articles in the business press, she gleans ideas for how her expertise in data privacy might be used more broadly in a corporate client's strategy. She then researches companies that her firm already serves, and writes a one-page memo to the appropriate partner outlining what she can offer specifically to that partner's client, and how her expertise solves a particular problem. Chris admits that the effort takes time, and not all of her colleagues are receptive to what they see as self-promotion. On the other hand, some are extremely grateful—enough that the tactic has so far resulted in multiple joint pitches for new work, and a couple of ongoing relationships with partners.

Second, *take advantage of your firm's equivalent of requests for information (RFIs).* With this approach, you're putting an existing system to a new (and valid) use. Here's how one partner described it:

> We have an internal system called Global Request that people can use when they have an opportunity or client question. To get input from others, he or she can write a specific request to a subgroup or the whole firm. Our firm has thousands of professionals, and several hundred partners. If you send to all partners, then you get three or four responses on average. If you get an answer that is well articulated, then next time you have this topic, you go directly to them, which is a benefit for both of you.
>
> But unless you have provided feedback and insights on twenty to thirty global requests, you aren't likely to see benefits in terms of work referrals. When I was a more junior partner, I pushed myself to try to answer as many queries as possible. Whenever I had anything to add, I tried to share it, or at least refer them to someone. I pushed myself more than just when it was convenient. I got an amazing response to my inputs, and it resulted in getting called to help on specific proposals, presentations, and so on.

Third, *initiate the relationship*. Invite influential colleagues onto your own client projects. Here's an illuminating example: Kevin, a veteran consulting partner, transferred from a boutique telecommunications firm to a generalist firm so he could apply his operations expertise to a wider array of clients. Soon after joining the new firm, Kevin identified three partners who were widely seen as prime players in other practice groups. He invited each to lunch, and before each meeting, he spent hours conducting due diligence about his prospective tablemates: studying their published papers, reading up on their clients, and talking to partners in their own practice who'd worked with them. Not surprisingly, those colleagues found those lunches interesting and productive.

Within his first year of joining his new firm, Kevin found an opening to hold joint meetings at his client with each of those partners; one developed into a small but promising stream of work. The three partners—not only the one who derived immediate benefits—grew to appreciate Kevin's deep expertise and client-handling skills. They understood and admired his determination to stay at the firm and build a thriving business.

Over time, those partners began telling others of their impressions of him, and his prospects began to develop for work on colleagues' clients across a range of industries. The initial trick, Kevin explained, was for him to learn enough of their domain expertise to be able to identify specific opportunities for them in his own client settings, and credibly start discussions about those opportunities.

And finally, *be an exemplary team player*. If you want referrals to come your way, you have to make the most of your reputation-building opportunities. Deliver what you committed to on time, without reminders. Communicate immediately if a real emergency delays you, but don't make excuses, and definitely don't blame underlings. Clarify expectations and your circumstances up front, such as travel plans that will make it hard for teammates to contact you. It may seem self-evident, but it bears underscoring: partners who refer work to you may be using that project as a tryout to see if you're ready for prime time.

"When given the chance to work on a high-prestige client for a high-profile partner," one collaborating contributor told me,

"I choose to overinvest in that project to display my professional skills at their best. It will certainly mean sacrificing somewhere else—usually giving up nights and weekends—but it's worth it to develop my standing as a go-to guy."

Develop your ability to dig into the client's toughest issues

I touched on the subject of skill building in chapter 3. Here, I want to make the same point in the context of contributors who are "just" team players. Do you want the opportunities that collaboration offers? If so, whether you "own" the client or not, you share the responsibility for unearthing opportunities.

If you don't have formal business training, you need to get familiar with the core business concepts that underpin your client company's strategy, operations, or commercial environment. You don't need an MBA to start a conversation about the client's competitors—but you'll certainly be better equipped to *continue* the conversation if you've learned some of these business fundamentals. Executive education courses that are geared to professionals in your specific field—law, accounting, and so on—are likely to preselect the most relevant core concepts, and help you figure out how to put your new knowledge into practice most easily.[8]

In addition, consider pairing up with someone in your firm who has a reputation for being great at holding "business insight" conversations with clients. This person might be another partner, but doesn't have to be. Think about striking an informal alliance with someone in your business development or marketing function, for example. Those individuals can be treasure troves of untapped wisdom, and many are thrilled to help make an impact directly on clients.

All of this will help you develop skills, confidence, and a reputation for tackling complex problems, even as a contributor. And in turn, that preparation—combined with your track record in this new realm—can help you decide how far you want to go in this new venture. If you persist and succeed, you by definition will become a seasoned collaborator.

Tackling the producer-manager dilemma

Taking the steps outlined above will help you reap the benefits of collaboration sooner and more reliably; in essence, they help you increase the *returns* from collaboration. But the final hurdle that many contributors have to clear before committing to more proactive, cross-practice, or cross-geography collaboration is the *investment* portion of the ROI equation: how to find time for this endeavor when they're already working flat out to contribute their own expertise on work that flows to them.

"If I have to start learning to spot and tackle more complex problems at my client," you might think, "won't it just lead to more hassles?" Contributors rightly worry about how they can possibly shoulder new responsibilities and bigger administrative burdens associated with growing their account teams—all while continuing to contribute at their traditionally high levels of quality and productivity. This challenge is the budding collaborator's version of what is often called the producer-manager dilemma: the challenge of generating and executing work while managing a client account and other professionals.

Budding collaborators can take some fundamental steps to stay focused on the most productive client and team priorities. Here are three approaches you can try, summarized as *managing your clients*, *managing your team*, and *managing yourself.*

Managing your clients

The core idea here is that stronger, more transparent client relationships will allow you to prioritize better and put more focus on areas that yield the highest value.

First, *agree on and manage task expectations*. At the outset, invest enough time to make sure you and your client both understand why you're suggesting a collaborative approach. Setting explicit objectives can save enormous time and rework later because you won't need to waste time explaining why, for instance, your colleague from a distant office (who has exactly the right specialist knowledge) shows up on the bill. Documenting these expectations gives you an easy way to onboard newcomers to the project, which is a critical timesaver because collaborative efforts are often more fluid than solo ones.

Document progress so that the client feels empowered and in control. Be up front when problems arise. The earlier you say, "We've spotted an issue but know how to resolve it," the more the client will trust you. One seasoned partner says that many of his responses to client emails are simply two words: "On it." Even this super-brief response tells clients that he received the instruction, and they know he'll follow up when he can provide more details about progress. Finally, be honest from the get-go about your own and your team's capabilities; it's far better to turn down work than erode trust.

Also focus on *learning the individual client's priorities, preferences, and fears.* Clients expect you to be sensitive to how they like things done, especially in terms of their communication preferences. Do they favor short, frequent email updates, or more comprehensive memos? Do they expect instant responses to emails? Do they hate to be interrupted during their kids' bedtime routine, but become available again after 9 p.m.? As you start collaborating on new accounts, get this information from the lead partner so that you can transition smoothly into a bigger role. Most collaborators say they know all of this about their key clients, but the client executives I interview often complain about a mismatch—probably because of a communication lapse between partners.

At a deeper level, do you know what your individual client's professional ambition is, and what it would take for her to achieve it? If your client's objective is also to keep learning in order to grow her area of responsibility, then your attempts to uncover complex issues and design collaborative solutions align closely with her goals. When you focus on what the client truly wants, you can make sure your own collaborative agenda adds real value and is not simply self-aggrandizing.

You also need to *involve the client in cocreating solutions.* Decades of psychological and organizational research show that people are more committed to ideas and solutions when they've been involved in their development. Surprisingly, people who wind up with objectively bad outcomes but who valued the process typically feel more satisfied than people who got favorable out-comes from a dubious process.[9] No, this tendency doesn't give you license to deliver mediocre service, but it does suggest that in the rare event that your work is not truly stellar, clients are likely to give you the benefit of the doubt if they've helped to cocreate the path.

You need, therefore, to collaborate with the client in all critical decision making—giving them real options, and not just conclusions you have already developed. Even if your team is tasked with developing a solution on its own, keep the client closely informed, create opportunities for them to ask questions, and provide reassurance about their fears and insecurities. By getting the client on your side, cocreation may also head off some of the us-versus-them mentality that creates stress. This lower pressure creates a virtuous cycle, because both you and the client are more likely to make sound decisions when facing less stress, which allows you to collaborate more effectively, which further reduces tension.

Managing your team

You can lower the cost of collaboration and create more time for your own highest-value activities if you invest in properly equipping and leading your account team. Note that you can take most of these actions whether or not you're the official leader—the best contributors find ways to facilitate collaboration from within the ranks. Again, I have three suggestions.

First, *supercharge the team through delegation*. The most motivated, engaged, and productive teams are ones whose members strongly agree with this statement: "At work, I have the opportunity to do what I do best every day."[10] Help to find an optimal match between each team member's capabilities and their tasks so that they are challenged but not overwhelmed. Delegation not only frees up your time, but also motivates the team to perform better. Meanwhile, you will increase your colleagues' skills, so that they can increasingly serve as your backup. Last but certainly not least, you'll also gain their loyalty.

A second tactic for efficient collaboration is to *hold frequent check-ins* to spot issues and course-correct early. For example: Deloitte recently launched an overhaul of its performance management system, which calls for weekly individual discussions between team leaders and each member. Deloitte stresses the interlinkage between performance management activities and a manager's core job: "For us, these check-ins are not *in addition* to the work of a team leader; they *are* the work of a team leader."[11]

It sounds counterintuitive, but investing in these brief conversations actually makes collaboration more efficient. The dialogue allows collaborative leaders to clarify priorities for the upcoming week, comment on recent work, and provide course correction, coaching, or important new information.

You might imagine that only juniors would crave these conversations, whereas partners would see them as meddling. In reality, though, most partners welcome brief phone calls, both to get updates about the client situation and to ask clarifying questions that will save time.

In many firms, people are not used to asking for input—perhaps because they believe the firm's "entrepreneurial" culture expects them to exhibit self-confidence and independence. Your job as a collaborative leader and contributor is to overcome those concerns, and provide nonjudgmental help until those behaviors become routine in your team. Whatever time you invest in short, frequent check-ins will allow you to be a more effective collaborator.

Finally, *empower the team to use each other, along with all of the firm's other resources.* If you had to draw a diagram of your team's communication patterns, what would it look like? Faced with this question, many account leaders and team members simply sketch a classic organization chart, with communication cascading downward through the hierarchy, as shown in figure 5-2. Others' drawings resemble a wagon wheel, with them as the center hub and team members as spokes. The best collaborations resemble a network, with potential communication lines connecting not only to the center, but also to and from all participants. This pattern signals that team members seek and provide help among themselves, freeing up the leader to focus on the most critical issues. To avoid

FIGURE 5-2

Team communication patterns

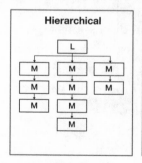

Hierarchical

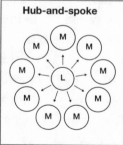

Hub-and-spoke

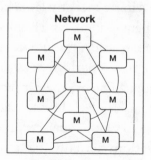

Network

	Hierarchical	Hub-and-spoke	Network
Benefits:	• Easy for leader • Efficient in the short term	• Leader retains control • Each member hears the same message	• Efficient—everyone engages only where necessary • Members inform and learn from each other • Leader can focus on highest-level issues • Empowered team members are more motivated and engaged
Risks:	• Disempowers lower staff • One-way flow inhibits innovation and feedback	• Leader becomes a bottleneck • Members are isolated from each other	• Information overload happens if ground rules are not followed

Note: L = Leader; M = Member

information overload in this kind of team, however, the leader needs to truly empower members to communicate directly with each other as needed, eliminating cover-your-backside tendencies to copy the leader or other team members on nonessential messages.

Also make sure the team is aware of the firm's resources beyond the team, and is comfortable collaborating with them. For example, many firms have underutilized communication specialists who can serve as a great sounding board when associates are writing the first draft of a client presentation. Similarly, many firms have (or have access to) industry experts, whose input may cut hours off a research project. You know the equivalent resources at your organization—and most likely, you know how to get great work from them. Model those behaviors for your team, especially by showing respect and empathy for those often underappreciated staff resources. The more you help your team effectively use resources, the more time you gain to invest in spotting and helping to deliver on high-value collaborative opportunities.

Managing yourself

My final suggestion for addressing the collaborative contributor's version of the producer-manager dilemma is to manage yourself.

First, *prioritize ruthlessly and realistically.* Decide what actions absolutely must get done in order to accomplish your client- and team-building objectives. As mentioned above, delegate where possible, especially the things that are good "stretch opportunities" for your team.

Next, *stick to your agenda.* It's natural for the best-intentioned plan to slip, especially when you're feeling overwhelmed. So each morning, review your priorities and recommit only to critical ones. Tackle the most important jobs (not necessarily the most urgent ones) first. Ideally, turn off your email and other outside-world intrusions while you're focused on concentration-intensive tasks. But since you're now working as part of a collaborative effort, remember to explain your temporary disappearance. For example, when I was working on this book, I put an automatic reply on my email that said:

> *I have email turned off this morning to focus on writing my book manuscript. Please excuse the delay in my response until I check email [at a certain time]. In case of an emergency, please call me on my mobile at [number].*

By telling people not to expect an instant reply, you buy yourself some time—especially because a large fraction of issues miraculously get resolved in the interim. Including your phone number on your automatic response definitely signals that you're willing to respond as needed—but also makes people think twice about whether their request truly needs immediate attention.

Mentally reframe activities. For those tasks that start to feel like a drag on your individual productivity, think hard about whether they serve "hidden" useful purposes. For example, the colleague you coach today may well use those skills to identify a sales opportunity. Of course, you shouldn't delude yourself—but you don't want to miss the silver linings waiting to be discovered.

Build a support network of people who know your goals and will give you the tough messages when you're going off track. The best networks include people at all ranks—superiors, peers, and subordinates—because each group has unique insights about how you're spending your time. Proactively seek their inputs at least once per quarter; put a recurring appointment on your calendar to reach out to them. Make sure you don't shoot the messengers who do point out your slippages—and of course, be prepared to reciprocate. What can you tell them about managing themselves?

And remember to *stay fueled*. When you're tired, hungry, or dehydrated, it gets easier to slip into comfortable patterns as a stand-alone contributor. Remember that your brain consumes up to a third of all the calories you take in. If you skip meals or succumb to junk food, you are inviting the kind of brain fog that makes it nearly impossible to spot complex, cross-discipline connections. Similarly, brain scans show how much of your gray matter switches off when you get dehydrated (like during a trans-Atlantic flight), so seemingly small steps like drinking lots of water turn out to be indispensable techniques for effective collaborators.

Finally, *sleep* is not a luxury, but rather, an essential success ingredient. Mental agility, focus, clarity, creativity, and memory all suffer without proper rest. An exhausted partner is also a pretty miserable team member—making it less likely that others will approach you with opportunities or feedback. Getting and staying in peak mental and emotional condition is essential for meeting your ongoing responsibilities, freeing up more time for collaboration.

How firm leaders can help

The strategies outlined in this chapter are intended to shorten the payback period for collaboration from the contributor's point of view. I've emphasized techniques that the motivated individual can adopt to hasten the point when benefits begin to outweigh costs.

Collaboration benefits not only the individual collaborator, but also the firm. Let me close this chapter, therefore, with steps that leaders can take to help contributors—and by extension, their firm—reap the benefits sooner.

Help diamonds in the rough to shine through

Contributors need tooth-cutting opportunities—their first foot in the door—which means in turn that they need account team leaders to take a chance on them. Particularly in firms that have grown through mergers, those lead partners may not be convinced that others (especially untested others) have their same levels of competence or professionalism. And this is especially true when we're talking about cross-discipline collaboration, because the more different someone's expertise is from one's own, the harder it is to assess the competence of or to trust that individual.

The stakes are high, and a partner once burned is going to be that much harder to lure back into a collaborative relationship. As one disappointed partner phrased it:

> Easily the largest impediment is setting up a client of mine with a colleague who will disappoint, in terms of either substantive lawyering or responsiveness. This situation has occurred with some frequency in my experience, and my sense is at an increasing rate. I have lost substantial clients and, more often, business as a result of this issue. I also have found some colleagues do a poor job of keeping me generally appraised, and/or involved, making it difficult to fulfill my role as relationship partner.

Given these sorts of perceived risks, how can you, as a firm leader, make sure that at least some legitimate referrals flow to people who may not be the "usual suspects"? One approach is to set up a series of low-pressure meetings where contributors can share concrete examples of times they've added value to the firm's clients. Especially for people who are generally uncomfortable blowing their own horn, these events normalize self-promotion and give them the chance to show off their expertise. These meetings are also great for allowing introverts to stand out. As one consulting partner, Janice, remarked, "I'm normally overshadowed by extroverts who can spout off their accomplishments at a moment's notice. If somebody rings them up or even mentions a potential opportunity, they're great at riffing—sort of tailoring their message on the fly. Personally, though, I need more time to prepare."

One reputation-building technique that is gaining popularity is the professional equivalent of "speed-dating" events: a group of partners get together, and each has five minutes, one-to-one, with a colleague to explain why the listener's clients should be interested in the presenter's specialist knowledge. This event is low cost, fun, and lively. But you can really only expect it to have lasting business impact if the group is carefully chosen to gather partners with high-potential opportunities. Hand-pick a couple of client-relationship partners with fast-growing accounts—the kind we advise contributors to cultivate—and get their personal commitment to attend with the intent to find at least one eager new member for their client team. Plus, everyone must show up prepared: each participant must research others' specific clients (which means they need the attendee list in advance), not just speak generally about their own expertise. These events seem to work best when all participants serve clients in a particular sector, such as life sciences or automotive or higher education, because then they have a natural core of shared knowledge to build on.

Here are a few other techniques you can use to help contributors build their profile and more readily reap the benefits of collaboration:

- Set expectations that client lead partners will ardently seek new team members from the ranks of the current contributors. To help these partners see the value to the account in building a set of highly committed professionals who are jumping at this chance to shine, draw on specific examples of where the technique has worked already—or better yet, ask the partners with success stories to do the proselytizing. Over time, reinforce your expectations by asking for specific examples of their progress, and if partners don't move the dial enough on their own, then set a formal performance metric and give it some teeth.

- Become an *honest broker*—someone who actively promotes low-profile professionals, but is known for giving the real deal. A partner in one firm I researched gave this example of how a leader's honesty in referring colleagues helped boost his confidence in the recommendations: "He has been unbelievably straightforward with me. In the past, he has said things like, 'Here are three people, and here is what I know about them. This person presents really well in front of clients, but doesn't roll up his sleeves and get into the details as much as others. This person is bright, sharp, and hardworking, but awkward socially. And this person is probably not the right choice if the deal is going to require weekends and holidays.' That honesty is very important."

- Assign practice managers or other business development staff the job of tracking contributors who have credible expertise in a specialist area or geography. Encourage contributors to get into the habit of updating development staff with sound bites from their own project work (including recommendations from the client or lead partner, if possible), and persuade lead partners to seek the development staff's input for sourcing new team members. This system works especially well for locating talent in far-flung locations, and it has the advantage of breaking up the old-boys' network. Again, the most credible way of advertising this system is for a few high-profile partners to use it and spread the word.

Boost contributors' ability to think like a client

Give aspiring collaborators the business-fundamentals skills they need to start and sustain a substantive conversation with a client. Research shows that adult learning happens 10 percent by formal training, 20 percent by observation, and 70 percent by experience and experimentation.[12] Surprisingly, even the best firms that invest heavily in training their junior professionals tend to downplay formal training for partners. Sure, they'll provide access to courses that are required for their professionals' continuing accreditation, and they often bring guest speakers to annual events like partner conferences. But how many firms deliver programs that focus on helping partners develop the capabilities and confidence to "think like a client"?

If you lead a firm where few partners have had formal business training, invest in giving them exposure to some core business concepts. You'll almost certainly delegate the design of these programs to experienced learning and development professionals, either in-house or external, but here are a few things to watch out for. First, make sure that the program is well rounded in giving partners exposure to fundamental concepts related to corporate strategy, finance, marketing, and organizational behavior. This cross-cutting approach is critical to get partners to think like clients who tend to say, "I have a business problem," rather than segment it by academic discipline.

Second, because the goal of these programs is to give partners the ability to *apply* the learning to their own clients, participants need both to understand the theory (in order to generalize from one client situation to another) and to practice using the new concepts. Scott Westfahl of Harvard Law School explains why executive education programs for lawyers need to be grounded in research, and his rationale applies equally well to many other kinds of professionals: "Executive education for lawyers needs to be research-based. Lawyers are inherently skeptical of theories and anecdotal evidence and are the world's most skillful debunkers of hypotheses. They have earned their standing by challenging assumptions, so executive education programs that shortcut the empirical knowledge will suffer."[13]

Third, make sure your learning and development specialists invest heavily in designing realistic vignettes so that partners have the chance to *practice* using the ideas in the low-risk setting of a training program. Set up the scenario so that one partner acts as the account handler and benefits from the chance to apply a concept during a simulated conversation with a client, while the partner who acts as the client benefits by learning how to take that perspective. Most grown-ups say that they hate role-playing, but feedback from executives suggests that these experiences are often the highlight of formal training programs.

Capabilities and confidence are also derived from internal support and external exposure. First, let's restate the problem. "I don't know how to approach client issues where I'm not the clear expert," is how some contributors phrase it to me. Or, "I can't steer conversations outside my core knowledge and comfort zone, which is what it takes to collaborate."

Part of the solution is simply tribal storytelling. Contributors need to learn how others improvise in the face of stress and uncertainty. I attended one meeting where a firm's managing partner told a revealing story. He had flown from London to Asia to accompany a tax partner to a meeting with the CEO of a major local client. After ten minutes and a nice cup of tea, the CEO flatly stated that he had no additional needs for tax advice, stood up, and thanked the partners for coming in. The managing partner interrupted— not rudely, but forcefully. "We're not here to sell you more tax advice," he told the CEO, "but rather to get to know your business needs. What's the biggest issue on your mind?"

The CEO sat back down, and said frankly that he didn't see how the firm could help with the biggest issue on his plate. In fact, he was totally preoccupied with trying to figure out how to keep his factories running after a neighboring country had embargoed the export of the exact type of fuel that could profitably power his plants. The managing partner nodded sympathetically and recommended that the CEO speak to a few of his partners with regulatory, international trade, and project finance expertise "simply to get a few new perspectives." In the end, the law firm ended up serving the client on a highly profitable, long-term engagement involving partners from multiple practice groups and offices.

Was there magic involved? No. Was there deep substantive knowledge on the part of the managing partner? Clearly not. The managing partner possessed, at most, a rudimentary understanding of regulation, trade, finance, and manufacturing. But he had abundant confidence to steer the CEO toward others in the firm who *did* have expertise in the necessary fields. The story had a visible impact on the junior people assembled in the room.

So my prescription here is to use the good storytellers among your firm's leadership to demystify and motivate. As you do so, be aware that in some organizational cultures—and even some national cultures—there's a reluctance to engage in this kind of storytelling. Senior leaders worry, for example, that by recognizing one colleague, they'll appear to be showing favoritism. But the goal, long term, is to help everyone develop their *own* stories. As a leader, you are simply modeling a key behavior that you hope your colleagues will emulate.

Finally, you can offer some of the most powerful learning opportunities when you offer direct exposure by going out into the field with your partners. Often, senior leaders like to have top-to-top conversations with clients, but if you exclude up-and-comers they'll never learn what it takes to have those conversations. When I was working in McKinsey's Johannesburg office, I saw firsthand how excellent leaders provide client exposure. The office's managing partner, Jon Cummings, worked closely with the CEO of one of the region's biggest companies. That executive used to call late-night meetings of a panel of his closest advisers—an investment banker, strategy consultant, PR expert, and a couple others. Jon often brought me along, and the banker brought his junior, too. While the top guns sat at the inner table hashing through the latest issues, we apprentices just listened—absorbing crucial lessons on everything from how clients interpret a shifting political climate to the ways to tactfully disagree with a professional peer (or with the client in front of others). In the next day or so, Jon and I would meet to rehash what we learned; over time I may have contributed a few meaningful insights, but mostly he mentored me for my benefit. If you can create these kinds of learning opportunities for your juniors, you will undoubtedly boost contributors' ability to think like a client.

Tigers collaborating on their stools

The preceding discussion, which focused on the senior leader's point of view, provides an easy transition to chapter 6, which aims at what I call the *ringmaster*. You know who you are: you're the one who keeps the tigers up on their stools, and makes them feel glad to be part of a successful collaborative show. As noted earlier, you have a special role to play in fostering collaboration.

So let's turn to examining and understanding that role.

[6]

Collaboration for Ringmasters

his chapter is aimed at the person I call the *ringmaster*. This term sounds both more dignified and more promising as a way of describing the leader of a professional service firm than the "cat herder" we hear so much about.[1]

The ringmaster runs the show and keeps the tigers up on their stools. The tigers present both opportunities and risks, which help keep the ringmaster's job challenging and interesting. There would be no show without the tigers, so the ringmaster has to make sure that they are happy enough to perform—and at the same time, hungry enough to pay attention.

In other words, compensation is key—and the analogy certainly holds in the realm of professional services. If collaboration is a goal, as I've argued it should be, then the firm's compensation system has to advance that goal. But as any experienced leader knows, motivating the stars—and everyone else who's critical to keeping the show going—takes far more than money.

Let's begin with a central premise of several earlier chapters: that serving clients with integrated, cross-practice offerings typically leads to a stable of "stickier" and more lucrative clients. Yet when we look around, some partners are obviously doing far more of this collaboration than others. This disparity begs an obvious question: Is one partner's willingness to bear the costs and risks of collaborating related to her firm's supportive compensation system? Conversely, is another professional's temptation to hoard work driven by an unsupportive compensation system? Is there a straight-line link between levels of collaboration within a given firm and its compensation system?

The answer to this last question is *not quite.*

Granted, a firm's compensation system plays a large part in shaping partners' behavior, and probably explains why some firms are, on average, more collaborative than others.[2] But this doesn't account for the difference in collaboration *between partners in the same firm*, where they're all (presumably) operating under the same compensation system. And the confusing truth is that *every firm has a wide range of collaborative profiles,* in terms of both the rainmakers who do and don't refer work to others, and the partners who are or aren't on the receiving end of those referrals.

Consider figure 6-1. It illustrates the experience of one typical firm, in which a third of the people referred work to other partners fewer than ten times during the course of my study (over several

FIGURE 6-1

Extent and distribution of partners' work referrals

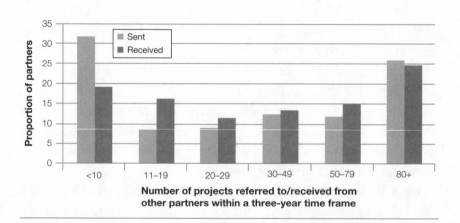

Number of projects referred to/received from
other partners within a three-year time frame

years), while a quarter of the other partners in the same firm referred work more than eighty times to their colleagues in that same period. When we dig deeper into the numbers, we see that a large proportion of the partners in the "under ten" group originated many projects, but simply worked on them solo, rather than getting other partners involved.

There's a parallel dispersion for people on the receiving end of those referrals: some partners very frequently get work referrals, whereas others receive them less than once per year. But why? If compensation were the sole or even primary driver of behavior— the way the tigers are kept up on their stools—wouldn't we see more homogeneous behavior from partners who all have the same incentives?

Another kind of evidence pointing toward the weak link between collaboration and compensation comes from so-called lockstep firms, in which a partner's salary depends 100 percent on her organizational tenure. Logically, such a system should explicitly promote collaboration. Because partners' compensation is a direct outcome of the firm's overall profit, each person should be motivated to broaden his or her business as much as possible, and should share work with whichever expert in the firm is most likely to profitably grow a client account.

But the reality is very different. In one lockstep firm I've worked with—let's call it Delta Associates—the partners' behavior defied the economist's concept of humans as consistently rational and narrowly self-interested agents who optimally pursue their own ends (*homo economicus*).[3] In fact, instead of sharing work across geographies and practices to optimize the client experience—and therefore profits—many partners hoarded work locally. My analyses of the firm's top global clients showed that some account leaders involved only partners and associates from their own office, even when those professionals weren't best suited for the work. These differences couldn't be explained by language, cultural barriers, or even a client-centric desire to minimize travel expenses. In some instances, the lead partner had the opportunity to involve a world-class expert from an office not only in the same country, but within driving distance—and didn't. The result was predictable: because of their local containment, these accounts grew more slowly than comparable accounts that weren't similarly confined.

Why such irrational behavior? The answers provide an interesting illustration of the law of unintended consequences. This lockstep firm tracked profit-and-loss figures at the office level, and published the figures quite prominently on their intranet. So even though the partners who hoarded work locally cost the firm potential revenues—and by extension, reduced their own share of the profits—they squirreled away work in order to pump up their local colleagues' utilization rates and office-level figures. In other words, they preferred the bragging rights about working in a highly efficient office over higher compensation from collaboration. The compensation system was ideal, in theory. In reality, though, it was badly undermined by metrics that promoted selfish behavior.

If people in the same firm, working under the same remuneration system, choose to behave differently—sometimes even against their own short- and long-term financial interests—then clearly, money isn't everything when it comes to influencing collaborative behaviors. Indeed, most psychologists (and increasingly, economists) argue that performance metrics, whether or not they're linked to compensation, drive behavior. "Human beings adjust behavior based on the metrics they're held against," flatly states Dan Ariely, a behavioral economist at Duke University. "Anything you measure will impel a person to optimize his score on that metric. What you measure is what you'll get. Period."[4]

In other words, even metrics that are carefully designed can become counterproductive, because they can direct people's actions in ways that leaders don't intend. Ariely recalls how a specific set of performance metrics during his days as a professor at MIT focused him more on boosting his teaching ratings than on the overarching objective that his managers envisioned:

> I was measured on my ability to handle my yearly teaching
> load using a complex equation of teaching points. The rating,
> devised to track performance on a variety of dimensions,
> quickly became an end in itself. Even though I enjoyed
> teaching, I found myself spending less time with students

because I could earn more points doing other things. I began to scrutinize opportunities according to how many points were at stake. In optimizing this measure, I was not striving to gain more wealth or happiness. Nor did I believe that earning the most points would result in more effective learning. It was merely the standard of measurement given to me, so I tried to do well against it.

So was it wrong for Delta Associates to track and measure performance by means of an office-based P&L? I'd argue not, because for the purposes of managing the firm, leaders do need this information. But, I'd further argue, *not all partners need this information*. In fact, some will function better without it.

Of course, some professionals will balk, chafe, and scoff at this idea. I hear these objections every time I make the case for selective disclosure in the context of a professional service firm. "Hey," they say, offended. "As a partner, I'm an *owner* of this firm! I *deserve* to know."

Maybe; maybe not. In the following pages, I explore ways that you—as a leader of the firm—can walk the fine line between transparency and information overkill, so that partners are adequately informed but not burdened by data that will mislead or misdirect them.

Let me preview those ideas briefly. To foster collaboration among your partners, you need to *focus on your firm's performance management system*, more than your compensation plan, as a critical lever to change and guide behaviors. If you want to tie some portion of partners' financial rewards to collaboration—that is, to the *way* they achieve their objectives, rather than just the outcomes themselves—then you need a credible, nonburdensome method of measuring their behaviors and holding them accountable. You need a system that can't be gamed, and also has some teeth.

No system will affect all partners' behaviors the same way. The smart, independent people who populate those firms—and who range, as we've seen, from solo specialists to seasoned collaborators to contributors—tend to want to do their own thing, and in fact are encouraged in that direction by the smart leaders of smart firms. At the same time, there *are* three things that ringmasters can do to influence behavior in the direction of collaboration. The first, introduced earlier, involves *measuring* collaboration. (What, exactly, are we looking for, and who is doing it well?) The second involves the *compensation* piece: an important, but not all-important component, for which I offer ideas about both design and implementation. And the third involves the use of *technology* in support of collaboration.

Let's look at each in turn.

Performance management: Measuring collaboration

As I just argued, the metrics you embrace for almost any organizational purpose are critically important. Choose those metrics wisely, and you have a shot at hitting your target. Choose them less wisely, and you are very likely to wind up where MIT did vis-à-vis its young faculty: in the realm of unintended consequences. In this section, I present eight guidelines for evaluating whether your performance management system fosters or inhibits collaboration.

Figure out what level and group in the firm you need to measure. The structure that already exists may go a long way toward determining whom you'll set metrics for. How are profits divvied up? Does the compensation system skew toward individual rewards, or does it also reward groups? Is the firm balkanized, or can it and does it act as a whole?

You may conclude that a wholesale overhaul of your firm's structure is beyond the scope of your mandate—or too big a mountain to climb at the moment. But if you conclude otherwise, consider moving toward a single profit pool for the whole firm, as advocated by David Maister and others.[5] Partners in elite firms like McKinsey, Egon Zehnder, and Sullivan & Cromwell swear that their firm's single system drives more-collaborative thinking and behavior. In recent years, some firms—like Ernst & Young in 2008—have taken the dramatic step of eliminating local P&Ls.[6] To the extent that your firm can move in that direction, you will greatly increase the opportunities to reward collaboration. In a single word, *unbalkanize.*

Then organize your professionals into groups that make sense to your core clients. After all, they consider themselves not as "purchasers of tax advice" or "consumers of IT services," but rather, as managers in a financial institution or retailer or hospitality group. The *industry sector* is the key driver for collaboration, because it allows your partners from different practice groups or functional areas to integrate their diverse expertise to collectively solve your clients' most complex, cross-disciplinary problems. Even if you choose to keep practice groups as the formal structure for reporting purposes (i.e., the sector head has no formal authority over people from other practice groups), you must give the sector-focused, go-to-market approach some teeth: consider allowing the sector head to give input on contributors' compensation, for example (more on this later).

Set the overall firm strategy, and then provide guidance for groups and individuals to set their own objectives. By "guidance," I mean that you are offering more than a suggestion, and less than a direct order. It's messier and more time-consuming than a "cascade," in which the firm's overall numbers are simply divvied up into increasingly smaller lots and handed down.

Why go this route? It ensures alignment, creates commitment and buy-in, and enables the people who know their opportunities best to set the objectives. It also reflects the reality of smart people in a high-end firm: they appreciate a framework and guidance, but want the autonomy to decide how to apply it.

How to get there? Use a holistic strategic planning review to decide where to focus your firm's resources and attention. The value of a sound strategic plan comes as much from its indication of where *not* to grow—and sometimes, where to cut. Once you've figured out the target sectors and clients, define the anticipated outcomes. The sector or practice group leaders can define the broad goals for the group, and individual partners can set their own objectives.

This may all sound extremely basic. If you've already got this case cracked, good for you! But most places I visit don't come close to this ideal state. For example, I was recently talking to the head of sectors at one of the world's largest professional service firms. "Imagine I'm an associate," I told that very senior person, "and I want to see what the energy sector is doing. Where do I go, and what do I see?" She spent literally twenty minutes rooting in her files for the relevant document—and what she finally found was nine months out of date.

At another firm I worked with, the leaders had no trouble laying their hands on the relevant documents. But after I read a sample of their plans at each level, I bluntly told them, "If I were you, I'd have no way of knowing at the end of the year whether people had actually met their objectives." The so-called plans consisted mainly of (1) a partner bragging about what he'd accomplished in the prior year, and (2) some vague objectives looking forward. If your goals aren't SMART (specific, measurable, assignable, realistic, time-bound), then they can't serve as a clear guide for decision making—either on the part of the partner who needs to prioritize activities, or on the part of leaders who need to hold people accountable.[7]

Focus on ends that can only be achieved through collaboration. In other words, make sure you're rewarding the "right" behaviors and not celebrating people who might best be described as high-performing jerks (or worse). Set objectives that require collaboration to be part of the "how"—and at the same time, avoid being inflexible or mechanical in your approach.

Transfer payments—for example, commissions for work referred by one group to another—have a certain appeal, but they tend to be blunt instruments, at best.[8] Because they are inflexible, and are likely to either overreward or underreward, they rarely work as intended. Likewise, mechanically calculating specific metrics—such as the number of referrals or multipractice pitches—leaves the system open to being gamed. To head off these kinds of problems, your firm needs a two-pronged approach. First, be sure to reward the *outcomes* of effective collaboration, such as rising levels of client satisfaction and retention, growth in revenue and profits from existing accounts, or the acquisition of new clients in target areas. For example, if you set a target of doubling revenues in a high-potential account, it will be almost impossible for anybody to achieve that by doubling the amount of tax advice they give existing tax clients; it will have to be accomplished by broadening the relationship, either cross-practice or cross-geography.

Second, set objectives that are driven almost entirely by a partner's business situation. One engineering firm leader explained this principle in practice: "We want to reward people who solve the business-critical problem. For example, there was huge attrition in one group, whereas most other groups had very high engagement. Holding everyone to the same standard would have made anyone shy away from the essential job of leading that underperforming practice. We needed to develop a metric by reference to their specific strategic priorities."

Is there a branch of your firm in a region where generating local clients is understood to be unrealistic? Focus their collaborative goals on helping inbound work to flourish, and value this outcome as highly as origination. Again, the right metric is situation-specific. But with appropriate guidance and oversight, specific metrics can support the firm's overall strategy of achieving broader collaboration.

Measure collaboration-related behaviors. To ensure that results are achieved in ways that are consistent with building a collaborative culture, you will need to include measures that capture partners' contributions to the kinds of nonbillable collaborative efforts described in chapters 3, 4, and 5, such as mentoring, sharing knowledge, and giving advice. Management consulting firm A. T. Kearney, for example, assesses its mentor and mentee pairs by having both individuals rate each other's effectiveness using the firm's formal evaluation system.[9]

In a similar vein, one law firm has made "collaboration and teamwork" the first of seven criteria in the Balanced Scorecard that they use to assess partner performance, and the performance of every partner is rated annually according to that criterion. Inputs include, for example, how many times a partner has shared knowledge to enable cross-practice pitches.

This firm also has an "appreciation system" whereby partners allocate kudos to other partners who have helped them be more successful, and this "soft metric" feeds into partner performance assessment and remuneration. This method tends to be slow-rooting, so bear with it. In this firm, people initially reacted with cynicism, referring to it as the "jelly bean" system. It gained acceptance only after the CEO used the system as the basis for identifying success stories that he told onstage at the firm's annual partner retreat. "We never heard 'jelly bean' again," he told me.

Taken together, these approaches help by creating a common language and clear reference points for performance discussions, bonus awards, and goal setting. They underpin what some partners now call a "culture of gratitude." The systems also allow the firm's leadership to reinforce the importance of collaboration and knowledge sharing in communications throughout the year, not just during compensation review season.

Remember that measuring inputs is critical when you want to reinforce specific behaviors—and especially when people are first getting used to them. It's also a way to reward people for getting and staying on the right path during that lag between investment and payback. Until good behavior is ingrained as a habit, you need to motivate people to continue on the collaborative path. Just be sure to combine input-related measures with outcome-related ones, as discussed earlier, to reinforce the point that collaboration is a means to other important ends.

Link objectives to day-to-day client work. This point sounds obvious, but many firms get it wrong: make sure that performance objectives are a part of the partner's "real" work, and not a frill. All too often, they're framed as major events in client service—like "hosting a conference" or "providing CLE training"—but those kinds of events are too irregular and exotic. They typically get crowded out by daily pressures: "Hey, the client asked me to do X, and X was billable, so I did it." Well, yes; but was it collaborative and cumulative?

If you've set clear objectives and a client *does* ask for X to be done, then there are really only three possible responses. If X is already linked to an objective, say yes. If you can honestly and productively adapt an objective to accommodate X, again, say yes. If X is clearly outside the strategy, say no. Politely.

Avoid measures that don't actually accomplish your collaboration goals—and especially avoid those that run counter to those goals. Embracing individualistic metrics when you're hoping for collaboration, as discussed earlier, is one such folly.[10] Time-based measures are also particularly pernicious. The more relentlessly a professional's performance is evaluated based on time, the more evident the opportunity costs associated with collaboration will become—and the more likely that a star will conclude that the time and effort demanded by collaborative work would be better spent developing his or her own book of business.

Stanford professor Jeffrey Pfeffer and the University of Toronto's Sanford DeVoe have demonstrated that people who are hyperaware of the value of their time get less pleasure from great art or classical music than others. It's a very relevant observation: even if partners are inclined to undertake collaboration for its psychological rewards—such as feeling connected with others, or giving back to the firm—the stress of making their billable-hours target may undermine their intrinsic motivation to collaborate.[11]

A time-based metric also runs counter to clients' goals of getting cost-effective, pragmatic, tailored advice. "It's amazing," one client told me, "how many fifty-page memos I get toward year-end when my lawyers need to beef up their billable hours." Ouch! Individual, time-based metrics are usually both anticollaborative and anticlient.

Build and use a personalized competency grid. This is a concept that I learned in my time at McKinsey, which has long used a system that allows people to play to their respective strengths—or "spikes," in McKinsey's distinctive parlance. To get started, ask your professional development staff to help partners define the core capabilities—say, five or six—that are necessary for success in their roles. Then you (or the group leader) sit down with each partner and agree on one or two that they will emphasize more than the others. They typically have to meet a minimum standard in all of the capabilities, and at the same time really develop a spike in one or two. In effect, you're allowing (and pushing) the individual to build on his or her strengths.[12]

This is a particularly effective way to foster collaboration, because it spotlights and values the various roles that are required to achieve effective cross-boundary work. For example, someone who spikes on functional specialist knowledge can be legitimately recognized as a strong contributor.

Use technology to help make it happen. Some new software packages can help make performance management powerful and palatable, if not fun. One that I've seen used to good effect is Objective Manager, which is designed to "get the most out of your people and teams with effective objective setting software" and "align people's objectives to your business plans and client plans."[13]

Simply stated, packages like this push objective setting down to the appropriate level—that is, the person who will actually have to *hit* the objectives—and thereby promote both ownership and transparency. When structured correctly, they reward specificity and punish laziness. The partner who uses at least eighty characters to describe the intended outcomes ("develop at least three new commercial real estate clients in the Middle East worth more than $500,000 apiece") is rewarded with a gold star in contrast to those who write—for example—"win more work." Guess what happens next? By and large, the people with the highest-quality objectives are much more likely to follow through, and much more likely to *deliver* against those objectives.

Of course there's a question of causality: the people who wrote SMART objectives using the software probably would have been stronger, more organized performers to begin with. But the point is that the software allows their objectives, and their progress against those goals, to become transparent to peers. Because others can see some of the "magic" behind high performance, the platform allows the stars to become better role models and inspiration for others—without spending any more time than they might have otherwise.

Here's how such technology helps: because updating is easy—partners should be able to access their plan from a smartphone, for instance—once someone makes progress toward a goal, he or she can post a brief update. This facility turns the online plans into living, breathing parts of a partner's workday, and helps people keep their objectives more firmly in mind. What's more, others on the team can see progress, which acts like a motivating success story. With nearly real-time updates, leaders can spot areas where their input would be more valuable—either by praising success or by offering to help underperformers. Far more effective than waiting for quarterly or annual reviews? You bet.

Excellent software packages also allow partners to see others' objectives, and this transparency often generates collaboration opportunities. So, for example, a partner pursuing that commercial real estate goal stated above could quickly search the system to see who else is pursuing Middle East clients and propose to join forces. Of course, software can only support collaboration as part of a robust performance management system—but I predict that it will become indispensable as technology-savvy professionals rise through the ranks.

Structuring compensation to support collaboration

Compensation is not collaboration's silver bullet—but it *can* be a silver dagger. In other words, even the best compensation system won't guarantee collaboration, while a poorly designed one can threaten it. One way it can pose risks is by reinforcing an individualistic, anticollaborative approach: "I'm the star in this group; the band behind me is merely backup." Poorly designed compensation schemes reward people who are bad for culture generally, and toxic to collaboration specifically. Meanwhile, they can demotivate contributors, who—as we've seen—are critical to the success of the firm's rainmakers. Rainmakers are crucial, but they can't produce if they have no team willing to work with them.

Bad compensation systems lead people to hoard work and fight over the credit (and financial rewards) for the work that they *do* share. In the almost-worst case, a compensation system that's seen as unfair drives away key revenue producers, who may take their clients with them. In the worst case, the firm gets forced into an unhappy merger with a competitor, or even collapses.[14]

So yes, compensation matters. While partners making less than the market rate may stay at a firm for a while out of a sense of loyalty, if the gap becomes too large, they are likely to go. Clearly, leaders need to accommodate rainmakers' demands—for symbolic reasons, as well as to meet individuals' financial needs. As one partner phrased it: "At the end of the day, after all of these things, the barometer is compensation, OK? Compensation sends incentives, it sends signals, it conveys culture. This is the language that we speak, it's the way we know how we're valued. We know everything by how we are compensated, by whatever the metrics are for compensation."[15]

At first, this statement sounds like it's all about money: *At the end of the day, it's compensation*. But note that qualifier at the end: it's really about the *metrics* behind compensation. That gets us back to the performance measurement techniques described in the preceding section, and the kinds of nonfinancial motivations described in earlier chapters. People work for far more than money—and that creates opportunity, when it comes to building a firm on a strategy of smart collaboration. Again, compensation shapes culture through the behaviors that it encourages and discourages. If a firm pays its contributors handsomely for helping to broaden and deepen a client relationship instead of devoting that time to (for example) landing new local clients, that speaks volumes about how much leaders value collaboration.

The ideas I present here are consistent with psychologist Frederick Herzberg's classic theory of motivation—first developed in a study of engineers and accountants—that described compensation as a "hygiene factor" that managers need to get right, but which is not itself a driver of motivation. "Motivation does not come from perks, plush offices, even promotions or pay," as Herzberg phrased it. "These extrinsic incentives may stimulate people to put their nose to the grindstone—but they will likely perform only as long as it takes to get that next raise or promotion."[16]

Here's a statement that I think every firm leader in the universe can agree with: changing the compensation system is one of the hardest, most fraught-with-peril decisions a professional service firm can make. No matter what steps get taken, there are always perceived winners and perceived losers.[17] So make deep surgical changes only where essential, and as a last resort. And before you undertake any kind of radical overhaul, check your system against the following three principles.

Compensation matters most when it is a person's only way of judging his or her worth. In one firm I worked with, nearly all consultants kept on their PC startup screen a shortcut to an Excel spreadsheet that they opened the moment they closed a new deal. It calculated their anticipated bonus down to the last cent. This frustrated the CEO to no end, because it left him so little latitude for adjusting pay to reward good behaviors. It didn't work so well for the people updating those spreadsheets, either. As one partner told me, "This place is a viper pit. The tracker's the only thing that gives me a sense of progress, since there's no feedback, no other way to get ahead, no way to know if Daddy loves me. It's like if you never expressed affection to your kids—they'd not only count the cookies you gave them, they'd count the crumbs."

In contrast, the best firms provide abundant psychological and social rewards. There's almost no limit to the forms these rewards can take—for example, recognition for excellent client work or firm-building initiatives, formal and informal feedback (even for partners), opportunities to represent the firm or practice at prestigious external events, getting teamed up with high-status colleagues, increasingly challenging and interesting client work, and—last but certainly not least—a brand name that people are proud to identify with. In firms that pay attention to these kinds of rewards, compensation still matters, but people pay far less attention to it than in places where "the number" is the only thing that's tracked.

Overemphasizing origination is countercollaborative. Often, the barrier to collaboration presented by professional firms' compensation systems stems from the outsized rewards given to selling instead of doing the client work. In the terms I used earlier, that means overrewarding solo specialists and devaluing contributors. Professionals who excel at developing clients and winning new work are typically—and in many cases, rightly—the most celebrated people in a firm: without them, there would be no clients to serve. But if this is taken too far, collaboration suffers.

Some firms reward rainmakers with a system that is akin to commission, whereby a partner receives a percentage of his gross sales (tellingly referred to as an "eat-what-you-kill" system). Other firms work on a tiered system—the more revenues an individual generates, the higher the percentage awarded to that person. The transparency of these sorts of compensation models is an advantage, since people know exactly what they need to do and how much they'll make in return. But they also discourage collaboration, because professionals who bring in a partner to help close a deal will need to split their commission. As one real estate broker told me, "The commission system stands in the way of collaboration, because I can make more money being greedy than sharing."

Because generating new business is harder, riskier, and more time-consuming than completing the work that someone else has sold, it usually makes sense to reward it accordingly. As firms compete with increasing ferocity for top rainmakers, they are increasingly likely to reward their most important revenue generators more highly than the average partner, and to pay them significantly more than the lowest-paid one. It becomes a very tough balance to strike—and if the firms get the balance wrong, then professionals become reluctant to contribute their expertise to work that other partners have originated.

In an extreme version of the system, the originating partner gets a cut of the fees forever. A version of this system was used, for example, by renowned Brazilian law firm Mattos Filho until quite recently.[18] Initially the policy made sense as a way to incentivize the founding partners to generate revenue for the fledgling firm. As the firm grew, however, many younger partners felt left out of the system because they saw very few opportunities to bring new clients into the firm. "When I started in this department, all the clients I got were already clients of someone else," remarked one young partner. "And the problem was, the 'partner owner' didn't even know the client. They had done some job in the past, but there was no ongoing relationship with the client."

I've already encouraged you to avoid radical surgery in the compensation realm whenever possible. But the leaders of Mattos Filho decided—rightly, I believe—that their circumstance created the exception to the rule. They undertook a significant overhaul of their system, moving away from the formulaic eat-what-you-kill approach to one that included a combination of objective, outcomes-based performance metrics and subjective decisions by a compensation committee. Changing the system was tough, time-consuming, and risky; a group of high-profile partners who resisted the changes defected en masse for a competitor. Ultimately, though, says the firm's managing partner, Roberto Quiroga, the firm achieved its goal of making the culture more collaborative by changing the system. It also enabled them to recruit some high-profile laterals, and in 2015 Mattos Filho was named Best Law Firm in Latin America by Chambers, which publishes a research-based ranking of firms by geography.

If your firm needs to rebalance the rewards between solo specialists and contributors, but in a less radical way than Mattos Filho undertook, you have several options. First, you might limit the period during which the origination credit is available, or require that eligibility for it is contingent on a partner having substantial ongoing involvement in a matter. Second, you can "multicount" origination credits: if a project is worth a hundred credits, rather than asking partners to split it fifty-fifty, give them each credit for one hundred. I know that sounds like book-cooking—ultimately, the firm can pay out only those profits that have actually been generated, right? Yes, but the difference with the multicount option is that people who collaborate extensively will be rewarded more than lone hunters. And as argued above, metrics drive day-to-day behavior more than annual pay, so not having to split credits makes an important psychological difference.

Finally, you might consider using a "top-up" fund to take some of the sting out of the investment that people make in providing excellent service to "other people's" clients.[19] For example, some firms set aside a pool of money that originating partners can draw on to reward colleagues who invest in building global accounts. No, those rewards typically do not boost compensation as much as origination credits do. But they can take the sting out of "merely" contributing, reduce the time invested in mental calculus, and off-set a contributor's sense of sacrificing himself or herself on some-one else's altar. They also communicate the importance and value of contributing to high-quality client service.

Relative compensation matters more than absolute pay. Science shows us the sometimes counterintuitive effects of relative compensation. Simply stated, a person's satisfaction with her finan-cial condition is based not on the amount of money that she earns, but on how much she earns compared to the people she regards as peers. One study suggested that people who make $40,000 a year and who know that their peers are making $35,000 are happier than those who are making $50,000 but know that their peers are making $60,000.[20] A celebrated study of Capuchin monkeys illustrated that even primates have a finely honed sense of justice: if they get cucum-bers for completing a task but then see a companion getting grapes (a higher-value reward) for doing the same job, they fly into a rage.[21]

Likewise, keeping partners satisfied is an especially difficult task when their compensation differentials get to be enormous. In the legal industry, for instance, the spread between highest- and lowest-paid partners in the *average* US firm was 10:1 in 2014—but that dispar-ity was a whopping 23:1 in some firms.[22] Think about it this way: if you're an average partner in that last firm and see that disparity, you will soon realize that it will take you almost *five months* to earn what the star in the big office down the hall makes in a week.

So transparency about partners' compensation cuts two ways. On one side, the *idea* of transparency has great appeal because it proves that leaders have nothing to hide. In truth, however, com-plete transparency almost never finds a home in successful pro-fessional firms. Leaders need discretion—for example, to reward exceptional but hard-to-quantify efforts on behalf of the firm, to allocate pay for a valued partner who underperformed while grieving for a lost loved one, or to make a partner "whole" after she has sacrificed her local practice to open a new office in a region that was risky but important for the firm.

So to foster collaboration, where should firms come out in terms of compensation-related transparency? I think the best answer is a *closed system that gets opened up selectively.* Why closed? "The advantages of a closed system," according to a report by one respected compensation consulting firm, "are that it consistently produces better morale, stronger teamwork, and more satisfaction with compensation."[23]

Richard Rosenbaum, the CEO of Greenberg Traurig, strongly endorses his firm's black-box system: "This allows us to run what is a large business in many disparate locations and practices without politics and without visible competition between our shareholders. This has been a major plus in our culture. It allows us to make decisions that make sense to the market."[24]

You may need to make at least some of the data available on an as-needed or as-requested basis. Firms that have moved in this direction find that there is a fairly predictable "weaning period." In the first year or two, quite a few partners ask to see the data. But once they've assured themselves that the compensation system is working in a reasonably equitable way, they stop feeling compelled to monitor it. In effect, they've gotten to where you need them to be: trusting you and the system, and staying on task.

Changing a compensation system

If you're convinced that you need to change your compensation system, here are a few tips to keep in mind.

Understand and plan for all the costs of this expensive move. Eminent professors James Baron and David Kreps categorize the price of changing a compensation system as "switching costs" and "legitimation costs."[25]

Switching costs, as the name implies, comprise all financial and other charges associated with changing an organizational process. For example, my students often suggest in class that a firm under discussion would benefit from a compensation system that rewards consultants based on project profitability instead of revenue. They often recognize the cost of developing, installing, and running accounting systems that would accurately capture the detailed data needed to calculate this metric.

What they fail to consider in this approach, however, is the further costs that would arise to train employees to input data, maintain the system and its interlinkages with legacy programs, produce reports based on the data, interpret those reports, provide feedback to others, use the data for decision making, and so on. I have counted twenty-two consequential actions that such a firm needed to undertake to implement even a modestly different compensation system. Switching costs are certain to be high—know them going in.

Legitimation costs are less tangible but no less important. Changes in the compensation system may be seen as misaligned with organizational norms—especially if those changes also disrupt the existing status hierarchy—which therefore may require leaders to put a lot of effort into legitimating them. And although these costs are almost impossible to quantify, they are nonetheless real.

Use a full-year transition in order to increase understanding— and therefore trust—of the new system. The leaders of Mattos Filho did this when changing their firm's compensation structure. To minimize the effects of the transition and increase buy-in, the executive committee agreed to slot everyone into the new system at a place equal to either their last year of compensation or the average of their last three years of compensation, at the partner's choice. By so doing, it assured that no one would be immediately penalized under the new approach, and it gave partners at least one year to learn new behaviors and meet new performance standards.

Deploying a collaborative technology platform

I referred to the use of technology earlier, in the context of performance measurement. Now let's take a look at how technology can be brought to bear on broader issues of collaboration.

By building a technology platform to help connect partners with the right opportunities and knowledge, you can mitigate many of the obstacles that stand in the way of contributors' increased involvement in cross-practice or cross-geography collaboration. One study estimated that for professional service firms, 98 percent of the benefits of these sorts of technology platforms stem from improvements in collaboration—distinctly different from the case in other industries, in which the benefits derive from (for example) consumer insights or marketing.[26]

Technology itself is not a stand-alone solution. Without supportive leadership, some degree of culture change, and close alignment with other activities—such as the kinds of performance management systems described above—even the best technology platform will simply fizzle out. But a growing number of professional service firms have successfully built and sustained internal IT systems that lower the costs and increase the benefits of collaboration by mimicking the best parts of popular social-networking applications.

What, exactly, *is* a collaborative technology platform (CTP)? Let's start with an example. Imagine that right after an insight-rich client meeting, partner Monica pulls out her phone and films a thirty-second selfie video about what she's just learned. She posts it to her account or sector team's site, and the headline of that new post pops up on the screens of all the team members. Later that day, they view it to get up to speed, and start building on Monica's insights.

The alternative? Using a traditional knowledge management system, Monica would wait until the project ended (if ever) to "codify key learnings." Perhaps in the case of really time-sensitive insights, Monica might email her teammates. But let's be realistic: this sort of ongoing communication is rarely standard operating procedure in professional service firms. Moreover, even when it happens, emails tend to get buried. Think back to the power of purposeful storytelling described earlier. Have you ever received an email that's been as lively and informative as even a "just OK" selfie video? People love the personal connection, even when mediated by video over a tiny phone.

Perhaps the biggest difference between a CTP and a traditional knowledge-management system is that the former is "social" in the same sense that Facebook and Twitter are: it connects individuals directly with each other, and makes their interactions available online to others. Rather than having the content curated by a website editor or database manager, excellent CTPs allow users to add or modify content themselves. They can comment on or respond to others' posts, rate or recommend existing content (e.g., by clicking the "like" button), download and distribute materials, and interact in real time.

The result, from a collaborative perspective? Well, here are some attractive outcomes: radically quicker ways to find the right expert, help for up-and-comers to promote their potential, and the democratization of access to the firm's knowledge and opportunities.

Maybe this sounds like a risky proposition to you—a near-complete loss of central control over a key data stream?

Yes, there are some risks, the biggest of which is that you will invest heavily in a bad system that nobody uses. (More on this subject later.) Other risks, such as client confidentiality and data security, are real, but by and large are manageable. Letting go—loosening the reins on data flow—actually poses minimal risk. You have to assume that your smart young leaders are responsible and have a finely tuned instinct for what information belongs where. And the truth is, your getting out of the way is exactly what it takes for a CTP to deliver on its potential.

How does a CTP help mitigate barriers to collaboration?

As noted in previous chapters, *competence trust* often gets in the way of collaboration. A lead client partner might hesitate to bring untested colleagues onto the account team because he's skeptical—or just plain ignorant—of their work quality or responsiveness. An effective CTP enables the partner not only to see these colleagues' self-proclaimed expertise areas—which is all that's available in a traditional knowledge-management directory—but also to vet their qualifications himself, by checking out what content they have authored and what role they've played in various client projects.

The transparency of the system also makes it difficult for people to take undue credit for their contributions. As one young partner put it, "I can *say* that I'm a thought leader in digital transformation, but on [the firm's CTP] people can actually go look and say, 'Ah, she's been involved in that discussion, and she's part of these groups, and look what she's authored and bookmarked—that's credible.'"

The curious lead partner might also get a sense of a prospective team member's responsiveness by seeing how timely and sophisticated he or she was in replying to queries. Finally, the platform acts as a passive referral network. People can see whom others have worked with, as well as the people who "like" or endorse their work. In most cases, of course, the platform is only a starting point: afterward, the partner will pick up the phone and assess a prospective team member before making an actual referral. But the ease and speed of finding a trustworthy partner significantly lowers one of the main barriers to collaboration.

From the other direction, a technology platform can also help a would-be contributor do her homework regarding the client service leader who's referred work to her. Will that partner run the team effectively and give her opportunities and credit? She can get a reasonable sense by examining the partner's record of contributing to the platform, providing feedback, acknowledging others' (especially juniors') part in successes, and so on.

Inefficiency is another frequently cited barrier to collaboration. The involvement of too many people can result in duplicated efforts and slow decision making. But when teams use a CTP, their actions, decisions, and rationale tend to become more transparent and searchable. It becomes easier for people to access and understand the *process* of the project. This, in turn, allows people to specifically target their communications only to the people who need to know. At the same time, that communication is freely available on the project record, which helps eliminate reply-all, "cover your butt" behavior. As one team member put it: "Platforms allow better sorting and filtering. Say you're on ten project teams. You need to know what's going on, so you're cc'd on all emails from all ten teams. You might only *need* to see one or two of those emails per team, but nobody thinks about the list. Or if they do, it's in a CYA sort of way. But in a networking platform, people can filter stuff. You get the messages in context, only when you want them. You can consume more communication because it has a *structure*."

CTP benefits by constituent group

Let's take another slant on CTPs by considering them from the perspective of some of the constituent groups represented in chapters 3, 4, and 5.

For example, your firm's highly visible experts—your gurus—may worry that a CTP will make them too accessible, and that they'll be inundated with expertise requests. In fact, in many cases, the opposite turns out to be true. One such partner noted that his firm's social platform actually made him *more* efficient, because suddenly he was "scalable" in a new way: "Whereas I previously fielded all sorts of basic inquiries, now—less than a year after we rolled out our CTP—I'm always 'available' through videos and my posts, and they're easy to find and use. So actually most of the dumb questions now get answered without bothering me, and I'm a lot more targeted about where I spend my time."

In the same spirit, one of the easiest ways to convince your highest-earning partners—the ones with the biggest account teams—to start using a CTP is to let them know how it can help to reduce their massive administrative burden. How does a CTP help in this regard? It becomes a self-service repository for all kinds of client-specific information, and new or prospective members of the team can be steered toward that repository to get themselves up to speed.

It's about enhancing efficiency and sharing expertise more broadly. In a recent report on CTPs, McKinsey noted:

> Today, a huge amount of relevant enterprise knowledge
> is locked up in e-mail inboxes. As more enterprise information
> becomes accessible and searchable, rather than locked up
> as "dark matter" in inboxes, workers could save not only
> [on] the amount of time they spend on writing, reading,
> and answering e-mail, but also on the amount of time
> spent searching for content and expertise. We estimate that
> total email use by interaction workers could be reduced by
> 25 percent, freeing up 7 to 8 percent of the workweek for
> more productive activities. With internal knowledge and
> information more available on social media, a typical inter-
> action worker could reduce information searching time by
> as much as 35 percent, which would return approximately
> 6 percent of the workweek to other tasks.[27]

How about solo specialists and seasoned collaborators? As we've seen, many individuals in these groups find that simply understanding and locating the firm's expertise poses one of the biggest challenges for collaboration. A well-implemented CTP can help enormously in this regard. As one firm leader told me:

> One of our consultants in Germany needed people with
> particular programming experience for one of our clients,
> but they had to be German speakers. Initially, he tried
> all his German contacts, phoned people, and he couldn't
> get anywhere, any way. So he posted something on an
> in-house forum focused on insurance clients. Somebody
> in London picks up the thread and mentions somebody
> on the West Coast who happened to know two people in
> Germany who could help. *That took 16 minutes.*

The contributors described in chapter 5 can also benefit greatly from having access to a CTP. Technology can help them do their homework regarding specific clients and potential relationship partners. A CTP also makes it far easier for contributors to respond to RFIs and build their reputations.

Finally, a robust CTP can also help boost contributors' skill at raising complex issues with a client. Think back to my description of storytelling as a way to inspire and instill confidence. A good CTP makes such storytelling organic: people hear about each other's successes "firsthand"—at least, in a virtual sense, which is a mode that many of them trust more than a "potted" version of reality from headquarters. Remember the example of Monica's video, at the opening of this section? Imagine the impact of a growing inventory of those kinds of success stories, especially as your millennials move into greater client service roles and find that they need their confidence boosted.

But will people use it?

Maybe you're one of those firm leaders who has invested in a knowledge-management system or customer relationship management database in the past, only to see it gather virtual dust. If so, you may be asking yourself whether people will actually use this system.

The answer, in many cases, is yes. One executive who has direct experience with both approaches explains why: "A traditional KM system is static and anonymous. It requires people to invest their precious time populating the database just in case some unknown Other needs the information at any point. But a collaborative platform lets someone respond to a specific human being—a colleague, no less—who needs that specific input at that exact time. It's way more motivating."

In other words, we humans find it more gratifying to respond "just in time" than "just in case." The former is about adding value; the latter is about covering your butt.

Unless you're the relatively unusual senior firm leader who has embraced social media in your personal life, you may be thinking that few of your really experienced (code for "older") partners will embrace, or even understand, the CTP way of sharing information.

Take heart: *The way you roll out the program can make a huge difference to adoption rates.* Do it well, and you can expect to bring professionals at all ages and stages on board.

Maybe looking at a specific example of a CTP rollout at a leading professional service firm best illustrates this point. Our subject company is PwC: a global accounting and consulting firm that employs more than 180,000 people and offers services across 157 countries. As an intensive knowledge business spread across so many locations, and with global clients expecting a joined-up seamless service, smooth and successful digital collaboration is critical.

In 2010, a group of global partners, working with the global knowledge function, helped to define an explicit goal: "To provide one common social networking and collaboration platform that accelerates our ability to connect with each other and collaborate together to create value for ourselves and for our clients." The end result of setting this goal was the launch of "Spark," a global social and collaboration network that has been widely adopted.[28]

"Within ten months of the initial launch, we had a hundred thousand active users," reports Paula Young, global head of knowledge at PwC. "On average, we are now getting 1.5 million page views per day." How did the firm achieve such enormous uptake? Young points to four key decisions that her team made:

- **Give up control in the design phase.** The then chairman of the firm, Dennis Nally, insisted that users—rather than any one functional area—design and control the system. "So I completely gave up control," reports Young. "We didn't have any governance groups. We didn't actually know how people would use the platform and realized that people might not know themselves. We wanted to experiment, as well as to listen, learn, and iterate."

- **Go where the energy is.** The team also knew it was important to select the right initial groups to work with, so they could share success stories that would help drive adoption for future waves. "We didn't always go for the most strategic parts of PwC to launch Spark," explains Young. "Instead, we went where there was a passionate partner who had a really clear idea of the value they thought they might get and who wasn't going to fall at the first hurdle."

- **Empower local sponsors.** CEOs from the twenty-one biggest PwC firms each chose a local leader to become their Spark Territory Sponsor. The firm invited each sponsor to choose how and when to launch Spark in their country and pick from the available toolkit of materials. For example, rather than launching Spark immediately, the Swiss Spark Territory Sponsors decided to piggyback it onto the appointment of their new chairman. They moved leadership communications and their intranet into Spark at that same time. Switzerland achieved 90 percent adoption in only a few days, and 100 percent soon afterward.

- **Tap into "advocates" at all levels.** The Spark Territory Sponsors were tasked with driving adoption locally, but, recalls Young, "We needed an army of volunteers on the ground to penetrate local teams, departments, and networks."

The Spark Advocate program was born. It aimed to involve tech-savvy, enthusiastic, open-minded individuals who would enjoy the chance to play with and improve Spark. "These are people on the ground, in every part of the organization: the guy on the security desk downstairs, the colorful character in Purchasing, and so on," Young explains. "You can always spot them—they're the ones who are going to show you the latest app with passionate enthusiasm."

Young invited these individuals to work with the system in beta form before anyone else got to see it. The response, she recalls, was amazing: "Not only did the majority say yes, they invited friends, colleagues, and acquaintances to sign up too. By the time of the soft launch, we had a community of more than three hundred advocates in place, with membership increasing by another hundred volunteers every week."

Within seven months of launch, Spark had nine hundred such advocates; less than two years later, there were eighteen hundred advocates in ninety-five countries.

So—getting back to our original question—has it stuck, or has it fizzled? Resoundingly, Spark has stuck. In a recent thirty-day period, 79.2 percent of PwC-ers, across 135 of the firm's 157 territories, used the system. Going back ninety days, the total rises to an amazing *95.5 percent* of the firm's staff. So yes—if you build it right, people will use it, and collaboration will be advanced.

Looking sideways at collaboration

Having devoted lots of space in this chapter to compensation, I now propose to take a somewhat abrupt step, in chapter 7, into a different realm—a field of endeavor in which collaboration is very much the wave of the present and the future, but in which compensation is a distinctly secondary consideration.

That field is elite medical research, which is commonly conducted by tenured or tenure-track faculty members. The salaries of those researchers are controlled by a central university compensation system, so salary bands are tight and bonuses are nonexistent. How can collaboration be fostered in such a constrained context?

The relevance of the lessons from this seemingly unrelated arena—so far from the worlds of business and professional services—may surprise you.

[7]

Looking Sideways
at Collaboration

Sometimes the best way to explore a complex business question—or for that matter, almost any complex question—is to take a sideways look at it. By *sideways*, I mean something other than a head-on approach. Can we bring our peripheral vision and our trained instincts to bear on this problem? Is there an analogy or metaphor that can shape our exploration in useful ways?

A few years back, I found myself asking such questions about collaboration. Was there another field of human endeavor in which the kinds of opportunities and challenges described in the preceding chapters come into play? Was there another realm that has its own rough equivalents of solo specialists, seasoned collaborators, contributors, and ringmasters? And was this a field from which we all could learn?

The answer, as it turned out, was yes. When I began asking these questions, I was based in Boston, where the other major industry besides education is medicine, broadly defined.[1] Not surprisingly, when I started looking for a new context to complement my traditional focus on professional service firms, I looked in the direction of institutions that conducted medical research. Very quickly, I found what seemed to be a promising organization for a sideways study: the Dana-Farber Cancer Institute.[2]

The context: Very different, with powerful parallels

An in-depth look at efforts by Dana-Farber's leaders to promote collaboration among its cancer researchers allows us to draw out overarching lessons for professional service firms later in this chapter. First, though, you might need some context for that case study.

When professional services guru David Maister argued in favor of developing a unified, "one-firm firm" culture in knowledge-industry firms—to reap the benefits of partners who are aligned toward achieving collective excellence and performance—he asserted that one of the keys was "downplaying stardom."[3] Over the years, following Maister's prescription and no doubt their own instincts, some organizations have taken well-publicized steps to move the spotlight off their individual stars. It's a tricky path to navigate: up to a point, stars bring luster and credibility to their sponsoring firms; past that point, they start taking too much oxygen out of the room, and distract from the real work of the firm. Organizations with strong cultures—including, for example, Harvard Business School and McKinsey—sometimes refrain from hiring or retaining the very biggest names, on the theory that the presence of such powerful individuals risks detracting from the dominant culture.

Nevertheless, many of the knowledge-intensive organizations I've studied tolerate—or even promote—some version of a "star culture," for the compelling reason implied above: stars can be a crucial source of distinction for a firm. This can be especially true in certain industries, or at certain stages in a firm's evolution. "In the engineering/consulting industry," as one contributor to my web-based forum noted, "iconic practitioners are often critical to start new practices or move an existing practice toward critical mass or 'blue chip' status. A cluster of icons in a practice or service area can have transformational effects."[4]

Similarly, in professional arenas like accounting—where firms sometimes struggle to convince clients that their product is more than a commodity—stars can play a crucial role. One accountant described a more nuanced approach: "We are still promoting 'stardom' wherever it makes sense as a differentiator in a narrow market, with few players (the Big Four) that are sometimes difficult to tell apart."[5]

What's the analogy to elite research institutions like the Dana-Farber? There, as we will see, faculty "stars" run more or less free-standing laboratories filled with postdoctoral researchers who are tackling some of the toughest problems related to cancer detection and treatment. In their role as the principal investigators on research programs, those stars play a critical role in winning grants from places like the National Institutes of Health. This funding, in turn, fuels a virtuous cycle: more money enables better research, which gets published in prominent journals, which brings greater prestige to the institution and the researchers, which attracts the highest-caliber talent, which increases the likelihood that the next grant applications will be successful. Meanwhile, the institution's fund-raisers market those stars and their successes to potential donors, thereby generating another welcome source of revenue.

I hope this all sounds at least vaguely familiar to you. Think back to the solo specialists described in chapter 3: successful professionals who hold great cards, and—up to a point—can call their own shots.

But let me raise the stakes a little bit. It's fair to hypothesize that the leaders of elite research institutions face even tougher challenges than their counterparts at, say, Bain (consulting), Grey (advertising), or Egon Zehnder (executive search). Places like Dana-Farber are absolutely *filled* with some of the world's best cancer researchers; even those who are not yet stars may be only one discovery away from being Nobel Prize–worthy. "Keeping the tigers on their stools" takes on a whole new meaning.

And who are these tigers? By the time someone gets a job offer at a place like Dana-Farber, he or she has typically spent as many as eight years in formal training beyond college to earn a PhD, an MD, or both. To run that extended gauntlet, young researchers have to be not only brilliant, but also exceptionally driven and politically savvy. They must not only earn great grades in multiple supercompetitive contexts, but also win a series of brutally competitive contests for internships, residencies, spaces on research teams, credits on publications, and so on.

So we shouldn't be surprised to learn that the researchers who end up as the stars at the world's leading research institutions aren't first and foremost team players. Collaboration among researchers can be challenging; competition tends to be the rule, rather than the exception. Seemingly little things—the size and location of one's lab, for example—denote prestige and signal one's position in the institutional hierarchy, and are therefore worth fighting over. As a result, administrators who have plenty of other things to worry about spend enormous amounts of time adjudicating turf battles.

But there's a catch—which again, based on earlier chapters, should sound familiar: like so many other knowledge-intensive arenas today, successful medical research increasingly depends on contributions from specialists who are willing and able to work across their expertise divides. It depends on people who can join forces, intellectually, to make themselves more innovative and productive.

At McKinsey and Dana-Farber alike, leaders impose high and paradoxical expectations on their professionals. To a great extent, everyone is supposed to *act* like a star. As a team leader at McKinsey, one of the aspects I coached juniors on most frequently was how to exhibit more "gravitas" in front of clients and partners. In their clients' eyes, too, those professionals are *supposed* to be stars—that's why they warrant rates that are sometimes many multiples of their clients' pay. To pull that off, you need to see yourself as a star, at least to some degree. That implies comparison with your peers, and a determination to look good in that comparison. So far, so good: the enterprise needs to cultivate internal energy and healthy competition for its long-term well-being. But at the same time, as I've argued in previous chapters, the enterprise needs to foster collaboration. *What got you here won't get you there.*

And nowhere is this more true than at places like the Dana-Farber Cancer Institute.

Collaboration and competition at Dana-Farber

The Dana-Farber Cancer Institute had its roots in the Children's Cancer Research Foundation, founded in 1947 by prominent pediatric pathologist Sidney Farber. It has since evolved into one of the world's leading institutions focusing both on the care of adult and pediatric cancer patients and on research to provide a better understanding of the disease. It also serves as the lead institution for the Dana-Farber/Harvard Cancer Center, a partnership among seven Harvard-affiliated hospitals and schools that together oversee some seven hundred clinical trials per year.

Research labs at Dana-Farber are led by principal investigators (PIs), who are Harvard faculty scientists. The PI is the intellectual visionary of his or her lab and has complete control over daily lab activities. Additional researchers in these labs represent most of the upper rungs on the educational ladder, ranging from undergraduates to physicians and postdoctoral fellows.

Even in the early years of the twenty-first century, there was almost no institutional guidance over the types of projects that labs undertook, which gave them tremendous autonomy over how they used institutional resources. The system was designed to encourage creative, talented scientists to study what interested them, whether or not those interests synched up particularly well (or at all) with the Dana-Farber's role as an academic cancer research center.

Inventing new approaches to research at Dana-Farber

Impressive economic growth in the United States in the late 1990s created a favorable funding environment for primary research, especially in the cancer field. By 2003, however, there was growing dissatisfaction among both government and private funding sources over the lack of translational therapies derived from the funding. Many research institutions anticipated, therefore, that the National Institutes of Health and other major funding sources would begin dialing back the generous grants they had been making up to that point.

Dr. Edward Benz, president of Dana-Farber since 2000, recognized these trends, and decided that research at his institution had to be conducted more efficiently. He thought that the effective translational therapy output of cancer centers would define institutional research success in the coming decade—a challenge that he described as part of a larger strategic planning process. To address this challenge, Benz envisioned collaborative organizational units of faculty and resources that would be formed and managed rigorously against a clear set of institutional goals. These units were called integrative research centers.

As soon as Benz outlined his vision, he began receiving the first of scores of proposals to establish research centers. To lead the effort in choosing centers and implementing their launch, Benz appointed a colleague, Dr. Barrett Rollins, as chief scientific officer. Rollins, an accomplished physician and scientist in his own right, saw his new role as twofold: first, implementing the constant stream of ideas emerging from the faculty; and second, making sure that those implementations were accomplished with *accountability*. Rollins saw the program as an opportunity to modify the scientific culture at Dana-Farber from one that solely celebrated individualism to one that also cherished broader institutional goals like collaboration. Collaboration, in turn, would produce science that advanced the institute's output at a quicker pace toward diagnostics and therapies.

That kind of transformation wasn't going to be easy. As Rollins recalls:

> Nobody in this environment had ever really written a business plan before. They looked at this as being just another example of institutional largesse going to the elect few. They said, "You've identified people who are running centers and you're just giving them money to run their labs? What's wrong with you guys?" And so, for the first couple of years, there was a real sense of insiders versus outsiders. It took a lot of presentations on my part to various groups to demonstrate the rigor behind the granting of the money.

Together, Benz, Rollins, and several other senior colleagues drew up a list of the first ten centers that would be created under the new strategic plan. Several years later, an eleventh center—the Center for Nanotechnology in Cancer, to which we will return shortly—was added.[6]

Structuring integrative research

The new integrative research centers applied the principles of project management to medical research—a new and unaccustomed kind of discipline for most traditional researchers. While one or more faculty members with content expertise would be designated as center leaders, membership in those centers could cross departmental lines—in other words, any faculty member interested in doing research in the center's area of study could join. But there was a catch, of sorts: the use of center resources by faculty who weren't members of that particular center required collaboration on projects with center members.

Each center leader was given an unprecedented amount of institutional financial resources to launch the activities of the center. But again, there were significant conditions. The centers had to meet specific metrics under a five-year budget stipulated in business plans that were submitted during the center approval process. Moreover, after five years, centers were expected to be financially independent of the Dana-Farber—on the assumption that their anticipated successes would win them outside funding. Another core business principle was that center funds could not be used for projects initiated in the leader's own lab, although he or she could be a "customer" of the center like any other faculty member.

In keeping with the managed approach to the new centers, all were, and are, subject to several layers of oversight. At annual oversight committee meetings, the center leader presents the progress of the center over the past year. Each committee member then evaluates the center quantitatively, assigning scores for performance against eight important metrics. The committee makes specific recommendations to center leaders, and reports its findings to chief scientific officer Rollins and the board of trustees.

The best-laid plans

The Center for Nanotechnology in Cancer (CNTC) was the eleventh integrated research center at the Dana-Farber. Established in 2010, the CNTC was viewed by Rollins and others as critical to the larger organization's scientific success, because it held the potential for both early detection of cancer (using nanoparticles and molecular imaging) and new treatments through tumor-targeting technology. Up to that point, engineering had been poorly represented in the Dana-Farber research portfolio; it was hoped that the CNTC would help address that shortcoming.

The CNTC's leader and chief faculty scientist was a talented and visionary researcher named Charlie Woods, who was a pioneer in the application of nanotechnology to treating cancer in the realms of both diagnostics and therapeutics.[7] When Woods submitted a business plan for the CNTC in 2010, therefore, Benz and Rollins quickly accepted it.

But despite his overall enthusiasm for growing Dana-Farber's capabilities in the nanotechnology realm, Rollins had reservations about Woods's leadership potential:

> Charlie is incredibly insightful as a scientist, very brilliant, but I think he'd be the first to admit that administrative skills are not his primary interest, nor his forte. So we knew that for this center, all of the vision part was fine: he certainly understood nanotechnology's broader role in cancer. But I was concerned about his managing the bits and pieces. Nonetheless, Charlie's "the guy" when it comes to nanotech and cancer, so we decided that the CNTC led by Charlie was a gamble worth taking.

Woods had his own reservations. At the time, he faced numerous professional pressures. The most important of these involved his personal career progression: he was on a "tenure clock" at Harvard Medical School. At Harvard, as at most academic institutions, junior professors are considered for promotion based on timelines, and they need to rack up a series of accomplishments deemed worthy of promotion within a set period of time. The promotion from associate to full professor—which Woods was now facing—tends to be the most challenging of all.

It wasn't long before the reservations held by both Rollins and Woods began to prove justified. Woods began a collaborative effort with a distinguished colleague in the field of neuro-oncology, and spent about $1 million of institutional money on specialized equipment to support that initiative, none of which had been included in the CNTC's business plan. Not long afterward, the collaboration collapsed amid mutual recriminations, with each scientist claiming that the other was seeking to control and take credit for the project.

More trouble was on the horizon. In July 2010, as the once-promising collaboration was falling apart, Woods received a phone call from the chief scientific officer of a biotech company who was convinced that the technologies that Woods had been developing would fit well with the company's expanding product pipeline. The company was prepared to offer up to $15 million in total research support to his laboratory—a truly princely sum. In keeping with the company's strategy, though, more than half of the funding would be contingent on developing variations on Woods's technology to detect noncancerous lesions of the brain, such as those resulting from strokes and parasitic infections. From Woods's point of view, this appeared to be a brilliant way to scale up the application of his nanoparticle. He happily agreed to the company's terms, and decided to allocate the funds directly to the CNTC instead of to his own lab budget.

On September 1, 2010, the CNTC oversight committee gathered for its first annual review of the center. Woods approached the meeting with mixed feelings. On the one hand, his center would be measured against a predefined set of rigorous metrics, some of which he clearly had not hit. The failed collaboration with the neuro-oncologist also loomed in the background. On the other hand, he had secured a $15 million commercial grant. Surely that success would outweigh any perceived shortcomings of the CNTC. With that in mind, Woods spent a half hour explaining to the committee his detailed plan for deploying the funds. Within three years, the CNTC would submit five new device applications to the FDA for brain-imaging diagnostic products.

At the end of his presentation, the conference room was silent. Finally, the committee chair broke the silence. "Well, Charlie," he began, "your ability to secure this amount of money is certainly impressive. But what have you been doing with this center all year?"

This first challenging question unleashed a flood of questions in a similar vein. Where was the staff that was supposed to be executing center operations? Where was the administrator who was supposed to manage this staff? Why hadn't the CNTC communicated any of its activities to other faculty or center administrators, in order to facilitate collaborative projects? Why had the center begun to pursue a line of diagnostics that was not focused on cancer?

At a meeting with Rollins later that same day, Woods boiled over with frustration. He told Rollins that he couldn't understand why the oversight committee had given him a failing grade, especially after he had brought so much industry money into Dana-Farber. The CNTC was *his* center, he said, and he needed enough autonomy to run it as he saw best. He demanded that Rollins get the committee "off his back"—and then stormed out of Rollins's office.

Rollins sat back in his chair, stunned. As far as the science went, there was nobody as good as Charlie Woods. But Rollins knew that the time had come to make decisions that were in the best interest of Dana-Farber. The early decision to focus the centers on collaboration, he felt strongly, was absolutely the right one. The complexity of the research problems at hand demanded no less. Over the previous year, Woods had clearly demonstrated his limitations as a collaborator. And according to the new rules of the game, the eleven centers had to be self-sufficient within five years: weaned off institutional resources, and adept at winning support from government, foundations, and donors—purely for cancer research. The chances of that happening with Woods as sole custodian of the CNTC were vanishingly small.

The institutional response

Although the crisis at hand involved the CNTC, Rollins realized Woods's center was only a case in point—that in fact, all eleven centers were vulnerable to the same kinds of problems that plagued the CNTC. As Rollins saw it, three things were needed to help the centers grow and prosper: *transparency* of project intake, *accountability* of the centers' members to the larger Dana-Farber, and the *alignment* of center activities with the institutional goal of advancing translational cancer research through greater collaboration among leading scientists. As Rollins recalls:

> At that point, although we entertained the idea, we decided that we couldn't remove Woods even though he hadn't delivered on the metrics we created for the centers several years prior. While many of the centers had achieved some success, many scientists still hadn't even bought into the system's philosophy surrounding collaboration, let alone institutional prioritization. We needed to prove first that centers could work well under the framework we designed before holding decorated scientists accountable to these metrics. And for this reason, it was a better idea to figure out a way for Woods to succeed under the center framework.

Of course, near-term discipline had to be imposed. Rollins talked at length with Woods about how the CNTC could move forward. The center had to build an administrative staff and a platform for communication with the rest of the Dana-Farber community. It had to focus its efforts on cancer therapies and not get distracted by the promise of unrelated riches. And because a large portion of the grant from the biotech company could not be used for cancer research, those projects had to be limited to Woods's own lab—meaning that he could no longer use center resources or personnel for those projects.

Woods spent several days in anger and denial, furious at both the oversight committee and Rollins. But he knew that he had a reputation to protect with a relatively small scientific community. He decided to stay and help lead a turnaround of the CNTC, and asked Rollins to help him recruit the necessary personnel.

Leadership was the immediate concern. Rollins addressed this issue by appointing one of Woods's longtime faculty colleagues,

Peter Lendale, as a coleader of the center. By so doing, Rollins was explicitly signing on an individual who was "more institutionally minded" than Woods and therefore would be more inclined to align center activities with larger Dana-Farber goals.

Rollins then asked Lendale and Woods to recruit a research scientist who could take responsibility for coordinating and executing the CNTC's research activities, as well as broadening its goals and scope. The research scientist role was specifically created as a Dana-Farber position—as opposed to a tenure-track Harvard position—to help center leaders in their project-management roles. As Rollins later explained, "The great thing about research scientists not being tenure-track faculty is that their motivation and incentives are different. Rather, they are evaluated on the basis of how they manage institutionally directed projects that come into the center. In the case of CNTC, we thought that a research scientist could allow us to revamp the business plan to do something that was more explicit around institutional responsibility."

Lendale and Woods decided to hire Louise Ratkin, a postdoc who had been working in Woods's lab for almost three years. Ratkin was an unusual scientist in that she was not particularly drawn to either the traditional academic environment or the pharmaceutical industry. The research scientist role at the CNTC promised the opportunity to conduct high-quality scientific work in a mission-driven context and still take on the managerial responsibilities that she also enjoyed. She readily accepted the position.

As one of her first tasks, Ratkin set up a project-intake mechanism that included an objective evaluations committee. This committee helped ensure that proposed projects not only had scientific merit, but also aligned with larger institutional goals. In addition, concrete milestones were agreed on at the projects' outset, to facilitate timeliness and efficiency. With the committee, scientists had to develop discrete budgets for each project, which were coordinated with project timelines and the center's overall budget. All of these checkpoints ensured that when a project was approved, its contribution to the center's mission—as well as its financial implications for the center—had been reviewed and documented. Ratkin also established a monthly billing cycle to track finances and ensure overall alignment with the business plan.

Lendale, Woods, and Ratkin also created a web-based platform to facilitate collaboration and marketing of the center's projects. This public resource was a startling departure from precedent, in that it provided near full disclosure of each project's goals to encourage more scientists to join the center's efforts—and to join those efforts in the right frame of mind. As Ratkin explains:

> I had a scientist come in and tell me that he wanted to collaborate with our center. In particular, he needed a very specific type of technology and he knew that we had it. He said, "I really want to do this, and I have some preliminary exciting results, but I don't want to share them with you just yet." And I kind of said, "Well, you know, our goal is to be collaborative, and while you certainly don't have to share the results with us, we can design a much better set of experiments if you are willing to actually talk to me about what you have." So he decided to share his results, and it was a great project. There is actually a clinical trial starting because of that.

As it turned out, the talk of collaboration was more than talk. Within a few years, the transformed CNTC had completed twenty-three projects and had another thirty-five projects under way—initiatives that included scientists from the Dana-Farber, Massachusetts General Hospital, the University of California at Los Angeles, and Case Western. Thanks to the thorough intake screening, moreover, the projects were consistently aligned with the Dana-Farber's institutional mission.

More broadly, and with the benefit of a half-decade's hindsight, Rollins believes that the integrative research center structure has proven itself. Of the Dana-Farber's dozen or so centers, only a few are generally seen as unsuccessful, a half-dozen have turned in an adequate performance, and three or four have been spectacular successes. But Rollins declares himself to be generally pleased with his experiment, pointing first to the *cultural* impact of the centers:

> After ten years of having these centers here, the culture of this entire institution has fundamentally changed.
>
> Nobody complains about centers anymore. I go to these faculty meetings, nobody complains anymore about the haves and the have-nots, as in, "People running centers have all these resources and the rest of us don't." There's no more of this cynical view. Everybody realizes that centers have changed the way we do work, made it easier for a lot of people to get access to complicated stuff, and nobody talks about this system going away.
>
> We now have over 120 people who are on the nontenure research scientist track. That's become a vibrant way for people to have a career here. Things are different.[8]

In assessing the output of the centers, Rollins resorts to business terminology. "We know which ones are successful," he says, "because they have a huge customer base, and people are very happy with the product."[9] One center has recently signed a multimillion-dollar contract with a pharmaceutical company to pursue a major initiative that jibes with the institute's overall mission. Another center has created such a demand for its MRI technology that Rollins and his colleagues are desperately searching for funds to buy an additional imaging system.

In Rollins's estimation, these are great problems to have.

Lessons from looking sideways at Dana-Farber

Let me open this discussion by emphasizing two points that are *different* about medical research before turning to the lessons for leaders of professional service firms.

First and most important, the kinds of financial incentives described in chapter 6 are simply not available in academia. In the same vein, for researchers on a tenure ladder, promotions in the academic setting are out of the hands of the organization's leaders. Ed Benz and Barrett Rollins didn't control Charlie Woods's advancement in any direct way. But this is good news for professional service firms. You have powerful tools at your disposal that should help you promote collaboration in ways that Benz and Rollins couldn't.

Second, the definition of the medical research "client" is markedly different. Medical researchers have to satisfy internal oversight committees, boards of trustees, outside funders, and—in the broadest sense—science and society. This is a sort of "collective client," with multiple heads, and it is a relatively patient client that understands false starts and dead ends. Not so among the clients of professional service firms! They expect pragmatic advice that they can implement *now*. And they may or may not re-up with your team, depending on the near- and middle-term results.

Nevertheless, there are obvious parallels between the challenges faced by the characters in the Dana-Farber case and their counterparts in the private-sector knowledge industry. Successful research today demands both specialization and collaboration, in part because the challenges being tackled are so complex—and getting more so every day. Like any senior leader in a knowledge-based firm, Rollins and his colleagues at Dana-Farber needed to find ways to convince powerful, portable, highly autonomous stars to change their behavior *well before* their competitive, siloed ways of working made them obsolete. In so doing, they faced a difficult challenge.

You face the same challenge. On the one hand, you must use persuasion and diplomacy to win over the autonomy-seeking professionals who largely control the firm's most important assets. On the other hand, you must manage your firm in ways that meet the increasing market demands to improve efficiency and competitiveness.

So what general lessons can we tease out of the Dana-Farber experience? How do you transform a competitive, star-driven culture into one that fosters cross-boundary collaboration? To answer these questions, I combine insights from the Dana-Farber case study with elements of the classic McKinsey model of influence, and suggest four specific levers of change.

Develop a compelling story

Before your partners and other colleagues will follow your collaborative lead, they have to see the *point* of the change. This means you have to develop the business case for collaboration, and use it to create buy-in. Of course, the story line will be different from setting to setting, but in general, collaboration is not just an aspiration or a nice-to-have; it's a strategic response to external change, and perhaps the path to survival.

Several years down his difficult institutional path, Rollins acknowledges that many of his scientists never bought into the new philosophy or way of working. What could he have done differently? First, he admits that he and his senior colleagues should have invested more time and resources to communicating how collaboration could make a significant difference to both the institution and the individuals involved.

In the private-sector analogue, this argues for developing a multipronged communication strategy. Because collaboration is by definition a collective effort, you need widespread buy-in across levels, roles, and tenure bands. In crafting a message about collaboration, therefore, you should spotlight benefits that may appeal to different people in your firm. For example, some senior partners will be motivated by the opportunity to shape a legacy by training a strong successor in each major account. Others will be drawn to collaboration's promise of creating a more inclusive organization, with opportunities for more diverse professionals. Some will be convinced by collaboration's financial outcomes—either because the collaboration shores up the firm's competitive position, or because profits will (eventually) flow to them as shareholders.

Figure out what motivates these professionals, and play up those attributes of collaboration in your personal communication with them. In the Dana-Farber example, Peter Lendale and Louise Ratkin are two kinds of contributors (in the language of chapter 5). Both are niche players, although Lendale—as a tenured "partner"—enjoyed a certain institutional stature that Ratkin did not. But remember: Ratkin didn't aspire to "partnership," as it is defined in academic medicine; she wanted to do great science and run some important projects. Like her counterparts in the for-profit sector, Ratkin makes her important contribution in part because she brings a different set of values and expectations to the table. Similarly in your firm, it's probably millennials whose aspirations conform least to traditional career tracks and role descriptions. Have you figured out how to tailor your message to motivate them? They're going to be an essential part of your change program, so get them onside before you lose them.

Sometimes storytelling requires proof of concept. In that spirit, consider testing small-scale versions of the collaboration initiative. Rollins admits that he and his senior colleagues were naive to launch ten new integrative research centers all at once, without any piloting or prototyping. Prototyping establishes a visible change that speaks for itself.

As you develop your story line, never underestimate the motivational power of small wins. Teresa Amabile, a social psychologist and Harvard Business School professor, examined twelve thousand daily diary entries written by hundreds of employees across many companies.[10] She found that the best predictor of these workers' desire to persevere on difficult, risky, and emotionally challenging projects was their sense of whether they were making noticeable progress toward their goals—even if progress was a relatively minor event, like having an encouraging meeting with a potential customer. Similarly, don't underestimate the power of vicarious wins. "When an army has the force of momentum," Sun Tzu wrote more than twenty-five hundred years ago, "even the timid become brave."[11] Make sure the whole firm understands the progress that is being made.

Model the desired collaborative approaches

Piloting is one way to introduce a new reality. So is modeling the desired behaviors. Employees want to see you and your senior colleagues—presumably, the leaders whom they admire—behaving in the new way. As Mohandas Gandhi put it, "Be the change you want to see in the world."

This aspect of leadership in a professional firm, like at the Dana-Farber Cancer Institute, is essential at multiple levels, including but not limited to the executive ranks. In a study I conducted of long-term change in the professional service firm context, I found that organizational stars—specifically, rainmakers whose client revenues were in the firm's top 10 percent—had the most influence over others' behaviors. When these people start modeling the behaviors you want to support, you are on the down slope.

Also remember that the most effective leaders may not be the most obvious ones. As two McKinsey consultants noted, "Our experiences working with change programs suggest that success depends less on how persuasive a few selected leaders are and more on how receptive the 'society' is to the idea. In practice it is often unexpected members of the rank and file who feel compelled to step up and make a difference in driving change."[12]

In one public relations firm I worked with, the core change leader turned out to be a relatively junior professional who was passionate about collaboration. He first educated himself so that he could deeply understand and articulate the business case—going so far as to devote all his vacation time one year to an executive development program. He identified a rationale for strategic change that convinced practice-group leaders in the firm, and used his knowledge and experience to bring along his peers. He organized workshops and focus groups, and got a budget to bring in outside experts to support the initiative.

Yes, his influence stemmed in part from the broad internal network he'd built working for the firm on three continents. Even so, he wasn't the most obvious suspect to spearhead a collaborative change effort. Like PwC's Paula Young—described in chapter 6—this firm's leaders were smart in going where the energy was, finding great people to model the change.

Reinforce the desired behaviors

The two guidelines outlined earlier are about getting people on board; the next challenge is keeping them there. This means that every relevant management lever that can be pulled has to work in support of collaboration—and conversely, no structures or processes can actively work against it.

I've already addressed performance management, compensation and other incentives, and technology, all of which must be lined up in ways that support collaborative behavior. In the same spirit, role descriptions should be clarified. Specifically, the *interrelatedness* of roles needs underscoring, and specific behaviors need to be "attached" to roles.

At Dana-Farber, Rollins and his senior colleagues should have clarified what their center leaders would do more of and less of, what their research scientists and project managers would do more of and less of, and so on. This is especially important if you're introducing new kinds of players into the account management structure: you need to help partners understand how to engage with these new players.

Let's face it: change management skills are probably not deeply ingrained in your partners (even if their job is helping other organizations change, it's sometimes hard to swallow one's own medicine). So you need to equip them to play that role. That means, in part, giving them a road map for the change, which can serve—at the very least—as a point of departure. It also means identifying and deploying project managers who have strong implementation skills, and again, explaining who they are and why they're there.

Aligning the formal systems and structures is an essential precursor to delivering more systemic change. *You can't fix culture*, as the cover of a recent *Harvard Business Review* proclaimed—meaning that attempts to directly transform organizational culture are fruitless unless leaders first tackle the structures to reinforce desired behaviors.[13]

Develop new collaborative capabilities and confidence

This focus on skills helps introduce my final point: for collaboration to work over the long term, your colleagues must have the collaborative skills to make the desired changes. It's simply not enough to point at a target and hope people can hit it. At Dana-Farber, Charlie Woods was given a leadership role for which his senior colleagues suspected he was ill suited. They went ahead anyway, and paid the price. I call this the "hope-for-the-best syndrome," and I see it all the time in professional service firms.

Leadership is critical to counter this syndrome. Leaders need to invest time on a one-to-one basis with the key implementers of the strategy, and support them with adequate training and coaching.

How can people best be equipped with the skills they need to make relevant changes in behavior? First, *give them time*. David Kolb, one of the world's foremost scholars of adult learning, argues that grown-ups can't learn merely by listening to instructions; they must also absorb the new information, use it experimentally, and integrate it with their existing knowledge.[14] In practice, this means that even your most willing partners will need plenty of time to develop the kinds of collaborative capabilities I have advocated.

Ideally—and yes, this is an especially long-term prescription—start developing collaborative leadership capabilities in your junior ranks. McKinsey, for example, provides associates with highly visible collaborative leadership opportunities early in their time with the firm, such as heading recruiting teams or planning business-unit retreats. Day to day, McKinsey project managers—who typically have three to five years' experience at the firm—run many aspects of the client relationship, including significant levels of interaction with clients. Build in collaboration at this level, and you are building for the future.

I hope the cast of characters in the Dana-Farber story seemed somewhat familiar to you. Ed Benz and Barrett Rollins are the "firm's" senior leaders—the ringmasters described in chapter 6. Charlie Woods sits somewhere in between the solo specialist and the seasoned collaborator discussed in chapters 3 and 4, respectively. The central evolution in the Dana-Farber story belongs to Woods, as he makes a painful transition out of the former category into the latter. The secondary evolution belongs to Rollins, as he lives through the uncomfortable experience of learning how his first collaborative structures were poorly designed—by him—and now need to be redesigned under pressure.

The parallels might not be exact, but the *dynamics* of the collaborative process at Dana-Farber are very similar to those in today's professional service firms. Collaboration starts slowly. It is intensely *human*, no matter how hard we try to corral it into systems and processes. It goes down blind alleys far more often than we like to admit. It is initially less productive and more expensive than its freewheeling, freestanding, single-silo counterpart.

But when it works, it works like nothing else. *What got you here won't get you there.* Collaboration gets you there.

The voice of the client

Throughout this book, I've made references to the client. What do clients of professional service firms need as they set out to solve their more complex and important problems—and how can they meet that need?

Chapter 8, the last in this book, turns to that perspective explicitly, and uses that opportunity to review some of the lessons learned in previous chapters.

[8]

Collaboration: Yes, Your Clients Care

Previous chapters have mostly taken a view from inside the firm, with occasional asides summarizing how a client might look at particular aspects of collaboration. This final chapter turns the telescope around by focusing mainly on the client's perspective.

My main assertion here is both simple and perhaps surprising: *Yes, clients want you, their professional service providers, to collaborate within your own firm*. They care about the quality of partner-to-partner collaboration. Why? Because they understand that your collaborative prowess is an important and valuable resource for them, too.

I'm not talking here about the quality of the working relationship between client and provider, or across multiple firms; or about the quality of the service that results from those relationships (although those are all extremely important, and I'll speak specifically to several of those points in the pages that follow). Rather, I mean how well your team members collaborate *with each other*. The savvy client assesses the quality of that collaboration, and this chapter explains when and why they are willing (and sometimes not) to pay more for productive collaboration within your shop.

There's a bigger picture. In all kinds of contexts, transparency is becoming more and more important. Why are so many restaurants now featuring windows that let you peek into their kitchens, or seating you as close as possible to the working chefs? Because customers have decided that they want to "be in the kitchen." They want to see how the sausage is made. Why are governments opening up once-secret databases and archives? Because the general public is demanding increased access to that information.

This same imperative for transparency has taken root across the broad base of sophisticated clients—not just in the United States, but around the world. Clients expect greater and greater levels of visibility into their providers' operations. Because they're investing in those relationships, they need to know that the firms who serve them are on financially, technically, and ethically solid ground for the long haul. If they like what they see, they're willing to pay more for access to that quality operation.

I'm guessing that some of my readers are conjuring up images of their toughest clients—their hardest-nosed, most bottom-line-oriented clients, who pride themselves on making a buck squeal—and those readers are, well, *skeptical*. Even if I've persuaded them in previous chapters that collaboration is good for their own firm, they're still pretty sure that the client they've just envisioned doesn't want to hear about collaboration, and certainly doesn't want to pay for it.

If so, they're probably wrong.

Over the past several years, I've conducted several extensive rounds of interviews with clients. These individuals represent widely varying roles and organizations, comprising CEOs, general counsels, board members (including heads of audit and risk committees), heads of procurement, vice presidents, and many more. The organizations they represent span almost all geographies, sizes, and sectors. They include publicly traded and privately held companies, as well as nonprofit and governmental institutions. And I went out of my way to interview clients who had a reputation for being tough negotiators, focused on measurable results—the kind of individual who, I'd been told, "wouldn't pay for collaboration."

That research revealed the opposite. It demonstrated that clients *care deeply* about the degree to which their external advisers collaborate with colleagues within their own firm, and are willing to pay for quality collaboration. Of course, there are caveats and conditions. First and foremost, we're only talking about *smart collaboration*: the problem at hand has to be complicated enough to warrant the input of multiple experts. Absent that complexity— as one senior client told me—there's no justification for additional expertise:

> I always get a little nervous when someone says, "I don't know about it, but let me bring in my expert." If I don't think it warrants an expert, then I think, "OK, this is an opportunity for you to hit me with more charges." In those cases, I usually get a so-called "specialist," but I'm not always sure what value they're adding, which gives me a nagging suspicion that I hadn't hired the right lawyer to begin with. In those cases, I interpret cross-selling as a chance to bring a buck.

This coin has two sides: First, clients must clearly understand the benefits of collaboration for them to be willing to pay for a team effort. Second, it's *your job* to help them understand those benefits—as early in the project as possible, and always before you bill them! Timing is key. It's easier and wiser to propose a collaborative team up front than to expand the team later on. As one client explained, "I want to have a team formed fairly early on, as opposed to added to over time. That shows me that the lead partner has thought through the issues and doesn't just pull in extra resources if suddenly he has better things to do. If I know what the team will be ahead of time and why each member is there, I never reject the idea of a team."

By the same token, clients draw a sharp distinction between what they consider a benefit to themselves as opposed to a benefit for the firm, and they're unlikely to pay for the latter. For example, they may well expect their advisers to "invest" in having more than one person on a call, while only billing for a single individual, so that the whole team can get up to speed quickly. Obviously, no client is going to knowingly pay for rework, duplication, or messy intrafirm communication that didn't add value. The better your project management, the fewer of these costs you'll need to eat.

These views speak directly to the issue of trust—the client's belief that you have their best interests at heart, over the long term. "If I trust them, that's the touchstone," a client told me. "In that case, I am always less focused on the cost than on the results."

Still skeptical? If so, consider this: clients uniformly told me that *they don't trust someone who purports to know everything.* They expect that there will be times when you will need to seek expert input from others, depending on the complexity of the problem at hand. Ask any CEO: the most dangerous advisers are those who are unwilling to say, "I don't know," and are unwilling to collaborate with someone who does.

To summarize: without a single exception, the clients I talked to emphasized that they *do* care whether their advisers collaborate effectively inside their own firm. In the following pages, I outline eleven reasons why that's true. For the most part, they're listed in terms of what I found to be the most important overall to clients— although certainly not all clients care about every one, or would rank them the same way I have.

Collaboration gives clients access to the best experts for the toughest problems

Business today is far more complex, more dispersed, and more global than ever before. As a result, companies can no longer rely on the advice of just one adviser with one specific area of expertise and a single frame of reference. Even as business crosses more and more borders, the laws, regulations, and cultural norms within those borders stubbornly persist, and a practice that's legal and acceptable in one country may not be in another. That fact alone puts a premium on collaboration. In addition, almost every significant business issue today is multifaceted: technical, environ-mental, regulatory, and more. It is increasingly rare to encounter a sizeable challenge that has only one dimension.[1] Again, solving these complex issues requires individual professionals—from con-sultants and lawyers to engineers—to work together with their col-leagues. As one chief in a pharmaceuticals company summed it up, "The more complex the issue, the more I expect my primary adviser to collaborate with other experts to ensure we're getting high-quality, strategic, accurate, appropriate advice."

But if you assume that collaboration matters only to the most sophisticated clients, you're wrong. Many midsized and smaller companies face new challenges and opportunities that would ben-efit from collaborative problem solving. Everyone understands intuitively that Jamie Dimon's challenges over at JPMorgan Chase probably need to be tackled by teams. But what about all those smaller banks that are dealing with a recent flood of regulations, and—in many cases—feel like it's almost impossible to keep up? "Depending on the mood of the examiners," a leader of one of those smaller banks told me, "we might be really good, or really guilty. I'd be desperately appreciative of an organization that would provide me timely information categorized in a way I could under-stand it." In short, managers in small and medium-sized compa-nies, nonprofits, and public sector organizations need and expect their external advisers to team up, precisely *because* their own operations are leaner. You have a larger, more accessible network of expertise, and they want you to use it.

Procurement is another realm that engenders skepticism about collaboration. Some professionals believe that once the client's pro-curement function gets involved, they'll no longer have the oppor-tunity to broaden their scope of service beyond the strict RFP. But here's what one global head of procurement for a major health care company had to say about that:

> Sure, a few of our business leaders sit up in their high
> chairs and say, "I know this business better than anyone,"
> and they tell the vendors, "This is exactly what I need."
> But the more forward-thinking ones—frankly, the ones

who are going to be more successful here—say, "These are my issues. Come back once a quarter just to help me understand what levers we can put into play to help me meet my goals." And they're open to wide-ranging conversations. Now, some vendors play more than others in that scenario. But the best ones recognize that our leaders seek more than is done at the moment, and they will enable us in procurement to help them get that.

As it turns out, those levers get pulled. That particular procurement head told me that his best guess was that between 15 and 20 percent of the new ideas put on the table by those broad-gauge vendors actually got implemented and moved up the value chain, with multiple benefits—including client revenues that climbed as well. Meanwhile, the service-providing firm learned how to do better and better work for that client, which led to new opportunities. "We are now able to leverage their broader knowledge and capability," he explained, "more than we would have known to ask."

Collaboration gives clients a deeper understanding of their own business

How does a business develop new ways of thinking about what it's doing? The truth is, your clients are often deeply siloed.[2] If you have colleagues who are advising in other parts of their organization *and* your team shares business intelligence with each other—that latter premise is, sadly, not a given in many busy teams—then you can use that information to enlighten your clients about important issues inside their own company. For example, has one division just negotiated a cut-rate contract with its software supplier that other divisions could also leverage?

Providing sectoral knowledge is another way your internal collaborative skills can work to great advantage. Your client may be a regional powerhouse looking to break out; it may be venturing into territories that you already understand. If you typically provide legal counsel to your client, for example, you may be able to augment that advice with insights from other fields. "If you can tell me just one thing that my competitor is doing better than we are," said an executive recently on a panel, "then I'll give you all the time in the world." So how good are you at leveraging insights from your colleagues who are serving different clients in the same industry?

One law firm that I've worked with maintains a staff of young MBA hotshots who have at least a passing acquaintance with the law, but also know a ton about the business realities of various economic sectors. In early client meetings, the lawyer in charge of the client relationship always brings along one or more of these whiz kids to help the client sort through opportunities and figure out what impending changes—including nonlegal ones—may mean for the company.

The result? The client gets a broader view of its own organization. By having multiple professionals who touch different parts of the company in coordinated ways and offer a robust knowledge base, that client should be able to think about complex issues in new and potentially valuable ways.

Keep in mind that clients are also becoming more collaborative within their own ranks. (People who used to be considered "back office" or—far worse—"cost centers" are now being called "business partners.") And functions that used to be discrete are now overlapping and even blurring together. For example, many businesses now have both a lawyer and a technology officer on the board who report to the CFO or CEO of the business, and who interact constantly with people from across the organizational ranks with the expectation of identifying not only risks (which was historically their job) but also opportunities (which requires collaboration). And as noted in previous chapters, those ranks are smartening up. As one CEO told me:

> Several decades ago, when the consulting firms were really taking off, they could make their money by exporting basic strategy ideas from one sector to another, as in "Here's a competitor analysis we developed for commercial banking; now let's sell it to insurance companies."

I know, because I was there doing it! But over time, banks filled their internal ranks with former consultants, and pretty much everyone has an MBA. So now we're much more sophisticated inside, and we expect our outsiders to bring us deeply focused, deeply customized knowledge. Their value-add comes from seeing *across* the competitive landscape.

Today, clients expect their outside consultants to be a source—even a wealth—of benchmark knowledge. For example: How are other banks in our circumstance handling their credit reserves? What regulatory changes on the horizon may affect that all-important calculation? Delivering these kinds of insights often requires collaboration not only among partner-level peers, but also between them and your firm's business support professionals—such as staff in marketing, business development, or practice group management—who have their ear to the ground, picking up sector-level intelligence. The better you are at internal collaboration, the more equipped you are to answer these kinds of questions—and the happier your client will be to pay your bill.

Collaboration enables global reach

Global reach is a phrase that is commonly used, but rarely parsed out. What does it mean, exactly, and how can your collaborative prowess serve your client in this regard?

First, global reach means multinational projects and deals. This is pretty straightforward: The client needs help in three countries at once on the same project, and counts on you to provide that help seamlessly. You are either equipped or not equipped to help, based on your prior experience with internal collaboration. Are you in a position to "export" the necessary work to trusted colleagues on the ground in those three countries, and then manage the project efficiently?

Second, global reach means helping a client with a country-specific project where it lacks sufficient capacity. Your collaborative skills give that client the convenience and assurance that comes with having a trusted contact in that country who has an insider's perspective on issues that would otherwise be opaque.

For example, a human rights lawyer told me the story of a major extractive company in Africa that found itself under a lot of investor pressure to expand its reserves, which it did by buying a gold company in another country. As it turned out, the acquired company had a terrible record of environmental abuses and human rights problems. How did this mess come to pass? The acquiring company did the deal through a big international investment banking firm—but the acquisition was handled strictly out of New York. The investment banker's legal counsel said, in so many words, "Hey—our job is to handle the law." From a purely technical, legal point of view, the purchase looked clean, but from the business and reputation sides, it was a bona fide disaster. Ironically, the bankers had a reasonably robust African practice that would have known the whole story and could have kept the ship off the rocks—if only those African partners had been involved. The acquiring company would have been glad to pay for those kinds of on-the-ground insights.

Global reach also comprises those companies that don't yet cross borders, and may never intend to. I interviewed one client in Brazil who runs an energy business. He told me, "I expect my adviser to say, 'Here are some problems we've become aware of because our African practice partner has seen it there, and it may be relevant to a Latin America transaction.' That's extremely valuable to us."

A leader of a European regional retail bank told me that his organization didn't do any business in the United States, and didn't expect to in the foreseeable future. "But I want my lawyers to help me understand the regulatory environment there, because it'll prepare us better for what might be coming here eventually," he explained to me. "At a minimum, I need to know what's going on so that I can make an informed decision that I *don't* need to worry. It's the unknown that provokes anxiety. I want my advisers to help me rest easier."

In the vein of *not* resting easier, a European telecoms client showed me the website of a consulting firm that his company calls on regularly. The website implied that the consultants had a deep penetration in, and understanding of, Silicon Valley. "But the people I deal with from that firm are clueless," he said with some frustration. He continued: "No, I'm not trying to engage with Silicon Valley directly. We have no aspirations there. But my consultants know our company is struggling with innovation. Why aren't they bringing me insights into how startups there manage to be so innovative? What's the process? What can we import?"

These clients realize the benefit of having a savvy, collaborative adviser close at hand. All of them, and perhaps some of your clients that resemble them, would happily pay more to rest easier and compete more effectively.

Collaboration fosters innovation

The case of the European telecoms executive just referred to raises the key issue of innovation. Clients are predisposed to think that teams are more innovative than individuals—no matter how talented and experienced those individuals may be. And, according to the research we reviewed earlier, that assumption tends to be correct.[3] So if that's their expectation, your firm needs to be prepared to meet it.

Even when the issue doesn't demand blue-sky thinking, you may still need to "small-i" innovate to appropriately customize your standard advice to the client's precise context and constraints. "They should adapt the way their advice is presented," one manager in a health care context told me with some frustration about his outside consultants. "We have to spend too much time to use it." Given how hard it is for professional firms to carve out a competitive advantage, shouldn't you collaborate with your colleagues to give your clients advice that is so tailored, it delights them? Collaboration can get you there.

Innovation can often add value beyond the scoped-out project. Until recently, that icing-on-the-cake mentality seemed optional, but more and more clients are starting to formalize the expectation. As one explained,

When we do new contracts with professional service firms, we put in a value-add clause. Most firms come back with very standard offers, like a couple of secondees or a software upgrade. Of course that's valuable and important to us, but it doesn't differentiate the firm. Maybe it distinguishes ones that *won't* do it. But the real opportunity to stand out is through collaboration. [What we] really want to know is, "What new are you bringing to the table? How will you go above and beyond to help improve our business?" We now expect firms to deliver a clear plan outlining how they'll deliver their expertise across our company. Increasingly this planning discussion impacts our decisions about short-listing, or giving additional work to existing providers.

Highly traditional firms are wary about agreeing to these clauses—fearing any kind of open-endedness in their contracts—and that skittishness may well be held against them. Clients want to work with firms that relish the opportunity to add value above and beyond the existing piece of work.

Most clients also understand that having new people arrive on the scene increases the chance of adding value through innovation. They doubt that something new and exceptional will arise through the individual who's been on the account for years. (Why wasn't he or she being exceptional already?) They want to see fresh blood. And they want to see evidence of what you've done that exceeds the terms of a contract with another client. If you can meet these criteria, you are far more likely to get short-listed when the next RFP is drawn up, or—better yet—you may be the only firm considered for that new work.

How do you foster innovation, which by definition is a departure from the tried and true? The very best professional firms are starting to take a "design thinking" approach to innovating within their client service offerings. Simply stated, you start small, test, discard the failed experiments while you pursue the promising ones, revise, test again, and so on.[4] This process is described explicitly in the contracting phase. The firm starts with X as the scope proposed by the client, and says in response, "Yes, of course we can quote for X. But we think that doing X+Y+Z—as a series of small and related experiments—holds way more promise for what you're trying to achieve."[5]

Clients get this. Yes, they understand that what you're proposing will benefit you, because it's a bigger assignment. But if they see the merits—with your help—then they may well modify the scope, at least to test the viability of an idea through a pilot project.

Collaboration leads to high-quality results and mitigates risks

As a rule, "more eyes on the work" assures quality and prevents avoidable errors. The bigger the business opportunity or challenge at hand, the more advantageous it is to bring multiple perspectives to bear—and clients understand this.

Of course, you have to avoid overdoing it. As an audit client put it: "There comes a point where 'collaboration' crosses the line into 'cover your ass.' I mean, I don't want to wait to have it checked, rechecked, and re-rechecked. Like on a draft report, I expect that the senior manager can show me the figures without sending it off to multiple partners for review. Or for that matter, that the partner I usually deal with can give me an opinion on a routine issue without consulting his tax expert. But for new or complicated questions? Yeah, sure."

You may recall the dabblers and lone wolves—two kinds of non-collaborative partners—whom I referred to in chapter 1. (Dabblers are partners who have a clearly defined area of expertise, but when their client comes to them with a problem outside that area, they decline to locate a colleague with the relevant expertise, and instead, "give it a go." Lone wolves are what they sound like: solo operators, often with sharp teeth.) Clients may not use these terms, but they understand clearly that there are downsides to working solely with noncollaborative representatives of your firm. Your job is to show them a more attractive alternative—and in the process, reduce your own risk of malpractice or rogue behaviors.

Peer collaboration signals your broader collaborative capacity

You may not realize it, but clients view your interactions (or lack of them) with your own colleagues as a signal of whether you're willing and able to collaborate more generally. Working with your own partners ought to be relatively easy, they reason, so if you can't pull that off, then you're unlikely to collaborate in trickier situations. This is important to them for at least two major reasons:

- As companies pull more high-end work in-house—a growing trend in recent years—they lean ever more heavily on those internal resources, who in turn need to draw on the expertise of external advisers. They need confidence that you'll be an effective thought partner and low-friction technical adviser for their internal staff.

- Conversely, as clients send more low-end work out of the shop, through disaggregation and outsourcing, they need their advisers to work seamlessly with other firms. Working effectively across firms—especially those that are actual or potential competitors—is obviously trickier than collaborating with colleagues; if you can't do the latter, clients assume you can't do the former, either.

Sometimes, it's easy to forget that your clients wear multiple hats. For example, they have customers who are suppliers as well as suppliers who are customers, which means that they absolutely *have* to collaborate internally, and in a very disciplined way. "I'll give you a classic example," one client firm executive said to me:

> We were negotiating with the post office in the UK as both a customer and a supplier. We took a very aggressive stance when buying from them, and a very conciliatory approach when selling to them. Quite frankly, we were talking to the same person and giving them completely different messages. It was completely stupid, but happened because in days gone by we had discrete businesses with discrete targets.

So from my perspective, collaboration is absolutely crucial to the customer experience, yeah? We've cleaned up our house that way. And so when we see law firms who are pitching us, it's quite obvious which of those organizations are joined up, and which are just headed up by a rainmaker with his or her own selfish targets. I've got no time or patience for that anymore.

Remember that your clients, both current and prospective, may well be sizing you up based on your proven ability to work collaboratively—not only with them, but within your own firm.

Collaboration leads to consistency in service levels

You already know how frustrated clients get when one partner fails to follow billing guidelines, how much they push back on getting billed for time spent re-explaining the same issue to multiple partners, and how foolish you look when the client informs you about work that one of your own partners is already undertaking with them. So you might not be surprised at how often I hear clients talk about the "consistency of the customer experience"—both locally and internationally—as one of the key differentiators they notice between firms.

Here are some relevant quotes from clients:

"I want assurances that the quality of the service will remain high no matter where we are working with the firm."

"Consistency across offices is important. I need to know a firm has the mechanisms in place to ensure that across international and multioffice lines, the firm is doing the work consistently."

"Finding consistency from office to office and the ability for a firm to deliver across markets is a problem. I can remember using Firm XXXX in Mexico, and they were just *terrible* there."

"I asked my firm, 'As you set up those firm offices in Brazil, will you have a US-based partner spend time in that office to make sure the culture is there?' For me, I want to know that when I'm calling that person in São Paulo, he or she is going to understand where we are coming from. That makes me more comfortable."

Those quotes speak to geographical consistency, but consistency over time is also key from the client's point of view. Many clients are actually very skilled at succession planning, at multiple levels in the organization; they expect the same from you. In chapter 3, we called out the reasons why firm leaders should pay attention to client transition plans and consider implementing a system of "laddering"—that is, matching up your professionals at each rank with client counterparts of a roughly similar experience. Now we're giving you the rationale based on the clients' point of view: they are equally concerned about smooth transitions across generations of their service providers. In fact, this issue is seen as so critical and problematic in some companies that it has risen to the board level. If they're already that sensitive to the issue of intergenerational collaboration, they must expect you to pay attention to it, as well.

Collaboration promotes simplicity

In an increasingly complex world, clients seek simplicity wherever they can find it. Purchasing a broader range of services from a smaller number of providers is one way of getting there.[6] A decade ago, this trend was mainly limited to the biggest, most sophisticated clients with powerful procurement functions. These days, many smaller clients are moving toward what is often called a "core provider" model. When collaboration broadens how the client views your firm, you reinforce or expand your position as a core provider.

It seems clear that this trend will only expand and intensify. Few single-service firms—even those offering bargain-basement pricing or guru-level expertise—will be exempt. As one high-tech executive described his company's approach to hiring professional service firms:

> We think the competitive benchmark should be a couple dozen suppliers, tops. We're WAY, way, way over that. Think of the costs we incur creating vendor profiles, getting accounts payable set up for this new supplier, all the hassles and the room for error. Think about how much totally useless time we spend briefing one vendor after another about billing guidelines and such. What a waste.
>
> Conversely, if we're using a firm for some but not all their services, then it's a real opportunity—for us and them.

Is your firm prepared to pounce on that opportunity? If you're an account leader, do you understand which of your clients are moving in this direction, and are you prepared to initiate discussions that tie your firm's collaborative experience to clients' need to simplify? You can position this move as a win-win by explaining that you understand your obligation to provide a steady stream of value going forward. Tell them that when they build a strategic relationship with *your* firm, you will take responsibility for keeping the pencils sharp. In fact, your cross-sectoral experience (made possible in part by your collaborative skills) positions you well to understand what great service means, what it should cost, and how to tailor it specifically to their needs. In effect, you can help them get smarter about building the strategic relationships they're looking for.

In some corporations, the person tasked with achieving their simplification goal is not the same person as the one buying your service. If this disconnect means that your pitch falls on deaf ears, then enlist your firm's managing partner to engage in a top-to-top discussion about how your broader service offering could meet their own strategic objectives: collaboration promotes simplicity.

Collaboration fosters responsiveness

One reason why business is increasingly complicated today is that it moves so much faster than it used to. Clients need to be able to pick up the phone (or whatever faster technology has just been introduced), describe the signals they've just received, and get a quick answer from the right person who's plugged into that particular issue and knows just where to go to get additional perspectives.

Again, the savvy client doesn't necessarily expect *you*, as an individual, to have all the answers all the time. But he or she does expect you to have the necessary depth and breadth of understanding to serve as the first contact, and to ferret out the expert fast. One securities lawyer described this challenge in compelling and very concrete terms:

> A client called me one day at 2 p.m. saying, "Look, our stock dropped 40 percent. There's no reason for it. I just got a call from the New York Stock Exchange, and they're going to suspend trading. They want us to put out a press release. What do I do?"
>
> When you get that type of call, it's not really a good time for you to say, "What an interesting question! We're going to research it and get back to you with an answer as soon as we can." Either you know the answer yourself, or you have to reach out to one of your colleagues who knows the exact answer and is willing to *drop everything* to collaborate with you.

One experience like that teaches the client the value of collaboration within your firm. The right answer to the New York Stock Exchange question—delivered *fast*—will cement your ties with the client, and open up new ways for you to bring collaboration to bear on the relationship going forward.

Collaboration increases efficiency

Everybody needs to do more with less. In that spirit, clients don't want to pay your firm to reinvent solutions that somebody inside already knows. They want you to save money by transferring learnings—the wisdom your firm has gained across multiple clients and sectors. They expect you to deploy the right resources at the right price—for example, shifting work to lower-cost juniors in another locale. Both kinds of transfers are fairly obvious examples of circumstances in which clients welcome effective collaboration to save costs.

But partners may shy away from discussions about ways that teaming up can actually increase efficiency. As the CFO of a major law firm put it, if there is a budget for the work, the firm should include the cost of collaboration in the budget, and seek approval up front from the client. If the client objects, seize that opportunity to educate him or her about the potential benefits of collaboration to his or her organization. Again, timing is all-important. "I won't pay for a stranger showing up on my bill," one tough-talking client told me. "If you're planning to bring in someone for a specialty consultation, you've got to clear it with me in advance. But if you tell me you need a ten-minute conversation with an expert rather than researching it for two hours, I'd welcome that!"

Of course, you then have to deliver efficiently. Be aware that the savvy client is going to be looking at the number of people billing against the account. If the overall number suddenly spikes, it suggests a lack of good collaboration, either because the work isn't being done efficiently, or because all of the people involved aren't working together effectively.

Most likely, the savvy client is also going to be scanning your invoices for cases in which someone has billed an extraordinary number of hours in a day. Why? Jennifer Daniels, the chief legal officer of Colgate-Palmolive, explains her rationale:

> Really good collaboration means people are working in a
> steady-state way where there shouldn't be too many crazy
> peaks and too many crazy valleys. By way of analogy, a
> factory that is humming along, doing what it's supposed
> to be doing without too much overtime and without too
> much under-time, is probably pretty efficient and prob-
> ably everyone knows what they're supposed to be doing.
> If I see a lot of spikes in a provider's bill, absent a trial or

other extraordinary circumstances, that usually is a sign
that someone hasn't planned well.[7]

It sounds paradoxical, but clients are very willing to pay good
money to achieve efficiency. Your experience with collaboration
delivers that outcome.

And finally: Collaboration builds strong bonds

At the outset of this chapter, I said that I would present the client's perspective on collaboration in the form of eleven assertions,
lined up in descending order of importance. Maybe you noticed the
hedge back there. "For the most part," I wrote, "they're listed in
terms of what I found to be the most important overall to clients."

For the most part. In fact, I've saved the most important assertion for last. It concerns what might be called the "human element."
Simply stated, collaboration builds powerful and productive relationships among people. Done right, it makes work more productive, interesting, rewarding, and fun—not just for you, but also for
the client, in the context of their relationship with you.

Having multiple smart people available to your client contacts
can be a *big deal* for them. It conveys, first and foremost, that you
value the relationship. It signals that they are important, and that
you will pull in all the needed resources to get their job done, and
done right. It says, *To us, you matter.*

Meanwhile, those people you are deploying on the client's behalf
are giving great advice—thanks to your collaborative prowess—
and helping that client rest easier. They're telling the client executives what they do and don't have to worry about. For a lot of
overworked managers out there in the world, that's just about
priceless.

In my experience, clients tend to return to the advisers who make
them calmer, and more confident that they know the way forward.
By providing the advice of your wise team, have you made their

path that much straighter? Did they put down the phone saying, "Jeez, I'm lucky I've got these guys on my side!"

Have you made them happier? No; the toughest of tough guys out there wouldn't talk, or maybe even think, like that. But it's definitely part of the bigger picture, and it's definitely made possible in part by collaboration. Think about it. Your partners are smart and interesting people. They are way more interesting than some of the other individuals whom the client deals with on a day-to-day basis. And as a team, they present to the client a whole collection of challenging, bracing, exciting, even offbeat perspectives. You can, and should, be a highlight of their day.

OK, let's not get carried away. Maybe it's time, in the final paragraphs, to switch back from the client's perspective to yours: the leader of an ambitious, world-class (or soon to be world-class) professional service firm.

Your firm is almost certainly facing an irresistible force: client demand for new kinds of services. These are services that can only be provided by interdisciplinary teams of experts working together. Why are these kinds of broadly based teams needed? Because the issues faced by major corporations today are enormously complex, and getting more complex every day. Think of the megamergers that have been proposed in recent years, or high-profile corporate data breaches on a massive scale, or auto-safety recalls numbering in the millions and spanning the globe. No one consultant or lawyer—or even one functional area—can guide a client through such a challenging episode.

Meanwhile, if your firm is like most out there, it's populated with smart, successful, autonomy-seeking professionals who have built their careers and reputations based on their own individual achievements. They are *stars*—be they architects, accountants, lawyers, consultants, executive search experts, or other kinds of specialists. They may even agree that collaboration is a great idea—for everyone around them, and as long as it doesn't require them to change their own behaviors! But as I've described, the tide is turning against them, and *what got them here won't get them there*.

What will get them there? Smart collaboration.

As I've said throughout this book, collaboration is not a nice-to-have; it's increasingly a strategic imperative. The market for professional services is bifurcating into high-profit, customized work versus lower-end, routine work. Many professional sectors—indeed, much of the broader universe of knowledge work—will soon arrive at an hourglass shape. At the top of the hourglass, collaboration that spans specialties within your firm will allow you to earn higher margins, inspire greater client loyalty, mitigate lethal risks, and gain an important edge when competing for a shrinking segment of high-profit work.

At the bottom of the hourglass, collaboration is no less important for firms pursuing more routine work that is highly cost-competitive. Standardized tasks increasingly require new types of collaboration—such as team-based problem solving—that are efficiently supported by and intertwined with technology. Any firm that is trying to differentiate itself in this crowded end of the market needs its partners to engage in even more refined, more efficient collaboration.

How will your firm, and the professionals within it, succeed in today's and tomorrow's turbulent market? Of course, there are many answers. But one of the best is, *by embracing and practicing smart collaboration.*

NOTES

Introduction

1. I use the term *partner* in this book to refer to any senior member of a knowledge-based organization who has the sort of power and autonomy described here.

2. Henceforth, unless otherwise stated, I will use the word *collaboration* as shorthand for "smart collaboration."

3. From H. K. Gardner, "Leading the Campaign for Greater Collaboration within Law Firms," in *Leadership for Lawyers: Essential Leadership Strategies for Law Firm Success*, eds. H. K. Gardner and R. Normand-Hochman (London: Globe Law and Business, 2015). The managing partner in question chose to remain anonymous.

4. For a history of specialization in the legal field, see M. Ariens, "Know the Law: A History of Legal Specialization," *South Carolina Law Review* 1003 (1994); and T. Hia, "Que Sera, Sera? The Future of Specialization in Large Law Firms," *Columbia Business and Law Review* 541 (2002).

5. G. C. Hazard Jr., "'Practice' in Law and Other Professions," *Arizona Law Review* 39 (1997): 390.

6. 976 F. 2d 86—*Stewart v. Jackson & Nash*, 61 USLW 2206, 127 Lab. Cas. P 57,631, 7 IER Cases 1322, United States Court of Appeals, Second Circuit, http://openjurist.org/976/f2d/86/stewart-v-jackson-and-nash.

7. Professional service firms are hardly the only organizations that have subdivided into siloes; for a fascinating account of this phenomenon in many domains, see G. Tett, *The Silo Effect: The Peril of Expertise and the Promise of Breaking Down Barriers* (New York: Simon & Schuster, 2015). Like Tett (see p. 13), I believe that *silo* refers not only to physical structures and organizational subunits, but also to psychological "tribalism" associated with silos.

8. The first use of the term is believed to be in the first edition of a report from the US Army War College: R. R. Magee, ed., *Strategic Leadership Primer* (Carlisle Barracks, PA: Department of Command, Leadership, and Management, US Army War College, 1998).

9. Harvard Law School, Center on the Legal Profession, "Perspectives from a General Counsel: Jennifer Daniels of the Colgate-Palmolive Company," *The Practice*, September 2015.

10. See IBM, *Capitalizing on Complexity: Insights from the Global Chief Executive Officer Study*, at http://public.dhe.ibm.com/common/ssi/ecm/en/gbe03297usen/GBE03297USEN.PDF.

11. Research interview with author; permission to quote contingent on anonymity.

12. I have also written five Harvard Business School case studies of knowledge-based organizations that are grappling with issues of collaboration among highly autonomous professional workers, as well as multiple book chapters and articles in the *Harvard Business Review* and similar publications on the subject. See, for example, "When Senior Managers Won't Collaborate," *Harvard Business Review*, March 2015.

13. My data from several firms spans the 2008–2009 period—arguably one of the most difficult stretches in history for the knowledge industry.

Chapter 1

1. The material in this section is largely derived from my article "When Senior Managers Won't Collaborate," *Harvard Business Review*, March 2015.

2. This chart and some of the accompanying analysis first appeared in H. K. Gardner, "Why It Pays to Collaborate," *American Lawyer*, March 2015.

3. Research interview with author; permission to quote contingent on anonymity.

4. M. Boussebaa and G. Morgan, "Internationalization of Professional Service Firms: Drivers, Forms and Outcomes," in *The Oxford Handbook of Professional Service Firms*, eds. L. Empson, D. Muzio, and J. Broschak (Oxford: Oxford University Press, 2015).

5. When I started research interviews with clients, I used the word *loyalty* rather than *stickiness*, but was quickly corrected: as one executive said, "I'm not *loyal*, in the sense that I continue the relationship out of a sense of devotion or duty. I'm simply *stuck* with the firm that collaborates because it's hard to find a substitute." Other clients confirmed that the word *sticky* was more accurate.

6. B. Groysberg and R. Abrahams, "Lift Outs: How to Acquire a High-Functioning Team," *Harvard Business Review*, December 2006.

7. See for example, R. Reagans and E. W. Zuckerman, "Networks, Diversity, and Productivity: The Social Capital of Corporate R&D Teams," *Organization Science* 12 (2001): 502–517.

8. The study of collaboration's impact on patents and publications was published by S. Wuchty, B. F. Jones, and B. Uzzi, "The Increasing Dominance of Teams in Production of Knowledge," *Science* 316 (2007): 1036–1039. What is not entirely clear in the comparison, however, is whether yesteryear's "freestanding geniuses" were actually working in teams and simply taking all the credit.

9. S. Wuchty, B. F. Jones, and B. Uzzi, "The Increasing Dominance of Teams in Production of Knowledge," *Science* 316 (2007): 1036–1039.

10. C. A. Cotropia and L. Petherbridge, "The Dominance of Teams in the Production of Legal Knowledge," *Yale Law Journal Forum* 124 (2014): 18–28.

11. H. K. Gardner, "Performance Pressure as a Double-edged Sword: Enhancing Team Motivation but Undermining the Use of Team Knowledge," *Administrative Science Quarterly* 57 (2012): 1–46.

12. See, for example, how one client measures these aspect of its service provider's work: H. K. Gardner and S. Silverstein, "GlaxoSmithKlein: Sourcing Complex Professional Sources," Case no. 414–003 (Boston: Harvard Business School Publishing, 2013).

13. From "Leading Through Connections," a study of global CEOs conducted by IBM in 2012.

14. The contact to the procurement department at this company came through one of my former executive education students. Because of my concern for strict confidentiality about my research participants, I couldn't tell the lawyer about my interview with his client, and I didn't reveal his statements to the purchasing head. I hope they both read this book and come to an understanding of the missed opportunities.

15. American Bar Association, Standing Committee on Lawyers' Professional Liability, "Profile of Legal Malpractice Claims 2000–2003," 2005.

16. This analysis is derived in part from a 2006 speech to the ABA—"The Top Ten Causes of Malpractice, and How You Can Avoid Them"—by legal risk management coordinator Mark C. S. Bassingthwaighte. Bassingthwaighte offered some pithy (and relevant) advice to his audience: "Don't dabble."

17. This particular interviewee was especially keen to preserve anonymity, given how sensitive a topic we were covering. Yet, multiple individuals in similar external positions—regulatory authorities, insurers, trade associations— reported an increase in both deliberate malfeasance and unintentional errors, all of which were linked to noncollaborative behaviors.

18. Office of Compliance Inspections and Examinations, US Securities and Exchange Commission, "National Examination Risk Alert" II, no. 2 (2012).

19. Today's e-billing systems have evolved to become essential analytic tools for legal departments. They analyze incoming invoices and provide reports full of detailed data on outside counsel activities and billing rates. "What e-billing can do is unbundle all of the information that comes from traditional legal bills so that you have the ability to compare over a long period of time, from timekeeper to timekeeper or from firm to firm," says Pamela Woldow, general counsel at Edge International Inc. quoted in J. Beck and A. Byrne, "The 4 Best Technologies to Add to Your Legal Department's Toolbox," *Inside Counsel Magazine*, November 28, 2012.

20. B. W. Heineman Jr., "Big Isn't Always Best," *Corporate Counsel*, November 2008.

21. See M. Sako, "Outsourcing and Offshoring by Professional Service Firms," in Empson, Muzio, and Broschak, eds., *The Oxford Handbook of Professional Service Firms*; "Law Firm Allen & Overy Creating 300 Jobs in Belfast," BBC News, February 3, 2011; Jennifer Smith, "Law Firms Wring Costs from Back-Office Tasks," *Wall Street Journal*, October 7, 2012.

Chapter 2

1. D. H. Maister, *Managing the Professional Service Firm* (New York: Free Press, 1993), 18.

2. "Laterals" can include anyone who has some successful experience in the workplace—in other words, anyone who's not fresh out of school—but I tend to use the word to describe relatively senior people.

3. M. Bidwell, "Paying More to Get Less: The Effects of External Hiring Versus Internal Mobility," *Administrative Science Quarterly* 56, no. 3 (September 2011): 369–407.

4. One study showed that after professionals in the banking sector switched employer, their average performance fell by about 20 percent, and had not reached pre-move levels even five years later. See B. Groysberg, *Chasing Stars: The Myth of Talent and the Portability of Performance* (Princeton, NJ: Princeton University Press, 2012).

5. A. Press, "Special Report: Big Law's Reality Check," *American Lawyer*, November 2014.

6. "Lateral Damage: Failed Hires Cost London Dear," *The Lawyer*, February 2012.

7. These confidential estimates were supplied in my research interviews and by my board of contributors.

8. Groysberg, *Chasing Stars*.

9. Note that culture is typically the outcome or by-product of many of the formal systems and structures in a firm, and strongly related to the type of people employed. See J. W. Lorsch and Emily McTague, "Culture Is Not the Culprit," *Harvard Business Review*, April 2016.

10. When the US Army opened up its front lines to female soldiers in Afghanistan—even in limited ways—it suddenly acquired the ability to interact with the "other half" of the local population.

11. J. Eligon, "3 Weeks into Retirement, Morgenthau Takes a Law Job," *New York Times*, January 21, 2010.

12. A. Nanda and K. Morrell, "Egon Zehnder International: Managing Professionals in an Executive Search Firm," Case 9-700-133 (Boston: Harvard Business School, 2004).

13. Confidential interview with the US-based COO of an international consulting firm. His point of view was echoed in some similar conversations with a few leaders in law and engineering-design firms. But too many leaders still fail to put the brakes on lateral hiring, perhaps because they lack either the willingness or the ability to enforce a more centralized approach in their companies.

14. Nanda and Morrell, "Egon Zehnder International," 2; see also F. Gino and B. Staats, "Mary Caroline Tillman at Egon Zehnder: Spotting Talent in the 21st Century," Case 9-426-027 (Boston: Harvard Business School, 2016).

15. The study was the result of joint research between Universum, INSEAD Emerging Markets Institute, and the HEAD Foundation: *Understanding a Misunderstood Generation*, 2014, http://universumglobal.com/millennials/.

16. N. Kitroeff, "The Smartest People Are Opting Out of Law School," April 15, 2015, http://www.bloomberg.com/news/articles/2015-04-15/the-smartest-people-are-opting-out-of-law-school; J. Areen, "Lawyers as Professionals and as Citizens: Key Roles and Responsibilities in the 21st Century: Commentary," https://clp.law.harvard.edu/assets/Commentary-Judith_Areen.pdf.

17. For more on leverage structure, see D. H. Maister, "The Anatomy of a Consulting Firm," in *The Advice Business: Essential Tools and Models for Managing Consulting*, eds. C. J. Fombrun and M. D. Nevis (New York: Pearson, 2004).

18. Universum et al., *Understanding a Misunderstood Generation.*

19. Ibid.

20. These ideas and more were initially published in the chapter by S. Sheehan, H. K. Gardner, and H. Bresman, "Leading the Millennial Generation," in *Leadership for Lawyers: Essential Leadership Strategies for Law Firm Success*, eds. H. K. Gardner and R. Normand-Hochman (London: Globe Law and Business Publishing, 2015).

21. The idea that meaning (also known as "purpose"), mastery, and autonomy are essential drivers of human behavior—more so than financial incentives—has been popularized by D. H. Pink, *Drive: The Surprising Truth About What Motivates Us* (New York: Riverhead Books, 2011). There is also significant academic research supporting the idea.

22. See, for example, T. R. Mitchell et al., "Why People Stay: Using Job Embeddedness to Predict Voluntary Turnover," *Academy of Management Journal* 44, no. 6 (December 2001): 1102–1121; and J. Pearce and A. Randel, "Expectations of Organizational Mobility, Workplace Social Inclusion, and Employee Job Performance," *Journal of Organizational Behavior* 25, no. 1 (February 2004): 81–98.

23. Of course, this assumes successful experiences, which this book aims to help you shape.

24. Academic research on the topic includes, for example, R. M. Steers, "Antecedents and Outcomes of Organizational Commitment," *Administrative Science Quarterly* (1977): 46–56; R. Eisenberger, P. Fasolo, and V. Davis-LaMastro, "Perceived Organizational Support and Employee Diligence, Commitment, and Innovation," *Journal of Applied Psychology* 75, no. 1 (1990): 51–59. The idea has been previously applied to professional service firms in D. Maister and J. Walker, "The One-Firm Firm Revisited," http://davidmaister.com/articles/the-one-firm-firm-revisited/.

25. J. K. Harter, F. L. Schmidt, and S. K. Plowman, "The Relationship Between Engagement at Work and Organizational Outcomes," *Gallup Report*, February 2013.

26. M. Buckingham and A. Goodall, "Reinventing Performance Management," *Harvard Business Review*, April 2015.

27. AARs were originally developed by the US Army and have since been adopted by all US and many non-US military services, as well as a wide array

of other kinds of organizations. See US Department of the Army, "A Leader's Guide to After-Action Reviews," September 1993: http://www.au.af.mil/au/awc/awcgate/army/tc_25-20/tc25-20.pdf.

28. Two excellent books that focus on the power of learning are A. Edmondson, *Teaming* (San Francisco: Wiley, 2012), and D. Garvin, *Learning in Action* (Boston: Harvard Buisness School Press, 2000).

29. McKinsey is mentioned here because it is credited with pioneering the idea of "alumni relations" for professional service firms. But many other consulting, accounting, law, and financial service firms have similarly built programs to build mutually beneficial relations with former employees. See "Gone but Not Forgotten," *The Economist*, March 1, 2014.

30. See the full article at the McKinsey site: http://www.mckinsey.com/careers/our-people-and-values/alumni-a-community-for-life.

31. In the field of organizational behavior, the term *psychological contract* is used to describe the set of expectations and informal obligation that exist between an employee and employer. Employees or employers who perceive a breach (i.e., failure to deliver on what was promised) are likely to respond very negatively. In contrast, if professional service firms make it clear that the odds of making partner are low, then employees who are not promoted are more likely to remain loyal to the firm, despite the outcome. See, for example, D. M. Rousseau, *Psychological Contracts in Organizations: Understanding Written and Unwritten Agreements* (Thousand Oaks, CA: Sage, 1995); and M.-R. Parzefall and J. A-M. Coyle-Shapiro, "Making Sense of Psychological Contract Breach," *Journal of Managerial Psychology* 26, no. 1 (2011): 12–27.

Chapter 3

1. Marshall Goldsmith, a highly acclaimed executive coach, popularized this saying in his book, *What Got You Here Won't Get You There: How Successful People Become Even More Successful* (New York: Hachette Books, 2007).

2. An earlier version of this figure appeared in H. K. Gardner, "When Senior Managers Won't Collaborate," *Harvard Business Review*, March 2015.

3. We uncovered these answers by asking open-ended questions; we then coded and categorized them and tallied the responses. We did not give multiple-choice options, which risk "leading the witness."

4. This barrier echoes findings in the organizational behavior literature, such as D. Dougherty, "Interpretive Barriers to Successful Product Innovation in Large Firms," *Organization Science* 3, no. 2 (1992): 179–202.

5. E. Ramanathan and J. Coates, "Corporate Purchasing Project," Center on the Legal Profession, Harvard Law School, 2011, https://clp.law.harvard.edu/clp-research/legal-markets/.

6. Dunbar's number—roughly 150 people—is the presumed number of individuals with whom one can maintain stable social relationships, because that size network allows a person to know each person directly, as well as how each person relates to every other person.

7. See Tan's bio at B&M's website: http://www.bakermckenzie.com/ Loke-KhoonTan/.

8. I thank Jim Hever and Richard Oakes of 010 Consulting for introducing me to this partner and sharing their expertise about how to use a structured program to build credibility with clients.

9. Loke-Khoon Tan, interview with author, March 2015.

10. For a compelling review of related research, especially with regard to gender perceptions and unconscious bias, see I. Bohnet, *What Works: Gender Equality by Design* (Cambridge, MA: Harvard University Press, 2016).

11. For surprising insights and practical ideas about team launches in a setting that is perhaps even trickier than professional service firms—the US intelligence community—see J. R. Hackman, *Collaborative Intelligence: Using Teams to Solve Hard Problems* (San Francisco: Berrett-Koehler, 2011).

12. In 2007, the American Bar Association took an official position against mandatory retirement policies. A series of high-profile age-discrimination lawsuits against firms was turning the tide against such policies as well. See S. Flaherty, "BigLaw Finds New Roles for Older Attorneys Amid Age-Bias Woes," *Law360*, July 25, 2014, http://www.law360.com/articles/558493/ biglaw-finds-new-roles-for-older-attys-amid-age-bias-woes. Also see M. Cohn, "Mandatory Partner Retirement Becomes an Issue at Firms," *Debits & Credits* (blog), *Accounting Today*, September 19, 2014, http://www.accountingtoday .com/blogs/debits-credits/mandatory-partner-retirement-becomes-an-issue-at- firms-72047-1.html.

13. M. P. McQueen, "Study: Big Law Leaders Are Much Older Than Clients," *American Lawyer*, September 5, 2015.

14. I thank Hugh Verrier, chairman of White & Case, for these insights (multiple interviews with author in 2015), which were first written up in H. Gardner and R. Normand-Hochmann, "Competing via Culture: How to Give Clients a True One-Firm Global Service," *Managing Partner*, October, 2015.

15. I thank "Jones" for providing this insight and giving me permission to use the firm's disguised example.

16. I thank the client executive who introduced me to the term *laddering*.

Chapter 4

1. This story is recounted in many places, including, for example, in Susan RoAne, *Face to Face* (New York: Simon & Schuster, 2008).

2. L. Nash and H. H. Stevenson, "Success That Lasts," *Harvard Business Review*, February 2004.

3. Of course, this hinges entirely on your actually *being* a good team leader!

4. This section draws on the work of R. Wageman et al., *Senior Leadership Teams: What It Takes to Make Them Great* (Boston: Harvard Business School Press, 2008); R. Wageman and J. R. Hackman, "What Makes Teams of Leaders Leadable?" in *Advancing Leadership*, eds. N. Nohria and R. Khurana (Boston: Harvard Business School Press, 2010).

5. This section draws on an article I wrote with a colleague from INSEAD, Mark Mortensen, who is an expert at making virtual collaboration smoother. See "Collaborating Well in Large Global Teams," *Harvard Business Review*, July 2015, https://hbr.org/2015/07/collaborating-well-in-large-global-teams.

6. M. Mortensen and M. Haas, "The Secrets of Great Teamwork," *Harvard Business Review*, June 2016.

7. H. K. Gardner, "Coming Through When It Matters Most: How Great Teams Do Their Best Work Under Pressure," *Harvard Business Review*, April 2012.

8. When prompted to reflect on their own leadership style, most people initially default to thinking of their *ideal* approach, rather than the one that is truly instinctive. Instead, ask trusted people how they experience your behavior when you're seriously stressed. Subordinates may be unlikely to tell you the hard truth. Try asking a spouse, an adult daughter or son, or a long-term peer.

9. For a description of these kinds of team dynamics—what they are, and how to spot and mitigate them—see Gardner, "Coming Through When It Matters Most."

Chapter 5

1. Obviously, this can be one and the same person, playing either role on different projects especially over time—but for simplicity's sake, in this section I'll draw a sharp line of demarcation between the senders and receivers of work.

2. See T. P. Delong and V. Vijayaraghavan, "Let's Hear It for B Players," *Harvard Business Review*, June 2003.

3. Actually, only some partners admit their deficiencies; many others blame the client for not appreciating their prior attempts. In tabulating my survey results, I code those in this latter group as not doing it well enough.

4. The size of the increase depends on the type of firm, level of partner, and so on. In small domestic firms in developing countries, the increase may be mere thousands; in elite global firms, partners may see financial returns in the hundreds of thousands.

5. A significant body of research in the academic realm supports this common-sense finding. See, for example, R. Zinko et al., "Toward a Theory of Reputation in Organizations," *Research in Personnel and Human Resources Management* 26 (2007): 163–204; M. Schulte, N. A. Cohen, and K. Klein, "The Coevolution of Network Ties and Perceptions of Team Psychological Safety," *Organization Science* 23 (2012): 564–581; R. Cross and J. N. Cummings, "Tie and Network Correlates of Individual Performance in Knowledge-Intensive Work," *Academy of Management Journal* 47 (2004): 928–937.

6. The graph is based on the coefficients resulting from analyses of all partners, on average. Here I take those statistical findings and apply them to two illustrative partners.

7. A. Press, "Special Report: Big Law's Reality Check," *American Lawyer*, November 2014.

8. S. Westfahl, "Learning to Lead: Perspectives on Bridging the Lawyer Leadership Gap," in *Leadership for Lawyers: Essential Leadership Strategies for Law Firm Success*, eds. H. K. Gardner and R. Normand-Hochman (London: Globe Law and Business Publishing, 2015).

9. For example, psychologist Tom Tyler found that defendants in court cases were more satisfied with their verdict if they felt they were treated fairly, whether or not the jury ruled in their favor. T. R. Tyler, "The Role of Perceived Injustice in Defendants' Evaluations of Their Courtroom Experience," *Law & Society Review* 18, no. 1 (1984): 51.

10. J. K. Harter, F. L. Schmidt, and S. K. Plowman, "The Relationship Between Engagement at Work and Organizational Outcomes," *Gallup Report*, February 2013.

11. M. Buckingham and A. Goodall, "Reinventing Performance Management," *Harvard Business Review*, April 2015.

12. M. M. Lombardo and R. W. Eichinger, *Career Architect Development Planner*, 3rd ed. (Minneapolis, MN: Lominger Limited, 2000).

13. Westfahl, "Learning to Lead," 85.

Chapter 6

1. "Cat herder" conveys a sense of futility—an activity that is hopeless by definition—so I don't like the term.

2. To accurately analyze the effects of different compensation systems across firms—for example, how much more collaborative is a lockstep versus a merit-based firm—I would need time sheet, personnel, and financial data from about sixty or more firms. So far, that's beyond my reach.

3. See, for example, C. Tavris, "How Homo Economicus Went Extinct," *Wall Street Journal*, May 15, 2015.

4. D. Ariely, "You Are What You Measure," *Harvard Business Review*, June 2010.

5. D. Maister, *Managing the Professional Service Firm* (New York: Free Press, 1993).

6. See the firm's website for a timeline of the firm's integration process: http://www.ey.com/GL/en/About-us/Our-people-and-culture/Our-history/About-EY---Key-Facts-and-Figures---History---Timeline.

7. The acronym SMART has a number of variations, but I've chosen the one where A represents "assignable" to highlight that partners should write objectives for themselves individually—not, for example, the practice group or client team, unless they're the leader of that team, in which case they are still ultimately responsible for achieving the objective. Assignable objectives enable greater accountability.

8. Maister, *Managing the Professional Service Firm*.

9. H. K. Gardner, "Mentoring Senior Lawyers," in *Mentoring and Coaching for Lawyers: Building Partnerships for Success*, ed. R. Normand-Hochman (London: Globe Law and Business Publishing, 2014).

10. S. Kerr, "On the Folly of Rewarding A, While Hoping for B," *Academy of Management Executive* 9, no. 1 (1995): 7–14.

11. J. Pfeffer and S. E. DeVoe, "Economic Evaluation: The Effect of Money and Economics on Attitudes About Volunteering," *Journal of Economic Psychology* 30 (2009): 500–508; J. Pfeffer and S. E. DeVoe, "The Economic Evaluation of Time: Organizational Causes and Individual Consequences," *Research in Organizational Behavior* 32 (2012): 47–62. See also I. Campbell and S. Charlesworth, "Salaried Lawyers and Billable Hours," *International Journal of the Legal Profession* 19, no. 1 (2012).

12. For practical insights and additional resources about strengths-based professional development, see S. Westphal and C. Fletcher, "Accelerated Strengths Development," *Law Practice*, May–June 2013.

13. See the company's website at https://www.objectivemanager.com/.

14. D. Jargiello and P. Gardner, "Free Agent Dysfunction: Management Realpolitik for U.S. Law Firms," white paper, August 2010, www.lawfirmgeneralcounsel.com/.

15. Partner quote in M. C. Regan Jr. and L. H. Rohrer, "Money and Meaning: The Moral Economy of Law Firm Compensation," *University of St. Thomas Law Journal* 10 (2012): 79.

16. F. Herzberg, "One More Time: How Do You Motivate Employees?" *Harvard Business Review*, September–October 1987, 109–120.

17. H. K. Gardner and K. Herman, "Marshall & Gordon: Designing an Effective Compensation System (A)," Case 411-038 (Boston: Harvard Business School, 2011) and the related Instructor's Note.

18. L. Rohrer and J. W. Jones, "Reforming Partner Compensation at Mattos Filho (A)," Case 15-21 (Cambridge, MA: Harvard Law School, 2015).

19. If the concept of "my client" versus "others' client" is jarring to you—great! That means you probably have weeded out at least the language that symbolizes the worst sort of territorial behaviors. I use those terms to emphasize the mindset that is often associated with anticollaborative behaviors stemming from a system that overemphasizes origination.

20. The finding that relative, as opposed to absolute, income promotes higher happiness and well-being has been replicated in many areas of the world; the result holds true after the individual has reached a certain level of financial security to cover their basic needs. See for example, A. Ferrer-i-Carbonell, "Income and Well-Being: An Empirical Analysis of the Comparison Income Effect," *Journal of Public Economics* 89, nos. 5–6 (2005): 997–1019; Marist Poll Report, "Generation to Generation: Money Matters," April 13, 2012; E. Clark and A. J. Oswald, "Satisfaction and Comparison Income," *Journal of Public Economics* 61, no. 3 (1996): 359–381.

21. S. F. Brosnan and F. B. M. De Waal, "Monkeys Reject Unequal Pay," *Nature: International Weekly Journal of Science* 425 (2003).

22. A. Press, "Special Report: Big Law's Reality Check," *American Lawyer*, November 2014; see also ALM Legal Intelligence, *The 43rd Annual Survey of Law Firm Economics*, 2015 edition.

23. Rohrer and Jones, "Reforming Partner Compensation at Mattos Filho (A)," 12.

24. E. Wesemann and N. Jarrett-Kerr, 2012 Global Partner Compensation System Survey, Edge International, May 2012 (reported in Regan and Rohrer, "Money and Meaning," 93).

25. J. N. Baron and D. M. Kreps, *Strategic Human Resources: Framework for General Managers* (New York: John Wiley, 1999).

26. McKinsey Global Institute, *The Social Economy: Unlocking Value and Productivity through Social Technologies*, July 2012, http://www.mckinsey .com/industries/high-tech/our-insights/the-social-economy.

27. Ibid.

28. I thank Paula Young and others at PwC for providing internal documents and their time and insights during research interviews, all of which served as the source material for this section.

Chapter 7

1. Of course, biotech—arguably a robust offshoot of the education and health care sectors—is also a major force in the regional economy.

2. The Dana-Farber Institute's leaders were incredibly helpful to me as I conducted my research for a series of Harvard Business School cases focused on the institute. (Those cases, all published in 2012, are collectively called "Ganging Up on Cancer: Integrative Research Centers at Dana-Farber Cancer Institute," HBS case numbers 9-412-029, N9-412-098, and 5-412-112 [Boston: Harvard Business Publishing, 2012].) I am especially indebted to Dr. Barrett Rollins, the Dana-Farber's chief scientific officer, who shared his thoughts with me and agreed to show up as the (undisguised) central protagonist in my cases. My former student Dr. Shereef M. Elnahal deserves credit for unearthing the research opportunity at the Dana-Farber; he and Dr. Edo Bedzra played crucial roles in researching and writing of the HBS cases.

3. See D. H. Maister, *Managing the Professional Service Firm* (New York: Free Press, 1993), chapter 27.

4. I'm grateful to the member of my online board of contributors who offered this insight in one of our online discussions.

5. I thank the member of my online board of contributors who offered this insight in one of our online discussions.

6. The Center for Nanotechnology in Cancer is a composite, rather than an actual, center.

7. "Charlie Woods," "Peter Lendale," and "Lousie Ratkin" are composite characters in this case study. They are not real people, but a combination of real individuals at the Dana-Farber.

8. Barrett Rollins, interview by author, November 2015.

9. Barrett Rollins, interview by author, October 2014.

10. T. Amabile and S. Kramer, *The Progress Principle: Using Small Wins to Ignite Joy, Engagement, and Creativity at Work* (Boston: Harvard Business Review Press, 2011).

11. Sun Tzu, *The Art of War*, trans. Lionel Giles (New York: Cosimo Classics, 2010).

12. C. Aiken and S. Keller, "The Irrational Side of Change Management," *McKinsey Quarterly*, April 2009.

13. J. Lorsch and E. McTague, "Culture Is Not the Culprit," *Harvard Business Review*, April 2016.

14. D. A. Kolb, *Experiential Learning: Experience as the Source of Learning and Development*, 2nd ed. (Upper Saddle River, NJ: Pearson Education, 2015).

Chapter 8

1. Think, for example, of recent cases in the energy and mining sectors. Companies that relied solely on legal title, without determining whether key community stakeholders believed that title was legitimate, soon ran into trouble.

2. If any of your clients have undergone any M&A activity within the last two years, it's guaranteed that they are still learning about other parts of their own organization. Help your contact become a hero by getting him or her up to speed faster about opportunities, risks, and potentially helpful connections elsewhere in the company.

3. See, for example, R. Reagans and E. W. Zuckerman, "Networks, Diversity, and Productivity: The Social Capital of Corporate R&D Teams," *Organization Science* 12 (2001): 502–517; S. Wuchty, B. F. Jones, and B. Uzzi, "The Increasing Dominance of Teams in Production of Knowledge," *Science* 316 (2007): 1036–1039.

4. J. Kolko, "Design Thinking Comes of Age," *Harvard Business Review*, July 2015.

5. Professionals who are skeptical about the value of collaboration in clients that are dominated by a procurement function might be surprised to learn that this example was provided to me by a procurement manager!

6. Of course, this strategy has a limit: smart clients will always maintain a portfolio of professional providers so that they can lower the risk of becoming overly dependent on a single supplier. In some cases, such as auditing, there are related regulatory constraints to consider. Overall, though, most professional service firms can provide the expanded expertise that will meet their clients' need to simplify their vendor base.

7. Harvard Law School, Center on the Legal Profession, "Perspectives from a General Counsel: Jennifer Daniels of the Colgate-Palmolive Company," *The Practice*, September 2015.

INDEX

ABOUT THE AUTHOR

Heidi K. Gardner, PhD, is a distinguished fellow in the Center on the Legal Profession at Harvard Law School. She also serves as a lecturer on law and the faculty chair of the school's *Accelerated Leadership Program* executive course. She was previously on the faculty at Harvard Business School, and continues to teach executive programs there. Gardner has also been awarded an International Research Fellowship at Oxford University's Said Business School.

Gardner's research received the Academy of Management's prize for Paper with Outstanding Practical Implications for Management. She has authored or coauthored more than fifty book chapters, case studies, and articles in scholarly and practitioner journals, including several in *Harvard Business Review*. She is coeditor, with Rebecca Normand-Hochman, of *Leadership for Lawyers: Essential Strategies for Law Firm Success*, published in 2015.

Gardner studied Japanese at the University of Pennsylvania, where she graduated summa cum laude and Phi Beta Kappa. She earned a master's degree with honors from the London School of Economics and a second master's and PhD in organizational behavior from London Business School. There she won the Outstanding Student Leader Award, an honor conferred by the dean at graduation in recognition of her service to the London Business School community.

Throughout her career, Gardner has lived and worked on four continents. She was previously a management consultant for McKinsey & Company in London, Johannesburg, and New York, and a manager for Procter & Gamble. She also held a Fulbright fellowship in Germany, and studied and taught at Kansai Gaidai University in Japan. At present, she serves on the board of directors for The Second Step, a Boston-area nonprofit that addresses the problem of domestic violence.

With a passion for using robust research to develop pragmatic advice, Gardner works extensively with professional service firms and in-house professional departments in corporations around the globe. In addition to advising senior leadership teams and executive committees on strategic issues, Gardner has addressed more than ten thousand professional firm partners in more than twenty countries on the theme of smart collaboration.